When should I travel to get the best airfare?
Where do I go for answers to my travel questions?
What's the best and easiest way to plan and book my trip?

frommers.travelocity.com

Frommer's, the travel guide leader, has teamed up with **Travelocity.com**, the leader in online travel, to bring you an in-depth, easy-to-use resource designed to help you plan and book your trip online.

At **frommers.travelocity.com**, you'll find free online updates about your destination from the experts at Frommer's plus the outstanding travel planning and purchasing features of Travelocity.com. Travelocity.com provides reservations capabilities for 95 percent of all airline seats sold, more than 47,000 hotels, and over 50 car rental companies. In addition, Travelocity.com offers more than 2,000 exciting vacation and cruise packages. Travelocity.com puts you in complete control of your travel planning with these and other great features:

> **Expert travel guidance from Frommer's** – over 150 writers reporting from around the world!

> **Best Fare Finder** – an interactive calendar tells you when to travel to get the best airfare

> **Fare Watcher** – we'll track airfare changes to your favorite destinations

> **Dream Maps** – a mapping feature that suggests travel opportunities based on your budget

> **Shop Safe Guarantee** – 24 hours a day / 7 days a week live customer service, and more!

Whether traveling on a tight budget, looking for a quick weekend getaway, or planning the trip of a lifetime, Frommer's guides and Travelocity.com will make your travel dreams a reality. You've bought the book, now book the trip!

A New Star-Rating System & Other Exciting News from Frommer's!

In our continuing effort to publish the savviest, most up-to-date, and most appealing travel guides available, we've added some great new features.

Frommer's guides now include a new **star-rating system**. Every hotel, restaurant, and attraction is rated from 0 to 3 stars to help you set priorities and organize your time.

We've also added **seven brand-new features** that point you to the great deals, in-the-know advice, and unique experiences that separate travelers from tourists. Throughout the guide look for:

Finds	Special finds—those places only insiders know about
Fun Fact	Fun facts—details that make travelers more informed and their trips more fun
Kids	Best bets for kids—advice for the whole family
Moments	Special moments—those experiences that memories are made of
Overrated	Places or experiences not worth your time or money
Tips	Insider tips—some great ways to save time and money
Value	Great values—where to get the best deals

We've also added a **"What's New"** section in every guide—a timely crash course in what's hot and what's not in every destination we cover.

Other Great Guides for Your Trip:

Frommer's Toronto

Frommer's Canada

Frommer's Montréal & Québec City

Frommer's Vancouver with Kids

Frommer's Ottawa with Kids

Frommer's®

Toronto with Kids

1st Edition

by Jennifer Crump

Here's what the critics say about Frommer's:

"Amazingly easy to use. Very portable, very complete."

—Booklist

"The only mainstream guide to list specific prices. The Walter Cronkite of guidebooks—with all that implies."

—Travel & Leisure

"Complete, concise, and filled with useful information."

—New York Daily News

"Hotel information is close to encyclopedic."

—Des Moines Sunday Register

CDG Books Canada
Toronto, ON

About the Author

Jennifer Crump is a freelance journalist whose work has appeared in many Canadian and international magazines, including *Reader's Digest, Canadian Geographic, Michigan Living,* and *Worth.* She has enjoyed the sights and sounds of Toronto for most of her life but has a whole new appreciation for the city now that she can share its charms with her five daughters.

Jennifer has spent many school and summer vacations exploring North America with her husband, Alex, and her girls. She can be reached at jlc@nt.net.

Published by:

CDG Books Canada, Inc.

99 Yorkville Avenue, Suite 400
Toronto, ON M5R 3K5

National Library of Canada Cataloguing in Publication Data

Crump, Jennifer
    Toronto

(Frommer's with kids)

Includes index.

ISBN 1–894413–32–6
ISSN: 1499–1608

1. Children—Travel—Ontario—Toronto—Guidebooks.
2. Family recreation—Ontario—Toronto—Guidebooks.
3. Toronto (Ont.)—Guidebooks. I. Title. II. Series.

FC3097.18.C78 2001   917.13'541044'083   C2001–901475–9
F1059.5.T683C78 2001

Editorial Director: Joan Whitman	Cartographer: Mapping Specialists, Ltd.
Editor: Jennifer Lambert	Map Editor: Allyson Latta
Substantive Editor: Marcia Miron	Cover design by Kyle Gell
Director of Production: Donna Brown	Cover illustration by Kathryn Adams
Production Editor: Rebecca Conolly	Text layout: IBEX Graphic Communications
Copy Editor: Susan Broadhurst	Special Help: Susan Johnson

Special Sales

Contents

List of Maps

Acknowledgments

Many thanks to my expert researchers: Laura, Emily, Alexandria, Kathleen, and Danielle Crump for their companionship, advice, and ideas and for making this project fun. My deepest gratitude to my husband, Alex Crump, for holding everything together while we conducted this research.

Thank you to the many family and friends who contributed to this book, especially to Terry and Linda Burke who were always there when I needed them and to Donna Lavoie who always asked. And a very special thank you to Ann Douglas for her generous support and advice.

To my editor, Jennifer Lambert, thank you for granting me this opportunity and for the calm and steady guidance you provided throughout this project. Thanks also to Marcia Miron for her top-notch editorial efforts that brought us down the home stretch.

Finally, I want to thank media relations staffs at Tourism Toronto, Toronto City Hall, the Royal Ontario Museum, Canada's Wonderland, the Toronto Zoo, and the Children's Own Museum, who shared their insight and knowledge of Toronto with me.

—Jennifer Crump

An Invitation to the Reader

In researching this book, we discovered many wonderful places—hotels, restaurants, shops, and more. We're sure you'll find other. Please tell us about them, so we can share the information with your fellow travelers in upcoming editions. If you were disappointed with a recommendation, we'd love to know that too. Please write to:

Frommer's with Kids Toronto, 1st Edition
CDG Books Canada • 99 Yorkville Avenue, Suite 400 • Toronto, ON M5R 3K5

An Additional Note

Please be advised that travel information is subject to change at any time—and this is especially true of prices. We therefore suggest that you write or call ahead for confirmation when making your travel plans. The authors, editors, and publishers cannot be held responsible for the experiences of readers while traveling. Your safety is important to us, however, so we encourage you to stay alert and be aware of your surroundings. Keep a close eye on cameras, purses, and wallets, all favorite targets of thieves and pickpockets.

New! Frommer's Star Ratings & Icons

Every hotel, restaurant, and attraction listing in this guide has been ranked for quality, value, service, amenities, and special features using a star-rating scale. In country, state and regional guides, we also rate towns and regions to help you narrow down your choices and budget your time accordingly. Hotels and restaurants in the Very Expensive and Expensive categories are rated one star (highly recommended) to three stars (exceptional). Those in the Moderate and Inexpensive categories rate from zero (recommended) to two stars (very highly recommended). Attractions, towns, and regions are rated according to the following scale: zero stars (recommended), one star (highly recommended), two stars (very highly recommended), and three stars (must-see).

In addtion to the rating system, we also use seven icons to highlight insider information, useful tips, special bargains, hidden gems, memorable experiences, kid-friendly venues, places to avoid, and other useful information:

Finds *Fun Fact* *Kids* *Moments* *Overrated* *Tips* *Value*

The following abbreviations are used for credit cards:

AE	American Express	DISC	Discover	V	Visa
DC	Diners Club	MC	MasterCard		

FROMMERS.COM

Now that you have the guidebook to a great trip, visit our website at **www.frommers.com** for travel information on nearly 2,000 destinations. With features updated regularly, we give you instant access to the most current trip-planning information available. At Frommers.com, you'll also find the best prices on air fares, accommodations, and car rentals—you can even book travel online through our travel booking partners. At Frommers.com you'll find the following:

- Daily Newsletter highlighting the best travel deals
- Hot Spot of the Month/Vacation Sweepstakes & Travel Photo Contest
- More than 200 Travel Message Boards
- Outspoken Newsletters and Feature Articles on travel bargains, vacation ideas, tips & resources, and more!

Introducing Toronto for Families

Toronto is a city for everyone. It is a place where schoolchildren from across Ontario come for field trips, parents travel to enjoy a night of theater, and teenagers and university students gather to catch a concert and pick up some vintage or designer duds. This multifaceted city, with its rich mix of cultures, demands endless exploration.

It wasn't until I had children, though, that I came to appreciate all the city has to offer. I knew that Toronto had fabulous restaurants and was a stop on every major concert and theatrical tour, but I didn't know just how many of those restaurants welcomed children and how many of those theatrical productions were aimed at kids. I thought the city was attractive, but I didn't realize how much room there was to run in the city's many parks and how many ponds, trails, and playgrounds were tucked into those green havens. And now that I have five girls under 10, I've learned how much Toronto has to offer and just how much fun it can be for families.

Toronto is a city of extremes in a sense. Here, you can explore the wonders of a nature trail and, later the same day, climb the world's tallest freestanding building. The city hosts world-class stage productions but also supports a vibrant independent theater scene. Top-rated restaurants line up alongside popular greasy spoons.

I can't think of a better way to explore Toronto than with a child, or five, in tow. Simply looking at the city through a child's eyes can be a wonderful experience— daily chores like riding the subway suddenly become an adventure. You may feel inspired yourself as you watch your kids develop a newfound appreciation for classical music, ballet, or opera at one of the many performances for children held in the city. They'll show you their artistic side while making crafts at Harbourfront, or give you a whole new appreciation for van Gogh at the Art Gallery of Ontario. I've written this book for families with tweens and under. There are certainly activities and attractions for teens too, but my focus is the experience that I've had with my girls as we've both visited and lived in the city.

Toronto has a wealth of activities and attractions that cater to young people— in fact, most of the city's major attractions are either designed for kids or have kid-friendly elements. But don't stick to the obvious activities for children. If you go out for a night on the town, there's no need to avoid the high-end restaurants—many chefs are happy to accommodate the picky palates of small children. Many of Toronto's hotels are also becoming more accommodating when it comes to satisfying their small guests. If you're missing something, chances are the concierge can get it for you. Torontonians in general are wonderfully unflappable when it comes to kids. Nursing moms are barely given a second glance, and nearly everyone waits to let anxious toddlers go ahead.

If you've been planning to introduce your kids to Japanese sushi, Spanish tapas, or Middle Eastern falafels, this is the place to do it. In Toronto, which has one of the most ethnically diverse populations in the world, you can get almost any kind of ethnic cuisine. To show your kids the world's cultures, take a stroll through Kensington Market, where you'll encounter a rich mix of languages and exotic fruits and spices, strange-looking sea creatures, and colorful clothing. You can delve further into Toronto's rich cultural heritage by touring the various ethnic neighborhoods. It's like taking a world tour without the expense—and you can do it in much less than 80 days.

Touring the many historic homes and buildings in the city will give your kids a rich lesson in Canadian history. My kids have a whole new appreciation for modern schools (and teachers) after visiting the Enoch Turner Schoolhouse. And writing with pencils doesn't seem half bad once you've tried writing with a quill and ink at Toronto's first post office.

If you take one of the many sightseeing tours offered in the city, chances are one or more of your fellow tourists will actually be native Torontonians. This is a growing city, one that is constantly changing and adding to its attractions, so that even resident Torontonians are forever discovering something new and exciting about their home.

For residents, it's often hard to decide which of the many festivals, parades, and special events to attend. They are held throughout the year and celebrate everything from Ontario agriculture to St. Patrick's Day to Greek cuisine to Caribbean culture. Something is being celebrated virtually every week in Toronto.

While in the summer and fall Ontario Place, Canada's Wonderland, and Harbourfront entice, in the winter the city boasts romantic outdoor skating rinks complete with bonfires, roasted chestnuts, and vendors selling hot chocolate. The city that spends several months each year knee deep in snow embraces winter and even celebrates it during Winterfest—a family festival of wintry pastimes with entertainment and activities for the kids. For those less entranced by the cold, the 10-kilometer (6 mile) long concourse beneath downtown, known as PATH, allows residents and visitors to work, shop, and access their apartments or hotels without ever having to don a coat.

Many Torontonians flee the city on summer weekends for cottages up north, but the Toronto Islands and the Beaches can offer as much appeal—without the drive. On summer weekends, the city hosts its most child-friendly activities. Crafts and activities, concerts, and dances are held at venues across Toronto on virtually every holiday.

No matter when your family decides to visit the city, take my advice and allow your child to take the lead. There's no better way to experience Toronto.

Just the Stats

- Population of 2.5 million
- Area of 632 square kilometers (244 square miles)
- North America's fourth-largest financial center, with the continent's third-largest stock exchange
- World's third-largest theater center, behind New York and London
- Canada's most popular tourist destination, with 21 million visitors in 1999

- One of Canada's most popular destinations for immigrants, with 80,000 immigrants arriving in 1997 from 169 countries and 51% of the population made up of immigrants
- A rich city of languages, with over 100 languages spoken in Toronto, and one-third of residents speaking a language other than English at home
- Site of North America's longest continuous underground pedestrian system, connecting 1,100 stores and restaurants, 48 office towers, 6 major hotels, and several entertainment venues

1 The Best Toronto Family Experiences

- **The View from the CN Tower:** It is nothing short of magnificent. Arrive on a clear day and you'll be able to see Niagara Falls. If nothing else, the kids will have a blast scaring the daylights out of you as they bounce on the glass floor 1,100 feet above the ground (see chapter 6, p. 91).
- **Skating at Nathan Phillips Square:** Toronto abounds in artificial skating rinks during the winter months, but this one beside City Hall in the heart of downtown is always popular. The trees are strung with lights, and vendors selling snacks and hot chocolate join the skaters rinkside. In the summer, the rink becomes a giant reflecting pool (see chapter 7, p. 132).
- **Cycling on the Toronto Islands:** Toronto families have escaped to the islands since the early part of the 19th century. Today it is still a wonderful refuge from the hectic pace of the city. Cars are not allowed and there are miles of walking and cycling paths leading to the amusement park, beaches, and historic lighthouse. The ferry ride to the islands is a special treat for kids (see chapter 7, p. 125).
- **Wandering through Riverdale Farm:** Meet the pigs, sheep, goats, cows, and horses that call this working replica of a 19th-century farm home. This rural delight is mere minutes from downtown (see chapter 6, p. 114).
- **Playing at the Adventure Playground in High Park:** Besides being an absolutely awesome place to play, this playground is a testament to the hard work of the thousands of volunteers who helped design and build it. The playground has attractions for almost every age group. You can also explore the rest of the park with its gardens, zoo, historic home, and train (see chapter 6, p. 114).
- **Watching the Horse Show at the Royal Agricultural Winter Fair:** There is something especially elegant and fascinating about the Royal Winter Fair that keeps children enthralled year after year. In fact, for many Toronto families visiting the fair is an annual event. My mother remembers going with her parents and I, in turn, went with mine (see chapter 8, p. 143).
- **Hanging Out at Ontario Place:** You'll find as many Torontonians here in the summer as you will visitors to the city. It's a wonderful spot in which to cool off after a long, hot day, and the magnificent rides and games are a huge kid magnet (see chapter 6, p. 96).

- **Shopping at the Eaton Centre:** There are better bargains to be had elsewhere in the city, but you have to visit this gorgeous mall at least once. More than 300 stores and restaurants lure Torontonians and travelers alike, and the spray shooting up from the indoor fountain delights little shoppers. It's also the place for teens to see and be seen (see chapter 9, p. 159).
- **Exploring Harbourfront Centre:** Set against the beautiful backdrop of Toronto Harbour, Harbourfront is a government-owned artistic and cultural center. Here you can rent a canoe, play at one of several playgrounds, eat your lunch on the patio at Lakeside Eats, and prowl the many galleries and shops along the quays (see chapter 6, p. 92).
- **Watching a Sunday Afternoon Ball Game:** Hockey may be Torontonians' game of choice, but there is something about a hot dog, a soft drink, and a Sunday afternoon ball game that all kids love. Sunday is also kids' day at SkyDome (see chapter 8, p. 140).
- **Spending a Rainy Day with the Dinosaurs at the ROM:** Actually, this is a lot of fun on a sunny day too. Amateur paleontologists can dig for bones in the Discovery Centre and then follow the dino prints up the stairs to the dinosaur exhibit. Kids who aren't into dinosaurs can explore the bat cave, check out a real mummy, or explore the night sky (see chapter 6, p. 102).
- **Meeting a Zookeeper at the Toronto Zoo:** The viewing area is almost always full when it's time to watch the elephants take their bath, but kids will also enjoy meeting other animals and their keepers. Many of the zookeepers set aside special times throughout the day to meet with kids (and adults) to talk about their animals. Times are posted at the park entrance (see chapter 6, p. 102).
- **Visiting Kensington Market at 5am:** If you can coax the kids out of bed at this time of the morning, the sights and sounds as the market opens for the day will awaken your senses. Delivery trucks unload wares from every corner of the world, and the merchants pile their stalls high with tropical fruits, fragrant spices, and vivid textiles, bringing a sense of vibrancy to the city (see chapter 6, p. 115).

Toronto Snapshots

Share the history of Toronto with the family as you discover something new around each corner:

1793 British soldiers build a fort at the newly created town of York, a muddy, mosquito-plagued outpost on the edge of the Canadian frontier.

1812 Toronto's population reaches more than 700 and includes farmers as well as a brewer-baker, blacksmith, watchmaker, chair-maker, apothecary, hatter, and tailor. Yonge Street is a 33-mile-long oxcart trail.

1813 Fourteen American warships invade York, blow up the fort, and torch the Parliament buildings.

1834 York is now known as Toronto, and a group of wealthy elites known as the Family Compact controls the city. Members of the Family Compact begin to build many of Toronto's stately mansions.

1837 Toronto is the scene of a violent rebellion in which 700 men, dissatisfied with the city's floundering economy, march on the city. Most of the city's 10,000 citizens stay home while two of the leaders are caught and hung.

1845 Toronto is a cosmopolitan city—steamboats chug along the lake and most of the main streets boast gas lights and sewers.

1872 Toronto is a hive of commercial activity, with large agricultural machinery firms, clothing factories, publishing plants, and metal foundries sprouting up across the city. Eaton's and Simpsons department stores are in business supplying city matrons with their dry goods.

1892 The streets are far cleaner as the last horse-drawn streetcar retires from duty and is replaced by an electric streetcar, heated inside with a coal stove.

1954 Toronto's new subway system runs along Yonge Street from Union Station to Eglinton Avenue.

1975 An influx of immigrants from Asia, Africa, India, Pakistan, the Caribbean, and Latin America enrich the ethnic diversity of Toronto's population.

1998 The six cities that made up Metro Toronto are merged to create the megacity known as Toronto. The city is one of the most ethnically diverse in the world and more immigrants arrive daily. Skyscrapers jostle for room with the 150-year-old St. James Cathedral and the CN Tower.

2001 Toronto launches its bid to host the 2008 Olympics but loses out to Bejing.

2 The Best Hotel Bets for Families

For complete reviews, see chapter 4, "Family-Friendly Accommodations."

- **Best View:** This very much depends on what it is you would like to view. The best view of the city skyline, including the awe-inspiring CN Tower, is from the floor-to-ceiling windows at the **Inn on the Park** (1100 Eglinton Ave. W. ℂ **877/644-4687** or 416/444-2561). The best view of the harbor and Lake Ontario can be had at the **Westin Harbour Castle** (1 Harbour Sq. ℂ **800/ WESTIN-1** or 416/869-1600), where my own children have whiled away the hours watching merchant ships navigate the lake and ferries take people across to the islands.

- **Best Pool:** Without a doubt the best pool for families in Toronto is the **Sheraton Centre Toronto's** gigantic indoor/outdoor extravaganza, at 123 Queen St. W. (ℂ **800/325-3535** or 416/361-1000). The deep end of the pool is located outside and is open year-round. My eldest girls were thrilled to be able to swim outside while huge snowflakes fell around them. The pool also boasts a huge complement of pool toys, from life jackets to noodles.

- **Most Family Friendly:** The **Delta Chelsea** (33 Gerrard St. W. ℂ **800/268-1133** or 416/595-1975) provides everything from a great activity room to a family pool (they have another pool on the top floor for guests traveling without kids). They also provide a vast array of accommodations to suit just about any family, including suites with two double beds and a pullout queen-size sofa bed. Kids feel right at home here.

The staff at some of the more elegant hotels can sometimes make families feel uncomfortable, especially when the kids are on holiday and are more excitable than usual. However, at the **Four Seasons Hotel** (21 Avenue Rd. ℂ **800/268-6282** or 416/9640411) everyone from the valet to the housekeeping staff pays special attention to the tiniest guests. Even the formal, fur-capped valet will stop to ask the kids about their day.

- **Best Hotel Restaurant for Kids:** The **Studio Cafe** at the **Four Seasons Hotel** (21 Avenue Rd. ℂ **800/268-6282** or 416/964-0411), despite its reputation as the place where the business crowd does lunch, welcomes kids with open arms. A children's menu is provided, and the chef will also prepare just about anything your son or daughter is looking for. The **Market Garden** at the **Delta Chelsea** (33 Gerrard St. W. ℂ **800/268-1133** or 416/595-1975) also boasts a great kids' menu, which includes a pasta of the day. For kids who prefer their pasta from a can, they'll serve that, too. The restaurant is self serve, with chefs cooking a variety of dishes at separate stations. During the summer, the courtyard is open and kids can spend their time watching the fountain or chasing the pigeons that occasionally find their way here. Kids under 6 eat for free, and kids aged 6 to 12 eat for half price when staying at the hotel.

- **Best Room Service for Kids:** From pizza to haute cuisine, the **Fairmont Royal York** (100 Front St. W. ℂ **800/441-1414** or 416/368-2511) can supply your kids' every whim, 24 hours a day.

- **Tops for Teens:** Shopping teens might prefer the **Toronto Marriot Eaton Centre** (525 Bay St. ℂ **800/228-9290** or 416/597-9200) for its connection to Toronto's shopping mecca, the Eaton Centre, or the **Four Seasons Hotel** (21 Avenue Rd. ℂ **800/268-6282** or 416/964-0411), for its location in the expensive and fashionable Yorkville shopping area. For teens who prefer sports to shopping, the **Renaissance Toronto Hotel at SkyDome** (1 Blue Jays Way ℂ **800/228-9290** or 416/341-7100) is the place to be. Over 70 of its rooms overlook the baseball field where the Toronto Blue Jays play.

- **Tops for Toddlers:** The **Delta Chelsea** (33 Gerrard St. W. ℂ **800/268-1133** or 416/595-1975) is a good bet, with its thoughtful array of amenities for families with young children, including free use of strollers and an activity center. The **Four Seasons Hotel** (21 Avenue Rd. ℂ **800/268-6282** or 416/964-0411) also scores big: If you arrive with only your toddler, staff will supply you with everything from baby wipes to humidifiers.

- **If Price Is No Object:** My children were impressed by the **Four Seasons Hotel** (21 Avenue Rd. ℂ **800/268-6282** or 416/964-0411) when they entered our suite and discovered china plates of white chocolate teddy bears and cookies with their names written in chocolate. And they were completely won over by the child-sized bathrobes. The staff at this hotel, including the restaurant servers, will cheerfully get you anything you or your child may require.

- **When Price Is Your Main Object:** The **Strathcona Hotel** (60 York St. ✆ 416/363-3321) offers few frills but exceptionally good prices—right in the middle of downtown. If you would prefer to spend your money on sightseeing and souvenirs, **Victoria University residence** (140 Charles St. W. ✆ 416/585-4524) offers clean, comfortable budget accommodations in the summer months.

3 The Best Dining Bets for Families

For full reviews, see chapter 5, "Family-Friendly Dining."

- **Best Children's Menu:** As a break from the standard children's menu fare of burgers, chicken fingers, and french fries, the **Boulevard Café**, at 161 Harbord St. (✆ 416/961-7676), provides kids with an astounding choice of 10 items, primarily Peruvian dishes. **The Fish House** (144 Front St. W. ✆ 416/595-5051) offers kids an array of seafood choices.
- **Best Dress-Up Dining:** Kids love to dress up and it's fun to take them somewhere elegant at least once during a vacation. **Le Papillon** (16 Church St. ✆ 416/363-0838) is both upscale and family oriented. This Quebecois restaurant supplies kids with a downsized version of the adult menu, and what kid doesn't love crepes?
- **Best Outdoor Eating:** Dining outside is one Toronto experience that shouldn't be missed. The **Safari Bar and Grill** (1749 Avenue Rd. ✆ 416/787-6584) has one of the best and most popular patios in the city. **Wayne Gretzky's** (99 Blue Jays Way ✆ 416/979-PUCK) has a cool tropical-themed patio that boasts its own waterfall.
- **Best for People Watching: Peter Pan** (373 Queen St. W. ✆ 416/593-0917) is a popular Queen Street West restaurant. If you sit near the front windows you can watch the strange mix of folks who flock to the area, and if you're lucky one of the many Hollywood stars who frequent this eatery will drop in for a quick bite.
- **Best Ice Cream:** Near trendy Yorkville, **Greg's Ice Cream** (200 Bloor St. W. ✆ 416/961-4734) has some cool designer flavors, but if you want to try something a little different, buy a granita at the **Sicilian Ice Cream Company** (712 College St. ✆ 416/531-7716).
- **Best Chinese: Happy Seven** (358 Spadina Ave. ✆ 416/971-9820) offers both a North American–style and a more traditional menu for the adventurous spirits in your family.
- **Best Italian:** For the best upscale Italian cuisine, **Grano** (2035 Yonge St. ✆ 416/440-1986) is the hands-down winner, but the **Old Spaghetti Factory** (54 The Esplanade ✆ 416/864-9761) is a big hit with kids. Seating is provided in a real streetcar, and the menu offers an extensive selection of familiar Italian dishes.
- **Best Burgers:** The singing staff at **Lick's** (1960 Queen St. E. ✆ 416/362-5425) serves great takeout and sit-down burgers. **Wayne Gretzky's** (99 Blue Jays Way ✆ 416/979-PUCK) serves delicious charbroiled burgers with the number 99 seared into the buns.
- **Most Kid-Friendly:** Many of Toronto's restaurants are kid-

friendly, but **Fran's Diner** boasts a staff that actually seems to enjoy small guests—they even hang the kids' artwork on the walls. The diner has three convenient locations: 21 St. Clair Ave. W. (© **416/925-6337**); 45 Eglinton Ave. E. (© **416/481-1112**); and 20 College St. (© **416/923-9867**). The staff at the **Il Fornello** (576 Danforth Ave. © **416/466-2931**) in Greektown have won awards for being the most kid-friendly restaurant in the city.

- **Best Picnic Fare:** You can stock your picnic basket at any downtown deli. **Shopsy's** (33 Yonge St. © **416/365-3333**) and **Druxy's Deli** (1 Eglinton Ave. E. © **416/481-5363**) are both good choices.
- **Best Entertainment While You Dine:** The **Rainforest Cafe** (3401 Dufferin St., in Yorkdale Shopping Centre © **416/780-4080**) with its animated elephants, simulated thunderstorms, and fish tank archway provides the kids with lots to look at while they wait for dinner; the only problem is they won't want to leave. The same can be said for **Shopsy's TV Deli** (248 King St. W. © **416/599-5464**), where PlayStations are available at every table and 40-odd TVs blare overhead.
- **Best Retro Diners: Flo's Diner** (70 Yorkville Ave. © **416/961-4333**) is a homey retro diner with the best milkshakes in the city. It sits above the street by way of winding outdoor stairs. **Mars Restaurant** (432 College St. © **416/921-6332**) hasn't changed much since it opened in the 1950s, and the comfort food it serves up is just as wonderful today as it was back then.
- **Best for Fussy Eaters:** At **Marché** in BCE Place (61 Bay St. © **416/366-8986**), you can choose your ingredients and sauces and pile your own plate full of fresh, delicious food. It's the perfect place to bring your finicky eater.

2

Planning Your Family Trip to Toronto

Although my approach to most things in life tends to be fairly laid-back, I admit to voraciously snapping up information and planning like crazy when we are about to embark on a family vacation. In my experience, the key to enjoying a successful trip with your kids is to be ridiculously overprepared and planned down to the last minute. Then you must be ready to toss the entire plan out the window if something else strikes your family's fancy.

However you prefer to travel, you'll want to arrive at your destination with at least a general idea of what you and the kids would like to see and do. This book will provide you with a good glimpse into what Toronto has to offer for various age groups, and the sections below provide a few more sources of information to ensure that your trip to Toronto will be one that creates wonderful, lasting memories for your family.

1 Visitor Information & Entry Requirements

VISITOR INFORMATION

FROM NORTH AMERICA The best source for Toronto-specific information is **Tourism Toronto, Metro Toronto Convention and Visitor's Assocation,** Queens Quay Terminal at Harbourfront, 207 Queens Quay W., Toronto, ON M5J 1A7 (© **800/ 363-1990** from the continental United States, or 416/203-2600; www.tourism-toronto.com). Call before you leave and ask for a free information package, which provides sections on accommodations, sights, and dining. If you can, visit the website, which includes up-to-the-minute events information.

There are several other good websites you can visit to get a feel for the city before you arrive. **Toronto.com** (**www.toronto.com**), owned by the Toronto Star newspaper, has extensive listings of accommodations, dining,

shopping, and entertainment venues in the city. The *Toronto Life* magazine website (**www.torontolife.com**) provides comprehensive restaurant and entertainment listings as well as some fairly thorough city guides. The Frommer's website (www.frommers.com) is also an excellent resource.

For information about Ontario, contact **Tourism Ontario**, P.O. Box 104, Toronto, ON M5B 2H1 (© **800/ONTARIO** or 416/314-0944, or visit the TraveLinx site at www.travel inx.com).

The Canadian consulates in the United States do not provide tourist information. They will refer you to the offices above. Consular offices in Buffalo, Detroit, Los Angeles, New York, Seattle, and Washington, D.C., deal with visas and other political and immigration issues.

> ### ✐ Toronto's Parenting Papers
>
> Toronto's free parenting papers offer families a general feel for what the city has to offer. These helpful planning tools contain calendar listings of all the family-friendly events occurring in the city during the month.
>
> **Today's Parent Toronto**   This paper is included as a free insert in *Today's Parent*, a national parenting magazine. It is also available throughout the city at retail locations and libraries. You can send away for a copy to TPT! 269 Richmond St. W., Toronto, ON M5V 1X1 (✆ **416/596-8680**; www.todaysparent.com).
>
> **City Parent**   Toronto's own parenting magazine is distributed free in libraries, retail outlets, museums, and other places that kids and their parents might go. For information on subscriptions or single copies contact *City Parent*, 467 Speers Rd., Oakville, ON L6K 3S4 (✆ **905/815-0017**; www.cityparent.com).

FROM ABROAD   The following consulates can provide information or refer you to the appropriate offices:

- **U.K. and Ireland:** The **Canadian High Commission,** MacDonald House, 1 Grosvenor Sq., London W1X 0AB (✆ **0171/6273-3844;** fax 0171/728-6384).
- **Australia:** The **Canadian High Commission,** Commonwealth Avenue, Canberra, ACT 2600 (✆ **02/9364-3000**), or The **Consulate-General of Canada,** Level 5, Quay West Building, 111 Harrington St., Sydney, NSW 2000 (✆ **02/9364-3000**). The consulate-general also has offices in Melbourne and Perth.
- **New Zealand:** The **Canadian High Commission,** 3rd floor, 61 Molesworth St., Thomdon, Wellington (✆ **04/473-9577**), or the **Consulate of Canada,** Level 9 Jetset Centre, 44–48 Emily Place, Aukland (✆ **09/309-3690**).
- **South Africa:** The **Canadian High Commission,** 1103 Arcadia St., Hatfield 0083, Pretoria (✆ **012/342-6923**).

ENTRY REQUIREMENTS

DOCUMENTS   U.S. citizens and legal residents do not need passports or visas to enter Canada, but must show proof of citizenship (birth or voter registration certificate, naturalization certificates, or green card). Every person under 19 years of age is required to produce a letter from a parent or guardian granting permission to travel to Canada. The letter must state the traveler's name and the duration of the trip. It is essential for teenagers to carry proof of citizenship—otherwise, their letters are useless at the border.

Citizens of Australia, New Zealand, the United Kingdom, and Ireland must have valid passports. Citizens of many other countries need visas, which must be applied for in advance at the local Canadian embassy or consulate. For more detailed information, call your local Canadian consulate or embassy.

CUSTOMS   Most customs regulations are generous, but they get complicated when it comes to firearms, plants, meat, and pets. Fishing tackle poses no problem (provided the lures are not made of restricted materials—

specific feathers, for example), but the bearer must possess a nonresident license for the province or territory in which he or she plans to use it. You can bring in free of duty up to 50 cigars, 200 cigarettes, and 2 pounds of tobacco, provided you are at least 18 years of age. You are also allowed 40 ounces (1.14ml) of liquor or wine as long as you're of legal drinking age in the province you're visiting (19 in Ontario). There are no restrictions on what you can bring out, except, of course, those imposed by your country of origin.

For information about customs regulations, write to the **Canadian Customs and Revenue Agency** (formerly Revenue Canada) at 875 Heron Rd., Ottawa, ON K1A 0L8, or check out their website at www.ccra-adrc.gc.ca.

2 Money

Canadians use **dollars** and **cents,** but with a distinct advantage for U.S. visitors—the Canadian dollar has been consistently fluctuating between 65¢ and 68¢ in U.S. money, meaning that your American money will get you 32% more when you exchange it for local currency. This can make a great difference to your budget. The cost of goods in Canada is roughly on par with prices in the United States so the savings are real, not imaginary. Sales taxes are higher in Canada, although you should be able to recoup at least part of what you pay out in sales tax (see "Taxes" under "Fast Facts" in chapter 3, p. 43).

What Things Cost in Toronto	C $	U.S. $
Taxi from the airport to downtown	33.00	22.00
Express bus from the airport to downtown	12.00	7.90
Local telephone call	0.25	0.16
Double at the Four Seasons (expensive)	350.00	231.90
Double at the Delta Chelsea (moderate)	135.50	89.45
Hot dog and soda (from a street vendor)	3.00	2.00
McDonald's Happy Meal with Chicken McNuggets	4.25	2.80
Child's lunch at Druxy's Deli	5.90	3.95
Child's lunch at Le Papillon	9.95	6.60
Can of Coca-Cola	1.25	0.83
Package of Pampers	10.50	6.95
Package of no-name diapers	7.95	5.25
Can of ready-to-serve Enfalac formula	2.50	1.65
Roll of ASA 100 Kodacolor film, 36 exposures	8.00	5.28
Admission to Children's Own Museum (adults and children)	4.75	3.15
Admission to Omnimax Theatre (adults)	10.00	6.60
(children under 17)	6.00	3.95
Play-all-day pass to Canada's Wonderland (ages 7–59)	40.00	26.40
(ages 3–6 and 60+)	22.50	14.85
Subway (cash fare) (adult)	2.25	1.50
(child)	0.50	0.33

Paper currency comes in $5, $10, $20, $50, and $100 denominations. (There are $1,000 bills, too, but these are currently being phased out.) Coins come in 1-, 5-, 10-, and 25-cent and 1- and 2-dollar denominations (the Canadian government is considering introducing a $5 coin as well, possibly in 2002). The gold-colored $1 coin is a "loonie" (it sports a loon on one side), and the slightly larger gold- and silver-colored $2 coin is a "toonie." These nicknames are commonplace; Canadians seldom refer to the coins as $1 or $2 coins.

You can bring in or take out any amount of money, but if you are importing or exporting $5,000 or more, you must file a report of the transaction with Canada Customs. Most tourist establishments in Canada will accept U.S. cash, but the exchange rate is rarely a good one. To get the best rate, withdraw your cash from a Canadian ATM (most are hooked up to the Cirrus or Plus system) or exchange your funds into Canadian currency upon arrival. MasterCard and Visa are accepted almost everywhere, but be forewarned: Some companies are starting to impose a foreign-exchange fee for out-of-country transactions. Be sure to check with your credit card company first so you won't get any nasty surprises on your bill when you return home.

If you do decide to use American money while in Toronto, you should know how the conversion is calculated. Many times, especially in downtown Toronto, there will be a sign at a cash register that reads "U.S. CURRENCY 60%." This 60% is the "premium," which means that for every U.S. dollar you hand over, you get $1.60 Canadian. For example, to pay a C$15 tab you need only $9 in U.S. currency.

The Canadian Dollar, the U.S. Dollar & the British Pound

The prices cited in this guide are given in both Canadian and U.S. dollars. Note that the Canadian dollar is worth 30% less than the U.S. dollar, but buys nearly as much. As we go to press, C$1 is worth US66¢, which means that your C$200-a-night hotel room will cost only US$168 and your C$8 breakfast only US$5.

Here's a table of equivalents:

C $	U.S. $	UK £	U.S. $	C $	UK £
1	0.66	0.48	1	1.51	0.73
5	3.30	2.40	5	7.58	3.65
10	6.60	4.80	10	15.15	7.30
20	13.20	9.60	20	30.30	14.60
50	33.00	24.00	50	75.75	36.50
80	52.80	36.00	80	121.21	58.40
100	66.00	48.00	100	151.52	73.00

It used to be that you were well advised to purchase traveler's checks and carry a bit of extra cash ($200). Now that **ATMs** are almost everywhere—and often deliver a better exchange rate—I suggest you obtain money from them. Do try to limit your transactions because you will pay a fee for each ATM withdrawal. You can find ATMs at most banks. For the location of the nearest ATM that is connected to the **Cirrus** network, dial ℭ 800/424-7787 (a global access number); for Plus call ℭ **800/843-7587**

(U.S. only). On the Web, try **www. visa.com** or **www.mastercard.com** for the location of the nearest Plus ATM. Most ATMs will make cash advances against your Visa or MasterCard, but make sure you have your personal identification number with you.

For those who prefer the extra security of **traveler's checks**, almost all hotels, restaurants, shops, and attractions will accept U.S. dollar traveler's checks. Traveler's checks can be exchanged for cash at banks, and you'll most likely get a better exchange rate this way. As in the United States, most small businesses will not cash traveler's checks in denominations greater than $50.

American Express (© 888/269-6669 in the U.S. and Canada) is the most widely recognized traveler's check; depending on where you purchase them, expect to pay a 1% to 4% commission. Checks are free to members of the **American Automobile Association (AAA)**.

Citicorp (© 800/645-6556 in the U.S., or 813/623-1709 collect in Canada) issues checks in U.S. dollars or British pounds.

MasterCard International (© 800/223-9920 in the U.S.) issues checks in about a dozen currencies.

Thomas Cook (© 800/223-7373 in the U.S.) issues checks in a variety of currencies.

3 When to Go

THE CLIMATE

Spring runs from late March to mid-May (though occasionally there's snow in mid-April); **summer,** mid-May to mid-September; **fall,** mid-September to mid-November; **winter,** mid-November to late March. The highest recorded temperature is 40.5°C (105°F); the lowest, –33°C (–27°F). The average date of the first frost is October 29; the average date of last frost is April 20.

Toronto's Average Temperatures

		Jan	Feb	Mar	Apr	May	June	July	Aug	Sept	Oct	Nov	Dec
High	(°F)	30	31	39	53	64	75	80	79	71	59	46	34
	(°C)	–5	–4	4	12	18	24	26	26	22	15	8	1
Low	(°F)	18	19	27	38	48	57	62	61	54	45	35	23
	(°C)	–13	–7	–3	3	9	14	17	16	12	7	2	–5

HOLIDAYS

A wealth of activities and events for kids are normally scheduled during spring break (mid-March), the summer holidays, and Christmas, and, of course, on weekends throughout the year. Hotels often offer package deals during these times and extend their pool and playroom hours. Some hotels even plan special events around U.S. holidays—inquire about these when you book.

Toronto celebrates the following holidays: New Year's Day (January 1), Good Friday and/or Easter Sunday (March or April), Victoria Day (Mon-day following the third weekend in May), Canada Day (July 1), Civic Holiday (first Monday in August), Labour Day (first Monday in September), Thanksgiving (second Monday in October), Remembrance Day (November 11), Christmas Day (December 25), and Boxing Day (December 26). On these days, schools, banks, government offices, and most corporations are closed, and public transit may operate on holiday schedules. Only banks and government offices close on Remembrance Day (November 11).

KIDS' CALENDAR OF EVENTS

Parades, celebrations, and festivals are held in Toronto throughout the year, and most include something for the kids. Many are geared specifically toward families.

In a city in which almost 50% of the population was born in another country, you can expect some awe-inspiring ethnic festivals, and indeed these are among the best of the Toronto event circuit. But there are also kid-centered celebrations of reading, film, and dance that shouldn't be missed. If you can arrange to be in town during any of the following events, I recommend you try to sample at least a few.

February

Chinese New Year Celebrations. This festival is a great way to introduce the kids to traditional and contemporary Chinese culture. Performances include Chinese opera, dancing, and music and, of course, the kids' favorite—Chinese dragons. For Harbourfront information call ℂ **416/973-3000;** for Sky-Dome call ℂ **416/666-3838.** In 2002, the Chinese New Year starts on February 12.

Winterfest. Held simultaneously at Nathan Phillips Square (downtown), the corner of Yonge Street and Eglinton Avenue (midtown), and Mel Lastman Square (North York), this is a 3-day family-centered celebration of all things winter. The fun includes ice-skating shows, snow play, midway rides, and performances by some wonderful musicians. YTV, a youth television channel, usually hosts a special gathering for kids during Winterfest. Don't miss it. For information call ℂ **416/338-0338.** Usually around Valentine's Day. Free.

Toronto Festival of Storytelling. All kids like stories and these are some of the very best tales told by first-rate storytellers. This family-friendly festival at Harbourfront celebrates international folklore and features over 60 storytellers from around the world telling their legends and fables to rapt audiences. For information call ℂ **416/973-3000.** Last weekend of February.

March

Spring Break. Events across the city celebrate the kids' release from school for a week. Harbourfront, the Children's Own Museum, and the Art Gallery of Ontario are just a few of the venues offering special entertainment and craft sessions. Hotels tend to put on special deals and open up more of their services as well. Check out the kids' page at **www.toronto.com** for information on what's happening in the city during the week. Mid-March.

St. Patrick's Day Parade. This parade celebrates Irish culture and is a thrill even for those not old enough to drink green beer. It is always a delight for youngsters, and the leprechauns and talking shamrocks are a hoot. For information call ℂ **416/487-1566.** March 17. Free.

April

Sprockets International Children's Film Festival. This is a top-notch international film festival with a twist—it's specifically for children and features the best in children's films from around the world. Most of the programming has subtitles, and some interesting workshops and post-theater chats are offered. Cineplex Odeon Varsity Cinemas in the Manulife Centre, 55 Bloor Street W. For information call ℂ **416/967-7371.**

May

Festive Earth Spring Fair. This festival is dedicated to all things green. Highlights for the kids include hands-on discovery programs, music and storytelling performances, and a traditional maypole dance. The festival also includes a "green" marketplace, an arts and crafts sale, and an organic eatery. Riverdale Park East. Call © **416/469-2977** for details. Early May.

Milk International Children's Festival. This 9-day festival of the arts at Harbourfront, is Toronto's premier celebration for kids. Featured performances include live theatre, music and dance, comedy acts, and storytelling. For information call © **416/504-3977.** Usually begins mid-May.

Canadian Children's Reading Festival. This salute to the wonderful world of Canadian children's literature features readings, book signings, interactive exhibits, and a literary marketplace all at Ontario Place. Call © **866/663-4386** or 416/314-9900. Late May. Free with the cost of admission to Ontario Place.

June

The Toronto Lion Dance Festival. This is a wonderful celebration of Asian cultures, art, and mythology. The weeklong event includes thrilling lion and dragon dances, martial arts demonstrations, and other musical and dance performances. The "Lion Park," an interactive kids' area, includes face-painting booths, a bouncing tent, and more. For information call © **416/392-0335** or visit the website at www.liondancefest.com. Early June.

Toronto International Dragon Boat Race Festival. In this 2-day event, 200 teams from Canada, the United States, Europe, and Asia compete in over 100 dragon boat

---

ⓒ Canada Day Celebrations

Canada was granted independence from Great Britain on July 1, 1867, and the anniversary is commemorated in a wealth of events across the city. Toronto Tourism (© **800/363-1990**) can provide a complete listing of events and locations, but here are a few to get you started:

Canada Day at Queen's Park. Held at the site of the Ontario legislature, this is the premier celebration of Canada Day in Toronto and is centered around kids. Clowns, musicians, dancers, and games are part of the fun, and there is even a giant birthday cake! Be warned, though, that it can get busy—upwards of 25,000 people attend this event each year. Call © **416/314-7526** for information. Free.

Fort York Festival, Historic Fort York and Harbourfront. Revisit 1812 with this reenactment of the invasion of the Americans and the Battle of York. Puppets, jesters, duels, music, and country dancing help the kids get a real feel for life in the 1800s at this weekend-long festival. Call © **416/392-6907** for details.

Toronto Harbour Parade of Lights, Harbourfront. One hundred boats are decorated with flags and lights and paraded across the harbor to compete for more than C$40,000 (US$26,400) in prize money, which is donated to the boat owner's charity of choice. This evening parade is the highlight of what has now become a 5-day harbor event. Call © **416/941-1041,** ext. 234, for details. Free.

races. More than 30 multicultural performances are also part of the fun. All on Centre Island. Call © 416/598-8945 for information. Third weekend in June. Free.

Toronto International Festival Caravan. Take a trip around the world in just 9 days. Stroll 40 international "cities," featuring replicas of castles, markets, and village squares, at venues across Toronto. Kids can enjoy over 200 awesome stage shows and collect stamps on their passports at each "city" they visit. Call © 416/ 977-0466 or 416/977-0494 for tickets and event information. Late June.

Chin Picnic International. This event is billed as the largest free picnic in the world. And it is huge. Over 2,000 performers from around the world dance, sing, and tell stories to 250,000-plus visitors during this weekend-long celebration. Kids will especially enjoy the lumberjack shows and the kids' zone, which features a circus, a petting zoo, midway rides, and plenty of other kid-enticing entertainment. All at Exhibition Place. Call © 416/531-9991, ext. 3900. Last weekend in June/first weekend in July. Free.

July

Celebrate Toronto Street Festival. Four sites and multiple stages up and down Yonge Street present jazz, hip-hop, rock, and children's musicians. Stilt-walkers, jugglers, and fire-eaters seem to be on every street corner thrilling kids and other passersby, and a small midway adds to the festivities. Call © 416/395-0247. First full weekend in July. Free.

The Fringe: Toronto's Theatre Festival. This major summer theater event features close to 100 companies from around the world performing in 8 venues around the city. Some of the main-stage presentations are family-friendly, and the Fringe has recently added KidVenue to the offerings, with prices that parents will appreciate. KidVenue presents 8 children's theater productions, including comedy, musicals, and dance. Call © 416/966-1062 or visit www.fringetoronto.com for tickets and information. Mid to late July.

Beaches International Jazz Festival. All kids love live bands and lively crowds, and this festival has both. Combine great music with the kid-friendly, laid-back Beaches attitude and you have the makings of a perfect family day. Over 100 bands play on the main stage, street corners, balconies, and rooftops around the Beaches area. Call © 416/698-2152 or go to www.beachesjazz.com for details. Late July. Free.

Caribana. This 2-week celebration of the Caribbean definitely qualifies as Toronto's most colorful event. Presentations of arts and crafts, music, dance, food, and fashion culminate in the magnificent Caribana parade. A separate Caribana Jr. parade is also part of the fun and features hundreds of young participants in equally colorful and fantastic costumes. Call © 416/ 465-4884 for dates and details. Late July to early August.

August

Canadian National Exhibition. This is a national fair with international flair. The horse and dog shows, circuses, and band performances are favorites with kids, but it's the midway that really thrills them. There is also a smaller, tyke-sized midway and Kids World, featuring kid-friendly exhibitions and shows, as well as Kidstreet, an interactive playground. Call ☎ **877/676-7466** or visit the website (www.theex. com). Late August/early September.

September

City Parent Family Show. This weekend show offers a chance for companies and organizations to highlight their products and services for children. Kids will love the clowns and magicians and will leave with some great loot bags. This event draws many large international companies, as well as local retailers. Metro Toronto Convention Centre. Call ☎ **905/815-0017**. Early September.

Cabbagetown Festival. Billing itself as a small town in the heart of the city, Cabbagetown's annual festival is about as down-home as one can get in Toronto. This is where you'll find pancake breakfasts, corn roasts, square dancing, and street dances, all of which appeal to the kids. Call ☎ **416/921-0857** or visit www.oldcabbagetown.com. First week in September.

Word on the Street and KidStreet. The organizers' objective is to bring authors, publishers, and readers together, and they do so in amazing style. Over 250 booths are set up along Queen Street West, with stages featuring readings, music, and other entertainment. KidStreet is the family venue at the event and features children's publishers and kid-centric entertainment, including readings by top children's authors, musicians, puppeteers, and other fun stuff. There are plenty of giveaways as well. Call ☎ **416/504-7241** for information. Late September. Free.

October

International Festival of Authors. This is the largest literary festival in the world. Usually several children's authors are featured among the more than 100 authors who attend for readings, book signings, interviews, and awards. For details call ☎ **416/973-3000**; for tickets call ☎ **416/973-4000**. Third weekend in October.

Toronto Maple Leafs Opening Night. Toronto loves hockey, so it can be difficult to get tickets to this event. At the Leaf's home ice at the Air Canada Centre. For information call ☎ **416/216-1700**; for tickets call ☎ **416/872-5000**. Mid-October.

November

Royal Agricultural Winter Fair and Royal Horse Show. Held over 12 days at Exhibition Place, this is the largest indoor agricultural and equestrian competition in the world. Kids get a kick out of the gigantic veggies and fruits and the livestock displays. Educational booths for the kids are set up throughout the fair, and a petting zoo is also part of the fun. Call ☎ **416/393-6400** for more information. Mid-November.

Santa Claus Parade. Held early so that little ones have plenty of time to jot down their wish lists, this parade has been a favorite with kids since 1905. Besides the cool animated floats, the parade features clowns, marching bands, and, of course, Santa himself. Call ☎ **416/249-7833**. Third Sunday in November. Free.

Cavalcade of Lights. During this holiday celebration, the trees in and around Nathan Phillips Square at City Hall are lit up. You'll find everything to put your family in the holiday spirit, including ice skating, performances, and holiday music. Late November through December 31. Free.

December

First Night Toronto. First Night is a family-friendly, alcohol-free approach to ringing in the New Year. A C$8 (US$5.30) button admits you to a variety of musical, theatrical, and dance performances around the city. Concerts begin at 10pm. December 31.

4 What to Pack

Lake Ontario has a strong effect on the city, cooling it on summer evenings and warming it in the winter. The windblasts that occasionally whip through the downtown streets mean you should pack light jackets or sweaters for the kids (and yourself) for summer evenings.

On the other hand, during the summer high humidity levels can leave you and the kids wilting, and the city is subject to frequent heat waves. Dress everyone in lightweight, light-colored clothing and bring plenty of sunblock, especially if you're planning to visit any of the outdoor attractions, such as Ontario Place or the Toronto Zoo. Sunglasses, hats, and, of course, bathing suits are a must. I would also suggest you pack lots of comfortable tees and shorts, as well as at least one pair of long pants in case you encounter a cooler-than-normal evening. Most restaurants do not have dress codes, but if you plan to attend any of the big-venue theater events you will probably want at least one dressy outfit each for you and the kids.

Comfortable shoes are a necessity if you plan to see much of the city. Sneakers are a comfy choice for everyone, and definitely make the kids wear socks. It can be tough on small feet to slog around in sandals all day. You will probably be walking for a significant amount of the time, so strollers are a good idea, even for toddlers who are used to walking alone. They will tire eventually and strollers (as well as the cords that fasten to your wrist and your child's) are also the best way of keeping hold of your child on busy streets and the subway. The best strollers for travel-ing are the umbrella type, which fold easily and take up very little room.

In the winter, the weather can range from cool and refreshing to downright harsh. Although the downtown buildings tend to warm the air, the wind can quickly cool it down. Hats, mitts, warm coats, and leggings will keep the chill off. Occasionally the city will be hit by a big snowstorm and snow will cover the streets and sidewalks, but walking areas are usually wet and slushy rather than snow-covered. Definitely pack some comfortable, preferably waterproof walking boots.

If you have an infant or toddler, call ahead to your hotel to see what they can provide. Normally they will be able to outfit you with a crib, and some may supply a bath seat or highchair for your room. For baby's safety, you may wish to bring along a few electrical outlet covers. You can buy all the usual baby stuff in Toronto, but you'll save yourself a trip to the store by packing your own supply of baby wipes, diapers, formula, and bottles.

I also strongly suggest you bring along a small backpack with a change of clothing for your infant or toddler for the inevitable spills and accidents. You may want to top the bag up with a few small toys. Older kids can carry backpacks on their own with a supply of art materials, a favorite book, and their CD player or Game Boy to keep them occupied while traveling. You may want to discourage them from carrying their backpacks around the city, though, lest you end up trying to juggle several of them by yourself when they tire of carrying them.

5 Health & Safety

TRAVEL INSURANCE

Before you decide to purchase **travel insurance,** check your existing policies to see whether they'll cover you while you're traveling. Also ask your **health insurance** company whether your coverage extends to Canada. Some credit cards offer automatic **flight insurance** when you buy an airline ticket with the card. These policies provide insurance coverage for death or dismemberment in the event of a plane crash.

If you plan to rent a car, check your credit cards to see if any of them pick up the **collision damage waiver** (CDW) in Canada. The CDW can run as much as C$16 (US$10.55) a day and add as much as 50% to the cost of renting a car. Check your automobile insurance policy too; it might cover the CDW. If you own a home or have renter's insurance, see if that policy covers off-premises theft and loss while traveling. Find out what procedures you need to follow to make a claim. If you're traveling on a tour or package deal and have prepaid a large chunk of your travel expenses, you might want to ask a travel agent about buying **trip-cancellation insurance** from an independent agency.

If, after checking all your existing insurance policies, you decide that you need additional insurance, a good travel agent can give you information on a variety of options. Or, contact **Wallach & Company,** 107 W. Federal St., P.O. Box 480, Middleburg, VA 20118 (℡ **800/237-6615** or 540/687-3166). It provides a comprehensive travel policy that covers all contingencies—cancellation, health, emergency assistance, and loss.

HEALTH

If your children require **medication,** I suggest you bring a good supply along with you. Most medications commonly used in the United States and Britain are also approved for use in Canada, but not all are, and you're better off safe than sorry. As a mother of four girls who wear glasses, I also strongly suggest you bring along a spare pair if you have one. Glasses are easily lost or broken during the excitement of a trip. You can, of course, have your eyeglass prescription filled in Toronto, but it is an unnecessary disruption of your tour.

You may also want to pack plenty of children's Tylenol, aspirin, or Advil and your favorite cold medication, although all are readily available at drugstores in the city. The nausea-relieving drug commonly known as Dramamine in the United States and Stugeron in Britain is called Gravol in Canada and is sold without a prescription in pharmacies.

If you have a health **emergency,** Toronto is on the **911** system. The **Hospital for Sick Children** (Sick Kids) is located at 555 University Ave. (℡ **416/813-1500**). Emergency wards in the city, including the one at Sick Kids, tend to be very busy. If your child needs to see a doctor but you would prefer not to wait in the emergency ward, you have several options. You can visit one of the many walk-in clinics located around the city. Sick Kids maintains a list at www.sick kids.on.ca/Emergency/walkinclinic.asp, or call ℡ **416/813-5817.**

For **poison control** information call ℡ **416/813-5900.** The **Toronto Health Connection** (℡ **416/338-7600**) provides information on referrals, counseling, and other health issues.

SAFETY

Safety precautions that need to be taken in Toronto are essentially the same as those that should be followed in most large cities.

IF YOU BECOME SEPARATED Discuss this possibility with your kids ahead of time and have a plan. I'm not suggesting that you pin nametags on your children, but you might consider tucking a hotel address or telephone number into one of their pockets. One other piece of advice: If your kids do become separated from you, ask for help from officials immediately. Don't wait. They are often glad to assist and are as relieved as you are when it turns out that your little one was simply getting a drink from the fountain around the corner. I follow a fairly simple rule with my kids: I have to be able to see them and they have to be able to see me.

ON THE STREETS You'll probably see many Torontonians doing it, despite a recent crackdown, but don't be tempted to jaywalk. It's not worth it. Drivers in the downtown core have enough to worry about keeping track of other vehicles and cyclists without having to watch out for you and your children.

THE SUBWAY Toronto subways are relatively safe, but my kids and I follow a simple rule: The kids stand with me and with their backs to the wall. Keeping the kids away from the tracks keeps me sane.

FIRE Have the kids review the fire escape route posted on the back of the hotel door. On your way to the elevator, help the kids locate the stairs and discuss with them the dos and don'ts of fire safety. Surprisingly enough, most kids actually find this kind of info interesting.

6 Tips for Travelers with Disabilities

Toronto is a fairly accessible city. Curb cuts are well made and common throughout the downtown area; special parking privileges are extended to people with disabilities who have special license plates or a pass. The subway and streetcar trolleys, unfortunately, are not wheelchair accessible, but the city operates a special service for those with disabilities, **Wheel-Trans.** Visitors can register for this service. For information, call © **416/393-4111.**

The **Community Information Centre of Metropolitan Toronto,** 425 Adelaide St. W., Toronto, ON M5V 3C1 (© **416/392-0505**), may be able to provide limited information about social-service organizations in the city. It does not have specific accessibility information on tourism or hotels. It's available weekdays 8am to 10pm, weekends 10am to 10pm.

7 Getting the Kids Interested

The key to a successful family vacation is to involve the kids in every aspect, including planning. Kids are usually research junkies. Give them a few resources and they'll run with them.

The first thing you should do is get out the atlas. Let them find Toronto on the map and point out its relation to other destinations they are more familiar with. Trace the path you'll be taking to reach the city, and note any interesting landmarks you'll see along the way.

Send away for or, better yet, encourage the kids to write for information on the city from Tourism Toronto, Metro Toronto Convention and Visitor's Assocation, Queen's Quay Terminal at Harbourfront, 207 Queens Quay W., Toronto, ON M5J 1A7 (© **800/363-1990**) or from **Tourism Ontario,** P.O. Box 104,

Toronto, ON M5B 2H1 (© **800/ ONTARIO** or 416/314-0944). Also, look over the possible destinations and read the descriptions in this book aloud to your kids. Discuss with them what they would like to see. Check out chapter 6, "What Kids Like to See and Do," for detailed information.

Prime your kids about some of Toronto's famous landmarks: the CN Tower, the harbor, the islands, the skating rink at Nathan Phillips Square. You can find many good picture books on Toronto by browsing the shelves at your local library or bookstore. Or you can try the **Amazon** website (www.amazon.com) and the Canadian online bookseller, **Chapters Online** (www.chapters. indigo.ca).

If you are on the Internet, definitely surf with the kids over to the Toronto Public Library's **KidSpace** (www.tpl .toronto.on.ca/KidSpace/index.htm). The site has links to Web cams and other travel information, biographies of famous Torontonians, Toronto history, and even a few Toronto jokes.

Kids' Books Set in Toronto

Babies and Toddlers
- *Night Cars* by Buddy Jam (Groundwood/Douglas & McIntyre). When baby stays up all night, the sights he sees are simply enchanting.

Ages 2 to 5
- *Big City ABC* by Allan Moak (Tundra). Toronto as seen through the eyes of its children. Your kids will be enchanted.
- *Farmer Joe Goes to the City* by Nancy Wilcox Richards (Scholastic). Farmer Joe sets off for the city with a cow, a pig, some chickens, and some gophers to buy his wife a red birthday present. You'll never guess what he buys.
- *It's Raining, Yancy and Bear* by Hazel J. Hutchins (Annick Press). Yancy and Bear have some pretty cool adventures, including a trip to the Royal Ontario Museum during which Bear comes to life and Yancy becomes his toy for the day.
- *The Red Caterpillar on College Street* by Afula Cooper (Tundra). A collection of beautiful rhythmic poetry with many recognizable Toronto sites.
- *Take Me Out to the Ballgame* by Maryanne Kovalski (Scholastic). The lyrics and music for the famous song are included in this book, in which Jenny, Joanna, and their grandma set out for the big game and a big adventure.
- *Who Goes to the Park?* by Aska Warabé (Tundra). Lovely illustrations of Toronto's High Park in all its different seasons are accompanied by some beautiful poetry for children.

Ages 6 to 9
- *Jonathan Cleaned Up, Then He Heard a Sound:* or *Blackberry Subway Jam* by Robert Munsch (Annick Press). Slightly irreverent, always hilarious, this Canadian children's author is adored by kids. This book, which relates Jonathan's observations of the subway stop outside his window, is charming and insightful.

- *Merry-Go-Day* by Sheree Fitch (Doubleday Canada). All of the sights and sounds of the Canadian National Exhibition are brought to life in this richly illustrated book that begs to be read aloud.

Ages 9 and up

- *The Sky Is Falling* by Kit Pearson (Penguin Canada). It's 1940 and a young British girl is sent to Toronto to escape the war. These are her impressions of the city.
- *Treason at York* by John F. Hayes (Copp Clark). This novel, set in 19th-century Toronto, will bring the city's fascinating history to life.
- *The White Stone in the Castle Wall* by Sheldon Oberman (Tundra). A young boy is down on his luck until he gets the grand idea of selling some dirty gray stone to financier Sir Henry Pellat, who is building Casa Loma, Toronto's well-known hilltop castle. This book is set in early 20th-century Toronto.

Nonfiction

- *The Toronto Story* by Claire Mackay (Annick Press). An easy-to-read history of Toronto for all ages.

8 Getting There

BY PLANE

Wherever you're traveling from, always shop the airlines and ask for the lowest fare. You'll have a better chance of landing a deal if you're willing to be flexible about when you arrive and leave.

You may be able to fly for less than the standard advance (APEX) fare by contacting a ticket broker or consolidator. These companies, which buy tickets in bulk and sell them at a discount, advertise in the Sunday travel sections of major city newspapers. You may not be able to get the lowest price they advertise, but you're likely to pay less than the price quoted by the major airlines. Bear in mind that tickets purchased through a consolidator are often nonrefundable. If you change your itinerary after purchase, chances are you'll pay a stiff penalty.

But really, the best place to find a travel bargain is to shop online. See "Cyber Deals for Net Surfers" on p. 24.

WITHIN CANADA **Air Canada,** which also operates Air Nova, Canadian Regional, and Air Ontario, offers direct flights from all major and most minor Canadian cities. In 2000, Air Canada took over Canadian Airlines International, making the former Canada's only national airline. The central reservation number for all Air Canada–operated airlines is © **888/ 247-2262**. **Canada 3000** (© **888/ 226-3000**) flies from Vancouver, Victoria, Edmonton, Calgary, Saskatoon, Winnipeg, Thunder Bay, Ottawa, Montreal and Halifax, expanding its service in the summer months. Montreal and northern Canada, including Cambridge Bay, Iqaluit, Kuujjuaq, Nanisivik, Resolute, and Yellowknife, are served by **First Air** (© **880/267-1247**). **Royal Airlines** (© **888/828-9797**) operates between Ottawa, Montreal, and Toronto. For an often cheaper flight, you can fly into Hamilton on **WestJet** (© **877/956-6982** or 800/538-5696).

FROM THE U.S. Air Canada (© **800/776-3000**) operates direct flights to Toronto from most major American cities and many smaller ones. It also flies from major cities around the world and operates connecting flights from other U.S. cities. In 2000, Air Canada took over Canadian Airlines International and thus became Canada's only national airline.

Among U.S. airlines, **US Airways** (© **800/428-4322**) flies directly to Toronto from a number of U.S. cities, notably Baltimore, Indianapolis, Philadelphia, and Pittsburgh. **American** (© **800/443-7300**) has daily direct flights from Chicago, Dallas, Miami, and New York. **United** (© **800/241-6522**) has direct flights from Chicago, San Francisco, and Washington (Dulles). **Northwest** (© **800/225-2525**) flies directly from Detroit and Minneapolis. **Delta** (© **800/221-1212**) flies direct from Atlanta and Cincinnati.

FROM ABROAD   There is frequent service (direct and indirect) to Toronto from around the world.

Several airlines operate from the United Kingdom. **British Airways** (© **0345/222-111**), **Air Canada** (© **0090/247-226**), and **Air India** (© **800/442-4455**) fly direct from London's Heathrow. Air Canada also flies direct from Glasgow and Manchester.

In Australia, **Canadian International** (© **0800/802-245**) has an agreement with **Qantas** and flies from Sydney to Toronto, stopping in Honolulu. From New Zealand, **Canadian International** (© **0800/802-245**) cooperates with **Air New Zealand,** scheduling on average three flights a week from Auckland to Toronto, stopping in Honolulu, Fiji, or both. Air Canada has taken over Canadian International, but these arrangements are still in place; Canadian's offices are open and bookings can be made through them.

From Cape Town, South Africa, **Delta** (© **800/221-1212,** or 011/482-4582 in South Africa), operates via New York; **Air Canada** (call Cardinal Associates in Johannesburg at © **011/8808931**) via Frankfurt; **Swissair** (© **021/214-938**) via Zurich; and **South African Airways** (© **021/254-610**) via Miami or New York. Several airlines fly from Johannesburg, including **British Airways** (© **011/441-8600**) via Heathrow, **South African Airways** (© **011/333-6504**) via Miami or New York, and **Swissair** (© **011/484-1980**) via Zurich.

TORONTO'S AIRPORTS

Most flights arrive at **Pearson International Airport,** in the northwest corner of Metro Toronto. Once you're in the airport, ask for assistance at the Special Services desk. The hallways tend to be long for little legs, and Special Services can give you a lift in one of their motorized carts—something kids always enjoy even if they're not tired. You can also get baggage carts and baggage assistance.

There are medical clinics at all three terminals; ask security staff to direct you. There is also a small children's play area on the departure level.

Don't let anyone tell you that the airport is close to downtown—it's not. It's a 30-minute drive from downtown and even longer if you're traveling during the morning rush hour (7 to 9am) or the afternoon commute (4 to 6pm). A few commuter flights land at **Toronto Island Airport,** a short ferry ride from downtown.

AIRPORT TRANSPORTATION

On all levels of the airport and at all three terminals there are highly organized, staffed stands for taxis, limousines, and buses. A **taxi** costs about C$36 (US$23.75), or you might thrill the kids by splurging on a flat-rate limousine, which costs around C$38 to $40 (US$25.10 to $26.40). Two limo services are **Aaroport** (© **416/745-1555**) and **AirLine** (© **905/676-3210**). Many first-class hotels run their own limousines to and from the airport. Ask about this when you make your reservation.

The convenient **Airport Express Bus** (✆ 905/564-6333) leaves from the airport every 20 minutes, all day, and stops at all major downtown hotels, including Harbour Castle Westin, the Royal York, Crowne Plaza Toronto Centre, the Sheraton Centre, and the Delta Chelsea Inn. This is an especially good deal for families. Children under 12 ride for free, and the adult fare is C$12.50 (US$8.25) one way.

The cheapest option is to travel by **bus and subway**. You must take a bus from the airport to reach the subway system. The **TTC airport bus** (no. 58A) travels between Lawrence West subway station and Pearson. The total fare of C$4 (US$2.65) includes a C$2 (US$1.30) supplement due at the airport. No. 307 also leaves from Eglinton station on the Yonge line. For more information, call ✆ **416/393-4636.**

GO Transit operates bus service from York Mills/ Yorkdale stations to Terminal 2 at Pearson. Buses go every 60 minutes, seven days a week. For more information call GO Transit at ✆ **888/GET ON GO** or 416/869-3200, or visit their web site www.gotransit.com.

CYBER DEALS FOR NET SURFERS

If you have access to the Internet you can find some great deals on airfare, hotels, and car rentals. Have a look at your hotel's website, as hotels often post special deals and packages, or try some of the general travel sites. Travelocity (www.travelocity.com) and Expedia (www.expedia.com) will both allow you to search for the lowest possible airfare. Travelocity will also allow you to book specific seats for your flight. Both services allow you to make hotel bookings.

On Wednesdays **Air Canada**'s website (www.aircanada.ca) offers deeply discounted flights to Canada for the weekend. You need to reserve the flight on a Wednesday or Thursday and fly on Friday (after 7pm) or Saturday (all day) and return Monday or Tuesday (all day). Once you register with Air Canada's Web specials page you'll receive an e-mail every Wednesday listing discounts available for that weekend.

BY TRAIN

VIA Rail trains to Toronto operate as part of the Montreal–Kingston–Toronto corridor as well as the London–Toronto and the Ottawa–Windsor–Toronto corridors. Toronto's Union Station (✆ **416/236-2029**) is located at 65 Front Street West, right downtown. VIA Rail often has special fares, and booking in advance may also get you a substantial discount. For rail information, contact **VIA Rail Canada** ✆ **888/VIA-RAIL** (888/842-7245), www.viarail.ca.

Amtrak's *Maple Leaf* links New York City with Toronto via Albany, Buffalo, and Niagara Falls. It departs daily from Penn Station. The journey takes 11¾ hours. From Chicago, the *International* carries passengers to Toronto via Port Huron, Michigan, a 12½-hour trip. Note that these lengthy schedules allow for extended stops at customs and immigration checkpoints at the border. Both trains arrive in Toronto at Union Station on Front Street, one block west of Yonge Street, opposite the Royal York Hotel. The station has direct access to the subway, so you can easily reach any Toronto destination from there. Call **Amtrak** at © **800/USA-RAIL** or 800/872-7245.

From Buffalo's Exchange Street Station, you can make the trip to Toronto's Union Station on the Toronto/Hamilton/Buffalo Railway (THB). Connecting service is also available from other major cities along the border.

To secure the lowest round-trip fares, book as far in advance as possible, and try to travel midweek. Seat availability determines price levels; the earlier you book, the more likely you are to land a lower fare. Trains can be a wonderful way to travel with your kids. They can see the sights and have room to walk, if not run, around. It may lack the speed of air travel, but it sure beats being confined to a seat on a bus or in a car.

Once you're in Union Station, be sure to ask for assistance from the Red Caps if you need help with your luggage. Your train's conductor should be able to flag down a porter for you—ask before you pull into Union Station. If you have anything you want stowed during your visit to Toronto (pillows and blankets you had on the train, for instance), baggage storage is available on the departures level. Don't leave anything in the lockers at the station, as they are cleaned out every 24 hours.

BY BUS

Metro Toronto Coach Terminal (© **416/594-1010**) is located at 610 Bay Street, in the heart of downtown. There is also a station at the Yorkdale shopping mall at the GO Transit site (1 Yorkdale Rd. © **416/869-3200**).

Greyhound Canada (© 800/661-TRIP, or 800/661-8747) provides coast-to-coast bus service to Toronto.

Greyhound/Trailways (© **800/231-2222**) is the only bus company that crosses the U.S. border. You can travel from almost anywhere in the United States, changing buses along the way. You'll arrive at the Metro Toronto Coach Terminal downtown.

The bus may be faster and cheaper than the train, and its routes may be more flexible if you want to stop along the way. This can be a challenging way to travel with kids, though. Seating is cramped, toilet facilities are meager, and rest and meal stops are sporadic and rarely convenient. Be sure to bring along plenty of toys and snacks.

Depending on where you are coming from, check into Greyhound/Trailway's special unlimited-travel passes and any discount fares that might be offered. It's hard to provide sample fares because bus companies, like airlines, are adopting yield-management strategies, causing prices to change from one day to the next depending on demand.

BY CAR

Downtown Toronto can be approached from a variety of highways. From the east and west, Highway 401 brings you to the Don Valley Parkway, which takes you directly downtown via the Richmond Street exit or via the Gardiner Expressway. Approaching from the west, you can also take Highway 427 from Highway 401 and follow it down to the Queen Elizabeth Way (QEW). The QEW comes from the southwest via Niagara Falls, Hamilton, and Guelph and leads straight into the Gardiner Expressway along the lakeshore. From the north, Highway 400 meets Highway 401 just to the west of Toronto, then follow the signs for the Don Valley Parkway.

Hopping across the border by car is no problem—the U.S. highway system leads directly into Canada at 13 points. If you're driving from Michigan, you'll enter at Detroit–Windsor (via I-75 and the Ambassador Bridge) or Port Huron–Sarnia (via I-94 and the Bluewater Bridge). If you're coming from New York, you have more options. On I-190, you can enter at Buffalo–Fort Erie; Niagara Falls, NY–Niagara Falls, ON; or Niagara Falls, NY–Lewiston. On I-81, you'll cross the Canadian border at Hill Island; on Route 37, you'll enter at Ogdensburg–Johnstown or Rooseveltown–Cornwall.

From the United States, you are most likely to enter Toronto from the west on Highway 401 or Highway 2 and the Queen Elizabeth Way. If you come east from Montreal, you'll also use Highway 401 and Highway 2.

Here are approximate driving distances in miles to Toronto: from Boston, 566; Buffalo, 96; Chicago, 534; Cincinnati, 501; Detroit, 236; Minneapolis, 972, New York, 495.

Be sure to carry your driver's license and car registration if you plan to drive your own vehicle into Canada. It isn't a bad idea to carry proof of automobile liability insurance as well.

If you are a member of the American Automobile Association (AAA), the **Canadian Automobile Associations** (**CAA**) Central Ontario Branch in Toronto (© **416/221-4300**) provides emergency road service.

3

Getting to Know Toronto

Toronto is a remarkably easy city to get lost in. The streets are laid out on a loose grid, but that pattern seems to have been cheerfully abandoned by city planners at key spots around the city. Street names have a disturbing tendency to change as you drive along them, so that after you cross King Street West, Blue Jays Way becomes Peter Street and on the east side of Yonge Street, College Street becomes Carlton Street. Avenue Road changes its name no less than four times as you travel from north to south.

You can console yourself with the fact that even Torontonians find themselves lost from time to time. Don't be afraid to ask for directions—it won't necessarily mark you as a visitor. And, above all, enjoy the adventure of seeing a fascinating part of Toronto that you hadn't intended to.

Below you'll find all the information you'll need to get around in the city.

1 Orientation

VISITOR INFORMATION

For hotel, dining, and other tourist information, head to (or write to) **Tourism Toronto,** 207 Queens Quay W., Suite 590 (P.O. Box 126), Toronto, ON M5J 1A7 (© **800/363-1990** or 416/203-2600); www.tourism-toronto.com. It's in the Queens Quay Terminal at Harbourfront and is open Monday to Friday 9am to 5pm. Take the LRT (light rapid transit system) from Union Station to the York Street stop. The website has an up-to-the-minute city calendar and events information.

More conveniently located is the drop-in **Ontario Visitor Information Centre,** in the Eaton Centre on Yonge Street at Dundas Street. It's on Level 1 (one floor below street level) and is open Monday to Friday 10am to 9pm, Saturday 9:30am to 6pm, Sunday noon to 5pm.

If you're in the neighborhood, the **Community Information Centre,** 425 Adelaide St. W. (© **416/392-0505**), specializes in social, government, and health-service information for residents or potential residents, but staff members will try to answer questions for travelers. And if they can't, they will direct you to someone who can.

To pick up brochures and a map before you leave **Pearson International Airport,** stop by the **Transport Canada Information Centre** (© **905/676-3506** or 416/247-7678).

PUBLICATIONS & WEBSITES

Toronto has four daily newspapers: *The Globe and Mail,* the *National Post,* the *Toronto Star,* and the *Toronto Sun.* All have some local listings, but the best are in the *Star,* which lists events, concerts, theater performances, first-run films, and the like.

Even better bets are the free weeklies *Now* and *Eye,* both published on Thursday and available in news boxes and at cafes and shops around town. You can also pick up a copy of one of the free "subway papers," *Metro* and *FYI Toronto,* although the information in these papers is fairly limited.

Other good sources include the glossy monthly *Where Toronto,* which lists events, attractions, restaurants, and shops and is available free in most hotels and in some theater district restaurants. *Toronto Life* is a lifestyle magazine that contains comprehensive listings of kids' events, theater, speeches, and art exhibitions; its April issue always contains a dining guide. Serious shoppers will want to pick up the latest copy of *Toronto Life Fashion,* which is published six times a year.

If you have Internet access, log on to the **MyToronto** website (www.myto.net) for its extensive restaurant reviews, events listings, and feature articles. *Toronto Life's* website (www.torontolife.com) also reviews the city's best restaurants, including the most family-friendly choices. Its online City Guides, especially Where to Get Good Stuff Cheap and the Fashion Guide, will provide you with some interesting and excellent shopping suggestions. **Toronto.com** (www.toronto.com), operated by the *Toronto Star,* has well-organized events, shopping, and services listings, but occasionally items such as admission fees are somewhat out of date.

For specific information about children's entertainment and outings, the *Toronto Star* publishes fairly comprehensive listings in its What's On section, published every Thursday. **Toronto.com** (www.toronto.com) also provides pages with kid-friendly places to go and see, as well as a great holiday page that will tell you what is happening around the city during spring break and other school holidays. Other good sources for kid-specific information are *Today's Parent Toronto* and *City Parent.* Published monthly, these parenting papers contain useful listings of all children's events organized in the city each month.

CITY LAYOUT

The best way to become familiar with Toronto's city streets may be to ride *under* them rather than *on* them. The subway system follows the main arteries that divide the city: **Yonge Street,** from Lake Ontario to well beyond Highway 401 in the north, and **Bloor Street,** the major east–west artery, which cuts through the heart of downtown. Yonge Street also divides western cross streets from eastern cross streets; thus, Bloor Street East becomes Bloor Street West as it crosses Yonge Street.

Most Torontonians refer to "downtown" as the area from Eglinton Avenue south to Lake Ontario, between Spadina Avenue in the west and Jarvis Avenue in the east. To help you get your bearings in such a large area, I have further divided the downtown area into **downtown** (from the lake north to College/Carlton Street), **midtown** (from College/Carlton Street north to Davenport Road), and **uptown** (from Davenport Road north to Eglinton). Further north of Eglinton is refered to as **north Toronto.**

The first area, downtown, includes such family attractions as Harbourfront, Ontario Place, Fort York, Exhibition Place, and the Toronto Islands. This is also where you will find the CN Tower, SkyDome, Chinatown, Kensington Market, the Art Gallery of Ontario, and the Eaton Centre. Midtown includes popular family venues such as the Children's Own Museum, the Royal Ontario Museum, and the Bata Shoe Museum, as well as chic Yorkville, with its wonderful shopping and dining offerings. Uptown is a fast-growing residential and entertainment district with great dining and shopping venues sprouting up to serve the young, hip, and well-heeled. North Toronto is a rapidly growing area, with new theaters such as the Toronto Centre for the Arts, galleries, and some excellent dining. This is also where you will find Yorkdale Shopping Centre, a decidedly upscale mall with some lovely children's boutiques and the kid-friendly Rainforest Cafe.

Toronto is a vast, sprawling city, and although many of its prime tourist attractions are centered in the downtown core, the number of worthy attractions that lie outside this area is growing. Most notable are the Ontario Science Centre and the Toronto Zoo to the east and Canada's Wonderland to the northwest.

UNDERGROUND TORONTO   It is not enough to know the streets of Toronto—you should also know how to navigate the labyrinth of walkways beneath the pavement. If the weather is bad, your family can eat, sleep, dance, shop, and even go to the theater without having to brave the elements. You can also visit the Eaton Centre, the Hockey Hall of Fame, and many other attractions via the subway system, which is also linked to the underground walkway. Consult our map, "Underground Toronto," or look for the clear underground PATH maps throughout the concourse.

You can walk from the Dundas subway station south through the Eaton Centre until you hit Queen Street, turn west to the Sheraton Centre, then head south. You'll pass through the Richmond-Adelaide Centre, First Canadian Place, and the Toronto Dominion Centre, and go all the way to Union Station through the dramatic Royal Bank Plaza. En route, walkway branches lead to the stock exchange, Sun Life Centre, and Metro Hall. Additional walkways link Simcoe Plaza to 200 Wellington West and the CBC Broadcast Centre. Other walkways run around Bloor Street and Yonge Street and elsewhere in the city.

Kids usually find this walkway a fascinating place—on most days the concourse is as busy as the streets above and is even more so during cold and windy weather. However, trying to follow the PATH can make for an interesting lesson in navigation. If you take a wrong turn and end up lost, watch for the maps and signs hanging from the ceiling above the concourse and on most of the tunnel junctures.

FINDING AN ADDRESS   This isn't as easy as it should be. Your best bet is to call ahead and ask for directions, including landmarks and subway stations. Even the locals need to do this.

Toronto the Good

Although Toronto is today a modern cosmopolitan city, for many years it was known as "Toronto the Good" for its staunchly conservative laws, as the following historical events reveal:

- In 1897, by a slim vote the city allowed streetcar service on Sundays.
- In 1907, the Lord's Day Act forbade all public activity, except going to church, on Sundays.
- In 1912, a law banned tobogganing on Sundays.
- In 1947, the city reluctantly approved Toronto's first cocktail lounge.
- In 1950, sports events were finally permitted on Sundays.
- In 1960, movie theaters were allowed to open on Sundays.

Metropolitan Toronto

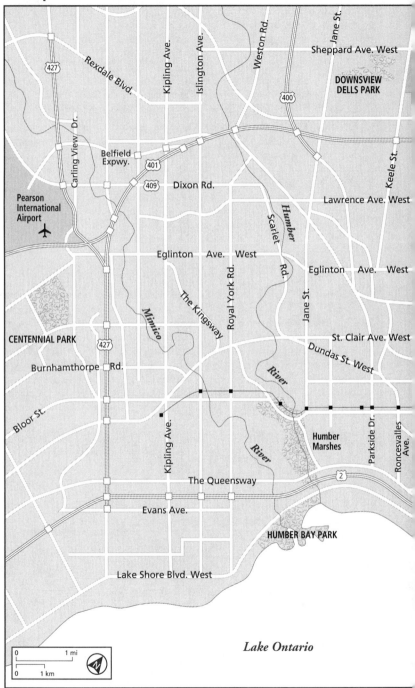

Lake Ontario

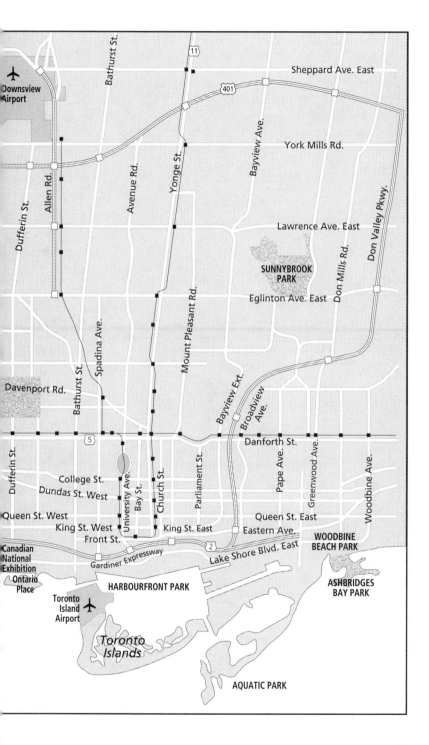

Underground Toronto

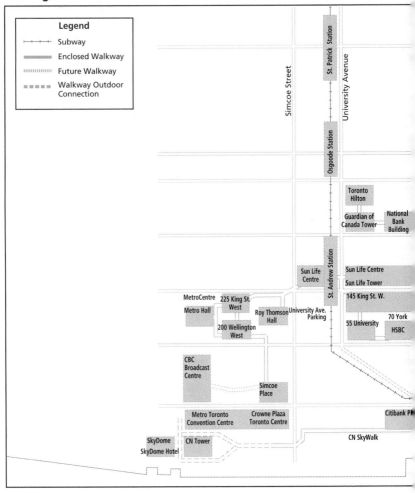

Legend
- ┝━━┿━━┥ Subway
- ▬▬▬ Enclosed Walkway
- ▥▥▥ Future Walkway
- ▪▪▪▪ Walkway Outdoor Connection

NEIGHBORHOODS IN BRIEF
Most of the following neighborhoods are in the downtown city center.

The Toronto Islands These three islands in Lake Ontario—Ward's, Algonquin, and Centre—are home to a handful of residents and no cars. The islands are a welcome haven from the hustle and bustle of city life for both Torontonians and visitors. Here you can in-line skate or bicycle along the extensive trail system, or have a picnic near Hanlan's Beach on Ward's Island or beside the Centreville Amusement Park on Centre Island. The islands also have facilities for boating and sailing. Ferries to the islands depart at the foot of Bay Street by the Westin Harbour Castle Hotel. Be sure to catch the right ferry—they all stop at different islands.

Harbourfront/Lakefront The landfill where the railroad yards and dock facilities once stood is now a

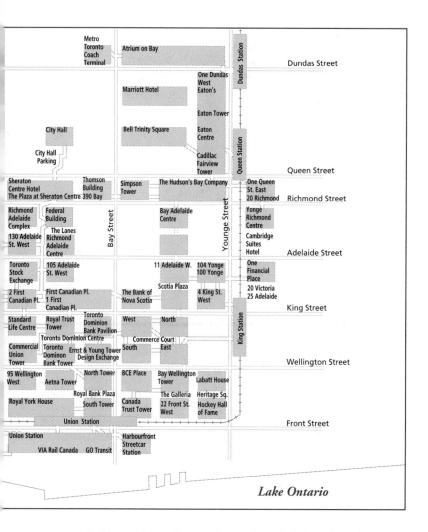

Metro Toronto Coach Terminal

Atrium on Bay

One Dundas West
Eaton's

Dundas Station

Dundas Street

Marriott Hotel

Eaton Tower

City Hall

Bell Trinity Square

Eaton Centre

City Hall Parking

Cadillac Fairview Tower

Queen Station

Queen Street

Sheraton Centre Hotel
The Plaza at Sheraton Centre

Thomson Building
390 Bay

Simpson Tower

The Hudson's Bay Company

One Queen St. East
20 Richmond

Richmond Street

Richmond Adelaide Complex

Federal Building

Bay Adelaide Centre

Yonge Richmond Centre

130 Adelaide St. West

The Lanes
Richmond Adelaide Centre

Bay Street

Yonge Street

Cambridge Suites Hotel

Adelaide Street

Toronto Stock Exchange

105 Adelaide St. West

11 Adelaide W.

104 Yonge
100 Yonge

One Financial Place

2 First Canadian Pl.

First Canadian Pl.
1 First Canadian Pl.

Scotia Plaza

The Bank of Nova Scotia

4 King St. West

20 Victoria
25 Adelaide

King Street

Standard Life Centre

Royal Trust Tower

Toronto Dominion Bank Pavilion

West

North

King Station

Toronto Dominion Centre

Commerce Court

Commercial Union Tower

Toronto Dominion Bank Tower

Ernst & Young Tower

Design Exchange

South

East

Wellington Street

95 Wellington West

North Tower

Aetna Tower

BCE Place

Bay Wellington Tower

Labatt House

Royal Bank Plaza

Royal York House

South Tower

The Galleria

Heritage Sq.

Canada Trust Tower

22 Front St. West

Hockey Hall of Fame

Union Station

Front Street

Union Station

VIA Rail Canada   GO Transit

Harbourfront Streetcar Station

Lake Ontario

wonderful waterfront playground. This is the home of Harbourfront, one of Canada's premier literary, artistic, and cultural venues, and Ontario Place, an amusement park/ entertainment complex popular with families.

Financial District Toronto's major banks and insurance companies have their headquarters here, from Front Street north to Queen Street, between Yonge and York streets. It's the location of Toronto's first skyscrapers; fortunately, some of the older buildings have been preserved. Ultramodern BCE Place incorporates the facade of a historic bank building in its soaring glass arcade design.

Old Town/St. Lawrence Market During the 19th century, this area, east of Yonge Street between The Esplanade and Adelaide Street, was the focal point of downtown. Today, the market is still going strong, and attractions like the glorious St. James Cathedral draw visitors.

Theater District   An area of dense cultural development, the theater district stretches from Front Street north to Queen Street, and from Bay Street west to Bathurst Street. King Street West is home to most of the important sights, including the Royal Alexandra Theatre, Princess of Wales Theatre, Roy Thomson Hall, and Metro Hall. Farther south are the Convention Centre and the CN Tower.

Chinatown   Dundas Street West from University Avenue to Spadina Avenue and north to College Street are the boundaries of Chinatown. Here you'll find a fascinating mixture of old and new. Hole-in-the-wall restaurants that have been in business for years share the sidewalks with gems of Cantonese and Szechwan cuisine and glitzy Chinese shopping centers.

Yonge Street   Toronto's main artery is lined with stores and restaurants of every description. It is sometimes seedy, especially between Dundas and Gerrard streets, but improves south of the Eaton Centre, and a massive restoration and cleanup project is underway.

Queen Street West   This stretch of Queen Street from University Avenue to Bathurst Street is youngish, hip, and home to many of the city's up-and-coming fashion designers, including several that cater to children. It offers an eclectic mix of antique stores, secondhand bookshops, designer boutiques, vintage clothing shops, and some modern megastores such as Gap Kids and Club Monaco Boys and Girls. The street has also built up a reputation as Toronto's gourmet ghetto, with some of the city's top bistros, trattorie, and cafes lining the street. There is some undeniably great food to be had here, but much of it comes

served with heaps of attitude—I've noted some exceptions in chapter 5, "Family-Friendly Dining."

Queen's Park and the University   Home to the Ontario Legislature and many of the colleges and buildings that make up the University of Toronto, this neighborhood extends from College Street to Bloor Street between Spadina Avenue and Bay Street.

Church Street   Between Gerrard Street and Bloor Street East along Church Street lies the heart of Toronto's gay and lesbian community. Restaurants, cafes, and bars fill this relaxed, casual neighborhood. Toronto's grandest cathedrals were built on Church Street in the 19th century.

Cabbagetown   Described by writer Hugh Garner in his novel *Cabbagetown* as the largest Anglo-Saxon slum in North America, this gentrified neighborhood of Victorian and Edwardian homes stretches east of Parliament Street to the Don Valley between Gerrard and Bloor streets. The sought-after residential district got its name because the front lawns of the homes occupied by Irish immigrants (who settled here in the late 1800s) were, it is said, covered with row upon row of cabbages. Toronto's only inner-city farm, Riverdale, is at the southeastern end of this district.

Yorkville   Originally a village outside the city, this area northwest of Bloor and Yonge streets became Toronto's Haight-Ashbury in the 1960s. Now, it's an haute, haute, haute district filled with designer boutiques, galleries, cafes, restaurants, and some of Toronto's most luxurious hotels.

The Annex   Like Cabbagetown, this area fell from grace for many years, but today much of it has been lovingly restored. The Annex stretches from Bedford Road to Bathurst Street, and from Harbord Street to Dupont Avenue. Many of the tremendous turn-of-the-century homes are still single-family dwellings, but others have been turned into charming duplexes and apartments. As you walk west it segues into the University of Toronto student ghetto.

Rosedale Meandering tree-lined streets with elegant homes and manicured lawns are the hallmarks of this residential community, from Yonge and Bloor streets, northeast to Castle Frank and the Moore Park Ravine. Named after Sherrif Jarvis's residence, its name is synonymous with Toronto's wealthy elite.

Koreatown The bustling blocks along Bloor Street West between Bathurst and Christie streets are filled with Korean restaurants, alternative-medicine practitioners such as herbalists and acupuncturists, and shops offering made-in-Korea merchandise. This neighborhood was one of the first Korean settlements in Toronto, though now it is primarily a business district.

Forest Hill Second to Rosedale as the city's prime residential area, Forest Hill is home to the prestigious private schools Upper Canada College and Bishop Strachan School. It stretches west of Avenue Road between St. Clair and Eglinton avenues.

Little Italy A thriving, lively neighborhood filled with open-air cafes, trattorie, and shops serves the Italian community along College Street between Euclid Avenue and Shaw Street. Trendy folk can't seem to stay away, which has driven up prices in this once inexpensive neighborhood.

The Beaches Communal, youthful, safe, and comfortable. These adjectives best describe the Beaches, just 15 minutes from downtown at the end of the Queen Street East streetcar line. A summer resort in the mid-1800s, its boardwalk and beach continue to make it a casual, family-oriented neighborhood.

The East End/The Danforth This continuation of Bloor Street across the Don Valley Viaduct is widely known as Greektown. Its main drag, Danforth Avenue, is lined with old-style Greek tavernas and hip Mediterranean bars and restaurants that are crowded from early evening until early morning. The densest wining and dining area starts at Broadview Avenue and runs four blocks east.

Eglinton Avenue The neighborhood surrounding the intersection of Yonge Street and Eglinton Avenue is jokingly known as "Young and Eligible." It's a bustling area and home to some of Toronto's top-rated restaurants and nightclubs. To the east it intersects with the 600-acre Sunnybrook park system and with the Ontario Science Centre.

North York Times are booming in this area, which until 1997 was a separate political entity from Toronto. Many companies have relocated their offices from downtown to the Yonge and Sheppard area, fueling the growth. The Toronto Centre for the Performing Arts is the major sightseeing attraction here, and there are a number of excellent restaurants to serve theatergoers. The area is set to become even more popular: A tunnel is currently being dug under Sheppard Avenue to make way for a new subway line.

2 Getting Around

BY PUBLIC TRANSPORTATION

The Toronto Transit Commission, or TTC (✆ **416/393-4636** daily from 7am to 10pm for information), operates the subway, bus, streetcar, and light rapid transit (LRT) systems.

FARES   One-way fares (including transfers to buses or streetcars) are C$2.25 (US$1.50) for adults and C50¢ (US33¢) for children.

For surface transportation, you need a ticket, token, or exact change. You can buy tickets and tokens at subway entrances and at authorized stores that display the sign TTC TICKETS MAY BE PURCHASED HERE. Bus and streetcar drivers do not sell tickets and cannot make change. Always obtain a free transfer *where you board the train or bus,* in case you need it. In the subways, use the push-button machine just inside the entrance. On buses and streetcars, ask the driver for a transfer.

THE SUBWAY   What kid doesn't like to ride in a fast train through a dark tunnel? This is the best method of family travel in Toronto—it's fast and surprisingly clean and quiet. It's also remarkably easy to use, especially if you're lugging a couple of kids around the city. The only drawback is that you'll have to carry strollers up and down the stairways that lead into the subways. There are some escalators but they are often shut down for maintenance. The subways will take you to most of the major downtown attractions

There are two subway lines—Bloor-Danforth and Yonge-University-Spadina—that basically form a cross. The Bloor Street east-west line runs from Kipling Avenue in the west to Kennedy Road in the east (where it connects with Scarborough Rapid Transit to Scarborough Centre and McCowan Road). The Yonge Street north-south line runs from Finch Avenue in the north to Union Station (Front Street) in the south. From there, it loops north along University Avenue and connects with the Bloor line at the St. George and Spadina stations. A Spadina extension runs north from St. George to Downsview station at Sheppard Avenue.

The LRT system connects downtown to Harbourfront. The fare is one ticket or token. It runs from Union Station along Queens Quay to Spadina, with stops at Queens Quay ferry docks, York Street, Simcoe Street, and Rees Street, then continues up Spadina to the Spadina subway station. The transfer from the subway to the LRT (and vice versa) at Union Station is free.

The subway operates Monday to Saturday 6am to 1:30am and Sunday 9am to 1:30am, with trains running about 2 to 5 minutes apart. For route information pick up a "Ride Guide" at subway entrances or call ✆ **416/393-4636.** Multilingual information is available. You can also use the automated information service at ✆ **416/393-8663.**

BUSES & STREETCARS   Where the subways stop, the buses and streetcars take over. They run east-west and north-south along the city's arteries. When you pay your fare (on the bus, streetcar, or subway) always pick up a transfer so you won't have to pay another fare if you want to transfer to another mode of transportation. For complete TTC information call ✆ **416/393-4636** or visit the TTC website at www.ttc.ca.

Buses and streetcars tend to be busier and more crowded than the subway, even during nonpeak hours. The steps into the streetcars and buses make them

Toronto Transit (TTC)

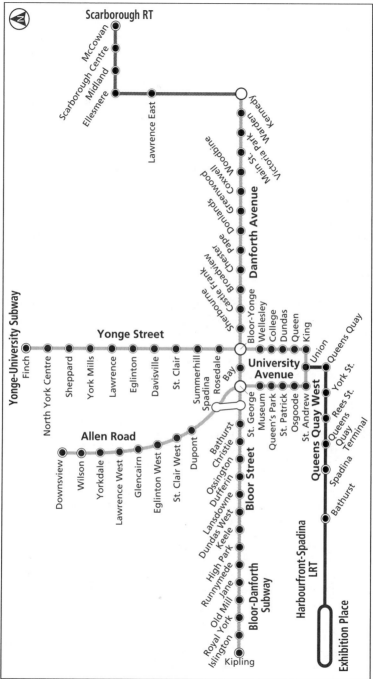

tricky to navigate, especially for small children and parents pushing strollers. Still, the entire TTC system is highly organized and efficient, making it easy for visitors to the city to travel to most of the city's attractions without having to go to the expense of renting a car or relying on taxis.

BY TAXI

Taxis are a more expensive option, but they are exceedingly plentiful and quick—except during rush hours. It's C$2.50 (US$1.65) the minute you step in, and C25¢ (US15¢) for each additional 0.235 kilometers (0.145 mile). Cab fares can quickly mount up, especially during rush hours, when you'll find yourself sitting at each intersection and plenty of times in between. You can hail a cab on the street, find one in line in front of a big hotel, or call one of the major companies such as **Diamond** (© 416/366-6868), **Royal** (© 416/777-9222), or **Metro** (© 416/504-8294). If you experience problems with cab service, call the **Metro Licencing Commission** (© 416/392-3082).

BY CAR

Even though Toronto is a sprawling city, with several major attractions on the far reaches of its borders, a car is not necessarily the best way to get around. In fact, Toronto has a reputation for being the worst city in Canada in which to drive. It is a reputation that is well earned. Driving in the city can be a frustrating experience. If you try to leave a little space between you and the car ahead, another vehicle will slip into it. Tail-gating and running red lights are such common problems that local government has installed cameras to monitor certain intersections. You should definitely avoid driving during rush hours—from 7 to 9am and 4 to 6pm, traffic on the major highways and arteries is often at a standstill. Downtown, the traffic generally crawls along at the best of times and there are frustratingly few intersections where vehicles are allowed to make left or even right turns—watch for the signs hanging over the intersections.

RENTAL CARS   If you decide to rent a car, try to make arrangements in advance. Companies with outlets at Pearson International Airport include **Thrifty** (© 800/367-2277), **Budget** (© 800/527-0700), **Avis** (© 800/331-1084), **Hertz** (© 800/654-3001), **National** (© 800/227-7368), and **Enterprise** (©800/736-8222). Some hotels have rental desks, and most of the major companies, as well as some of the less well-known ones, maintain locations at convenient points around the city. The rental fee depends on the type of car you want, but the starting point is around C$45 (US$29.70) per day, not including the 15% tax. This rate does not include insurance, although insurance is paid automatically if you use certain credit cards (check with your credit card issuer before your trip). Be sure to read the fine print of the rental agreement—some companies add conditions that will boost your bill if you don't fulfill certain obligations, such as filling the gas tank before returning the car. Keep in mind, also, that there is usually a steep fee when you rent a vehicle in one city and drop it off in another.

Tips Under 25 and Renting a Car?

If you're under 25, check with the company—many will rent on a cash-only basis, some only if you have a credit card, and others will not rent to you at all.

PARKING   Parking lots downtown run about C$4 to $6 (US$2.65 to $3.95) per half hour with a C$16 to $20 (US$10.55 to $13.20) maximum between 7am and 6pm. After 6pm and on Sunday, rates drop to around C$8 (US$5.30). Generally, the city-owned lots, marked by a bright green P, are slightly cheaper than private facilities. Observe the parking restrictions—otherwise the city will tow your car away, and it will cost more than C$100 (US$66) to get it back.

BY FERRY

Metro Parks operates ferries that travel to the Toronto Islands. Call ✆ **416/392-8193** for schedules and information. Round-trip fares are C$5 (US$3.30) for adults, C$2 (US$1.30) for children aged 2 to 12, and free for children under 2. The ferries operate from dawn until dusk and leave from the terminal on Queens Quay West, at the foot of Bay Street. Note that no cars are allowed on the ferry.

BY BICYCLE

Toronto is one of the best biking cities in North America. Getting around on two wheels is safe and many major streets have bike lanes. See "Cycling," in chapter 7, for more details. Tourism Toronto distributes a pamphlet that outlines biking routes. The Toronto Islands, the Beaches, Harbourfront/Lakefront, High Park, and Sunnyside (just south of High Park) are all great biking areas.

You can **rent bicycles** at Harbourfront (✆ **416/973-3000**), across from Queens Quay Centre, year-round; on Centre Island from **Toronto Island Bicycle Rental** (✆ **416/203-0009**) May to September; and year-round at **High Park Cycle and Sports,** 24 Ronson Dr. (✆ **416/614-6689**). Prices range from C$12 to $24 (US$7.90 to $15.85) per day.

✆ *FAST FACTS:* Toronto

Airport   See "Getting There," in chapter 2.

Area Code   Most Toronto telephone numbers use the area code 416, but the city has run out of numbers and has recently begun assigning the area code 647 to all new telephone numbers assigned in the city—regardless of where they are located. This means that you must always use an area code, even for local calls. Outside the city, the area code is 905.

Babysitting   Hotel concierges can suggest reliable babysitters if there aren't any child-care facilities on site. In a pinch, call Care-on-Call (✆ **416/975-1313**), a 24-hour service.

Business Hours   Banks are generally open Monday to Thursday 10am to 3pm and Friday 10am to 6pm. Most stores are open Monday to Wednesday 10am to 6pm, Thursday to Friday 8am to 9:30pm, and Saturday and Sunday 10am to 5pm.

Car Rentals   See "Getting Around," earlier in this chapter.

Currency Exchange   See "Money," in chapter 2. Generally, the best place to exchange your currency is at an ATM or a bank. You can also change money at the airport, but at a less favorable rate.

Dentist For emergency services from 8am till midnight, call the Dental Emergency Service (℃ **416/485-7121**). After midnight your best bet is the Toronto Hospital, 200 Elizabeth St. (℃ **416/340-3948**). Otherwise, ask the front desk staff or concierge at your hotel.

Doctor The staff or concierge at your hotel should be able to help you locate a doctor. You can also call the College of Physicians and Surgeons, 80 College St. (℃ **416/967-2600**, ext. 626), for a referral between 9am and 5pm. There are good walk-in clinics located around the city—see "Health & Safety," in chapter 2. See also "Emergencies," below. Doctor in the House provides a doctors housecall service 7 days a week, from 8am to midnight within the Toronto area. The housecall fee is fully covered by the provincial health plan, call ℃ **416/398-100**. Telehealth Ontario offers free telephone access to registered nurses, 24 hours, 7 days a week (℃ **866/797-0000**).

Documents See "Visitor Information & Entry Requirements," in chapter 2.

Driving Rules See "Getting Around," earlier in this chapter.

Drugstores Most pharmacies offer free delivery, and some are open until midnight or 24 hours. Drugstores are common throughout the city—see "Drugstores," in chapter 9.

Electricity It's the same as in the United States—110 volt, 50 cycles, AC.

Embassies/Consulates All embassies are in Ottawa, the national capital. They include the Australian High Commission, 50 O'Connor St., Suite 710, Ottawa, ON K1P 6L2 (℃ **613/236-0841**); British High Commission, 80 Elgin St., Ottawa, ON K1P 5K7 (℃ **613/237-1530**); Irish Embassy, 130 Albert St., Ottawa, ON K1P 5T1 (℃ **613/233-6281**); New Zealand High Commission, 727–99 Bank St., Ottawa, ON K1P 6G3 (℃ **613/238-5991**); South African High Commission, 15 Sussex Dr., Ottawa, ON K1M 1M8 (℃ **613/744-0330**); and the U.S. Embassy, 100 Wellington St., Ottawa, ON K1P 5T1 (℃ **613/238-4470**).

Consulates in Toronto include the Australian Consulate-General, 175 Bloor St. E., Suite 314, at Church St. (℃ **416/323-1155**); British Consulate-General, 777 Bay St., Suite 2800, at College St. (℃ **416/593-1290**); and U.S. Consulate, 360 University Ave. (℃ **416/595-1700**).

Emergencies Call ℃ **911** for fire, police, or ambulance. The Toronto General Hospital, 200 Elizabeth St., provides 24-hour emergency service (℃ **416/340-3946** emergency, or 416/340-4611 for information). See also "Hospitals," below.

Hospitals In the downtown core, the Hospital for Sick Children, 55 University Ave. (℃ **416/813-1500**), specializes in pediatrics. Also downtown are the Toronto General Hospital, 200 Elizabeth St. (℃ **416/340-3946** for emergency, or 416/340-4611 for information); St. Michael's, 30 Bond St. (℃ **416/864-5094** for emergency, or 416/360-4000 for information); and Mount Sinai, 600 University Avenue (℃ **416/586-5054** for emergency, or 416/596-4200 for information). Uptown there's Sunnybrook Hospital, 2075 Bayview Ave., north of Eglinton Ave. (℃ **416/480-4207** for emergency, or 416/480-6100 for information). In the eastern end of the city, contact Toronto East General Hospital, 825 Coxwell Ave. (℃ **416/469-6435** for emergency, or 416/461-8272 for information).

Hotlines/Helplines   AIDS & Sexual Health Hotline (✆ **800/668-2437**). Assaulted Women's Help Line (✆ **416/863-0511**). Distress Centre suicide prevention/family problems (✆ **416/598-1121**). Kids Help Phone for kids and teens (✆ **800/668-6868**). La Leche League of Toronto for breastfeeding support (✆ **416/483-3368**). Medical Information Line: Hospital for Sick Children (✆ **416/813-5817**). Parent Help Line for 24-hour advice for parents and caregivers (✆ **888/603-9100**). Poison Information (✆ **416/813-5900**). Rape Crisis Centre (✆ **416/597-8808**). Telehealth Ontario 24-hour access to registered nurses (✆ **866/797-0000**). Toronto Prayer Line (✆ **416/929-1500**).

Internet Access   Internet access is provided at all Toronto Public Library branches (see "Libraries," below), and some hotels offer Internet access. You can also visit a cybercafe such as the Cyberland Cafe, 257 Yonge St. (✆ **416/955-9628**), although cybercafes are difficult to find in downtown Toronto.

Laundry/Dry Cleaning   Most hotels have either laundry or dry cleaning service, but if not, laundromats are common throughout the city. Bloor Laundromat, 598 Bloor St. W., at Bathurst St. (✆ **416/588-6600**), is conveniently located. At the Laundry Lounge, 531 Yonge St., at Wellesley St. (✆ **416/975-4747**), you can do your wash while sipping cappuccino and watching TV in the lounge. It's open daily 7am to 11pm. Careful Hand Laundry & Dry Cleaners Ltd. has outlets at 195 Davenport Rd. (✆ **416/923-1200**), 1415 Bathurst St. (✆ **416/530-1116**), and 1844 Avenue Rd. (✆ **416/787-6006**); for pickup and delivery call ✆ **416/787-6006**.

Libraries   The Toronto Public Library System has branches across the city. Some of the more conveniently located are City Hall Branch, Nathan Phillips Square, 100 Queen St. W. (✆ **416/393-7650**); Yorkville Branch, 22 Yorkville Ave. (✆ **416/393-7660**); and Locke Branch, 3083 Yonge St. (✆ **416/393-7730**). For further branch information, call ✆ **416/393-7000**.

Liquor Laws   The minimum drinking age in Ontario is 19. Drinking hours are daily 11am to 2am. Government-owned Liquor Control Board of Ontario (LCBO) stores are the only retail stores permitted to sell liquor, wine, and beer. Hours at individual stores vary, but most are open Monday to Saturday from 9:30am to 9pm and Sunday from 12am to 5pm.

Wine lovers will want to check out Vintages stores (also operated by the LCBO), which carry a more extensive, specialized selection of wines. The most convenient downtown location is at Queens Quay (✆ **416/864-6777**). The Wine Rack, 560 Queen St. W. (✆ **416/504-3647**) and 77 Wellesley St. E., at Church St. (✆ **416/923-9393**), sells only Ontario wines.

The Beer Store, owned and operated by Canadian beer companies, sells a range of domestic and imported beers. Again, hours vary, but most are open Monday to Wednesday 10am to 8pm, Thursday to Saturday 10am to 9pm, and Sunday 11am to 6pm. Two downtown locations are 614 Queen St. W. (✆ **416/504-4665**) and 350 Queens Quay W. (✆ **416/581-1677**).

Lost Property   If you leave something on a bus, a streetcar, or the subway, call the TTC Lost Articles Office (✆ **416/393-4100**) at the Bay station. It's open Monday to Friday 8am to 5pm.

Luggage Storage/Lockers   Lockers are available at Union Station and at the Eaton Centre. Another option is to leave your luggage at the Via Rail baggage station, on the departure level of Union Station. The fee is C$2 (US$1.30) per night.

Mail   Postage for letters and postcards to the United States is C60¢ (US40¢); overseas, C$1.05 (US70¢). Mailing letters and postcards within Canada costs C47¢ (US30¢).

Maps   Free maps of Toronto are available in every terminal at Pearson International Airport (look for the Transport Canada Information Centre signs), the Metropolitan Toronto Convention & Visitors Association at Harbourfront, and the Visitor Information Centre in the Eaton Centre, at Yonge and Dundas streets. Convenience stores and bookstores sell a greater variety of maps. Or try the Canada Map Company, 63 Adelaide St., between Yonge and Church streets (© **416/362-9297**), and Open Air Books and Maps, 25 Toronto St., near Yonge and Adelaide streets (© **416/363-0719**).

Newspapers/Magazines   The four daily newspapers are the *Globe and Mail,* the *National Post,* the *Toronto Star,* and the *Toronto Sun.* Eye and Now are free arts and entertainment weeklies. The free mini-newspapers Metro and FYI Toronto are available on the subways and elsewhere. In addition, many English-language ethnic newspapers serve Toronto's Portuguese, Hungarian, Italian, East Indian, Korean, Chinese, Caribbean, and Latin American communities. *Toronto Life* is the major monthly city magazine; its sister publication is *Toronto Life Fashion. Where Toronto* is usually free in hotels and some theater district restaurants. *City Parent* and *Today's Parent Toronto* are the city's two parenting monthlies and can usually be found in bookstores and in some kids' entertainment venues such as the Children's Own Museum.

Police   In a life-threatening emergency call © **911**. For all other matters contact the Metro police, 40 College St. (© **416/808-2222**).

Post Office   Postal services are available at convenience stores and drugstores; individual hours vary. Look for a sign in the window indicating postal services. There are also post-office windows in Atrium on Bay (© **416/506-0911**), Commerce Court (© **416/956-7452**), and the TD Centre (© **416/360-7105**).

Radio   The Canadian Broadcasting Corporation (CBC) offers a great mix of intelligent discussion and commentary as well as drama and music. In Toronto, the CBC broadcasts on 94.1 and 99.1FM. CHIN (1540AM and 100.7FM) will get you in touch with the city's ethnic and multicultural scene; it broadcasts in more than 30 languages.

Restrooms   Finding a public restroom is usually not difficult. Most tourist attractions have them, as do hotels (on the lobby floor), department stores, and public buildings. There are restrooms at the major subway stations (Union and Yonge/Bloor), but they are best avoided.

Safety   Toronto's adopted moniker, Toronto the Good, is a fair description, but you should still be careful and use common sense—especially if you have young ones in tow. Yonge Street and attractions such as Harbourfront, Ontario Place, and the Eaton Centre are extremely busy and it's easy for kids to become lost in the crowd. Consider putting your toddlers in a stroller or attaching them to your wrist on a lead—especially if they have a tendency to wander.

The Yonge/Bloor, Dundas, and Union subway stations are favorites with pickpockets. In the downtown area, Moss Park is considered one of the toughest areas to police. Avoid Allan Gardens and other parks at night.

Smoking   Smoking is banned in all Toronto restaurants, dinner theaters, and bowling centers except where a separate, completely ventilated smoking room is available. In 2004 all Toronto bars will also become smoke free.

Taxes   The provincial retail sales tax (PST) is 8%; on accommodations it's 5%. There is also an additional 7% national goods and services tax (GST).

In general, nonresidents may apply for a refund. They can recover the accommodations tax, the sales tax, and the GST for nondisposable merchandise that will be exported for use, provided it is removed from Canada within 60 days of purchase. The following do not qualify for a rebate: meals and restaurant charges, alcohol, tobacco, gas, car rentals, and such services as dry cleaning and shoe repair.

The provincial and federal sales taxes are administered separately and separate applications must be made to receive rebates on taxes paid.

The quickest and easiest way to secure a refund is to stop at a duty-free shop at the border. You must have proper receipts with GST registration numbers; photocopies of receipts are accepted for PST claims. You should also note that as of April 1, 2001, nonresidents must be able to prove that they are taking goods out of Canada—inspectors at all major airports and at land borders may ask to look at the goods for which you are claiming a rebate.

You can also apply for a rebate through the mail, but it will take about 4 weeks to receive a refund. For an application form and information, write or call the Visitor Rebate Program, Revenue Canada, Summerside Tax Centre, 275 Pope Road, Summerside, PEI C1N 5Z7 (✆ **902/432-5608**), well in advance of your trip. You can also contact Ontario Travel, Queen's Park, Toronto, ON M7A 2R9 (✆ **800/668-2746** or 416/314-0944).

Taxis   See "Getting Around," earlier in this chapter.

Telephone   A local call from a telephone booth costs C25¢ (US15¢). Watch out for hotel surcharges on local and long-distance calls; often a local call will cost at least C$1 (US65¢) from a hotel room. When making a local call in the Toronto area, you must always use the area code. The United States and Canada are on the same long-distance system. To make a long-distance call between the United States and Canada, use the area codes as you would at home. Canada's international prefix is 1.

Time   Toronto is on eastern time. Daylight saving time is in effect from April until October.

Tipping   Basically it's the same as in major U.S. cities: 15% in restaurants, 10% to 15% for taxis, C$1 (US65¢) per bag for porters, C$2 (US$1.30) per day for hotel housekeepers.

Transit Information   For information on the subway, bus, streetcar, and light rapid transit (LRT) systems, call ✆ **416/393-4636**.

Weather   Call the talking yellow pages (✆ **416/292-1010**) for a current weather report and lots of other information.

4

Family-Friendly Accommodations

Toronto has become a great favorite among both business and leisure travelers alike. While this increasing popularity has led to an astounding growth in the number of hotels in the city, it has also led to a rise in hotel rates, particularly in the downtown core. Even budget hotels in the downtown area often charge more than C$100 (US$66) per night. The 5% accommodations tax and 7% GST make the price even steeper, although the 7% GST is refunded to nonresidents of Canada upon application at customs or at refund centers located across the city.

Rates fluctuate widely depending on the season and availability. High season runs from April through October, but downtown hotels can fill up quickly (or become quite expensive) even in low season when a major convention comes to town. The irony of making hotel reservations in Toronto is that if you don't book ahead you may be unable to get the hotel you want; however, if you do book ahead you risk losing out on some of the last-minute deals offered when hotels are not fully booked.

The good news is that there are definitely bargains to be had. Belonging to a union, the military, a frequent flyer program, or an auto club can qualify you for a discount, as can working for certain corporations. A growing number of hotels offer discounts for families and seniors. As well, many hotels offer special weekend rates, especially during the winter, and package deals that might include such goodies as tickets to the theater or passes to Canada's Wonderland. Even if discounts aren't advertised, never be afraid to ask for a better deal.

There are also bargains to be had the farther north from the city center you go. You might consider staying at a less expensive location north of the city and making the trip downtown by subway or car. However, before making your reservation you have to decide how you plan to spend your time. If you want to trek around the popular shopping districts, visit Harbourfront, or catch a game or two at SkyDome, it may be worth paying the extra cost of a downtown hotel to avoid the headache of traveling for an hour or more on the subway. If you are planning to hit the Ontario Science Centre or Metro Zoo, you might consider staying in the eastern edge of the city. If Canada's Wonderland is the focus of your trip, there are plenty of decent options in the north and along the airport strip.

All the hotels listed here are family friendly, and staff understands the special packing and planning needs that go into a family trip. If you find you've forgotten a favorite toy or need a humidifier or high chair, just ask. Most hotel staff will be happy to find what you need.

A NOTE ON RACK RATES The prices quoted in this chapter are rack rates and represent some of the highest rates the hotels charge. I'll say it again, when booking a hotel reservation, always ask for special rates. If booking at a chain, call both the 800 number and the local hotel as you may get different rates. When traveling with your kids, make sure to enquire about a suite versus separate rooms. Often a suite is less expensive. Most hotels also have special kid rates.

A NOTE TO NONSMOKERS
Many Toronto hotels reserve floors for nonsmoking guests. Don't assume you'll get a nonsmoking room if you don't specifically ask for one. If you require a nonsmoking room, request it when you reserve and be sure to ask specifically for a nonsmoking floor if one is available.

BED & BREAKFASTS A B&B can be an inexpensive and comfortable alternative to hotel accommodations. But be sure to let the proprietors know you are traveling with children—the antiques and crystal figurines that adorn some B&Bs can make them unsuitable places for small children.

You can request a list of accommodations in the city from **Toronto Bed and Breakfast,** 253 College St., P.O. Box 269, Toronto ON M5T 1R5 (© **705/738-9449;** fax 705/738-0155; www.torontobandb.com). Doubles cost roughly C$80 to $135 (US$53 to

$89). The registry will process your registration and send you confirmation along with directions. Phones are staffed Monday to Friday 9am to noon and 2pm to 7pm. Another useful resource is the **Downtown Association of Bed and Breakfast Guesthouses,** P.O. Box 190, Station B, Toronto, ON M5T 2W1 (© **416/368-1420;** fax 416/368-1653; www.bnbinfo.com). Doubles range from C$75 to $140 (US$50 to $92). **Bed and Breakfast Homes of Toronto,** Box 46093, College Park P.O., 777 Bay St., Toronto, ON M5G 2P6 (© **416/363-6362;** www.bbcanada.com/toronto2.html) is an organization of 10 bed and breakfasts. Doubles range from C$70 to $125 (US$46 to $83).

ACCOMMODATIONS SERVICES
If you're having trouble finding a hotel, call **Accommodations Toronto** (© **800/363-1990** or 416/203-2500), which represents more than 100 member properties throughout Toronto.

FOR TRAVELERS IN NEED If you run into trouble once you're in the city, call the **Traveler's Aid Society** (© **416/366-7788**). This organization, which also maintains help desks at the bus and train stations and at the airport, provides shelter for people in crisis situations.

1 Downtown

Downtown runs from the lakeshore to College/Carlton Street, bordered on the west by Spadina Avenue and on the east by Jarvis Street. Many of Toronto's best family attractions are found downtown, and most others can be easily accessed from downtown via public transportation.

VERY EXPENSIVE

The Fairmont Royal York ⭐⭐ *Moments* The grande dame of Toronto has been restored to its original 1920s decor, reminiscent of the opulence of a luxury ocean liner. The hotel has a prime location, directly across from Union Station, the hub of Toronto's cross-country train, local commuter train, and subway service, and within a few blocks of Harbourfront. It is also connected to PATH, Toronto's underground walkway, so guests can access most downtown attractions without having to brave inclement weather.

Family-Friendly Downtown Accommodations

TORONTO

Downtown
Toronto

Best Western Primrose **1**
Cambridge Suites **2**
Comfort Suites **3**
Courtyard by Marriott **4**
The Crowne Plaza **5**
Days Inn Toronto
Downtown **6**
Days Inn Toronto Beaches **7**
Delta Chelsea **8**
Holiday Inn on King **9**
Neill-Wycik College Hotel **10**
Quality Hotel
(on Lombard) **11**
Renaissance Toronto Hotel
at SkyDome **12**
(Fairmont) Royal York **13**
Sheraton Centre
Toronto Hotel **14**
Strathcona Hotel **15**
Toronto Colony Hotel **16**
Toronto Marriott
Eaton Centre **17**
Westin Harbour Castle **18**

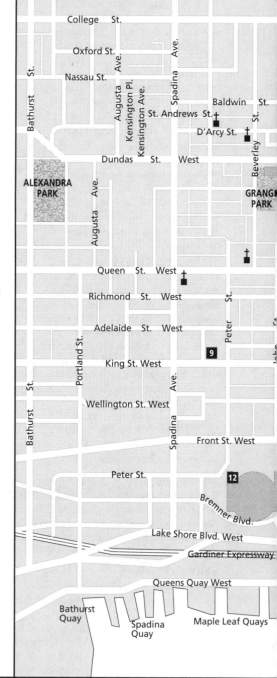

Legend
✝ Church
✉ Post Office
Ⓣ Subway stop

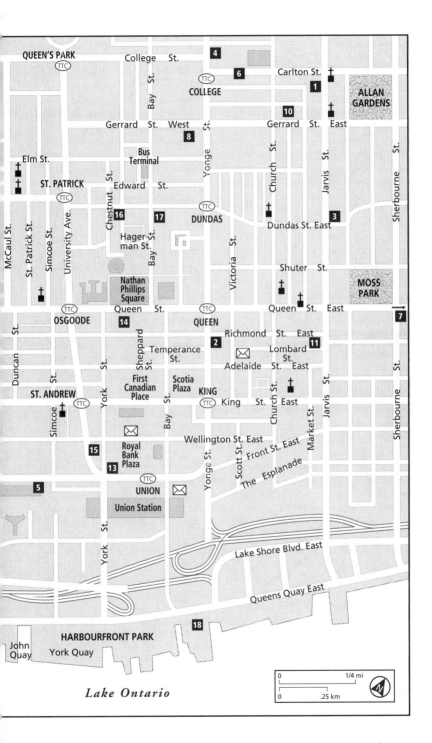

Budding princes and princesses will love the castle-like atmosphere of the hotel. In fact, several generations of Britain's royal family have stayed here, and the hotel even houses two resident ghosts (ask the concierge!). A special children's check-in is available, and kids receive a package of coloring books, crayons, game sheets, and bathtub toys.

A variety of room styles is available, some more spacious than others, and all decorated in reproduction antiques and plenty of brocade. Bathrooms are oversized and have an old-world appeal. There are no adjoining rooms, but families may opt for the premier rooms, which have two bathrooms and pullout couches. Cribs, rollaway cots, and playpens are provided free of charge, but because of fire regulations, cots are permitted only in certain rooms.

The hotel is extremely large and, because of its extensive conference facilities, very busy. As a result, the limited valet and self-parking fills up quickly. The staff is remarkably efficient and pleasant.

Surrounded by potted palms and lit by skylights, the lap pool allows you to swim with a view of downtown. While the pool is rather deep for nonswimmers, tiny tots can splash around in the small wading pool with three waterspouts. The exercise facilities are among the best in the city.

100 Front St. W., Toronto, ON M5J 1E3. © 800/441-1414 or 416/368-2511. Fax 416/368-2884. www.cphotels.ca. 1,365 units. C$169–$379 (US$112–$250) double; C$219–$449 (US$145–$296) and way up suite. Children under 18 stay free in parents' room. Crib/rollaway free. AE, DC, DISC, MC, V. Valet parking C$26 (US$17.15) weekdays, C$22 (US$14.50) weekends. Subway: Union. **Amenities:** 7 restaurants, kids' menu, 3 lounges with extensive wine lists; small heated indoor pool, wading pool, and whirlpool; extensive health club and spa; concierge 6am–10pm; tour desk; car-rental desk; elaborate business center; small shopping arcade with airline desks and travel center; salon; 24-hour room service; massage; babysitting; laundry/valet service; same-day dry cleaning; executive-level rooms. *In room:* A/C, TV w/ pay movies, dataport, minibar, fridge, coffeemaker, hairdryer, iron, highchairs upon request, Super Nintendo.

Renaissance Toronto Hotel at SkyDome ⊛   For the sports fan, these are rooms with a serious view. Seventy of the hotel's rooms overlook the field at SkyDome, so guests can watch a baseball game or concert from the privacy of their rooms.

For those who are athletically inclined themselves, a five-story health club and indoor pool are attached to the hotel. There is a lot of action off the playing field as well, since the hotel is close to the theater district and the CN Tower looms directly behind the hotel. However, if you just can't get enough of sporting events, the Air Canada Centre, the new home of the Toronto Maple Leafs and the Toronto Raptors, is nearby.

Although the view from rooms that don't overlook the stadium is less than spectacular, the hotel is still worth a visit. The small, nondescript lobby offers little hint of the oversized, stylish rooms above. Bathrooms are large if somewhat austere. There is a lot of room for the kids to play, and cots and cribs can easily be added to increase sleeping space.

1 Blue Jays Way, Toronto, ON M5V 1J4. © 800/228-9290 or 416/341-7100. Fax 416/341-5090. 346 units. C$199–$234 (US$131–$154) double; C$209–$334 (US$138–$220) suite; field-view rooms C$259–$379 (US$171–$250). Children under 18 stay free in parents' room. Crib free; rollaway C$25 (US$16.50). Weekend, theater, and baseball packages available. AE, DC, DISC, MC, V. Valet parking C$25 (US$16.50); self-parking C$18 (US$11.90). Subway: Union. **Amenities:** 3 restaurants (2 Continental plus the Hard Rock Cafe—American); large indoor pool; 5-story health club with Jacuzzi; concierge; car-rental desk, 24-hour room service; babysitting; laundry/valet service. *In room:* A/C, TV w/ pay movies, dataport, coffeemaker, hairdryer, iron.

EXPENSIVE

Cambridge Suites ★★ *(Finds)*   This all-suites hotel combines the comforts of home with all the luxuries expected of upscale accommodations. It is conveniently located in the heart of the financial district, close to all downtown attractions.

Although it attracts primarily a corporate clientele, Cambridge Suites also has much to offer families. If you run out of jumpers for junior, the hotel offers complimentary valet service and laundry facilities. Suites are bright and stylish, and all the rooms, including the bathrooms, are spacious. In-suite refrigerators, microwaves, and dinnerware allow you to prepare some of your own meals and snacks, and a few of the suites contain a full kitchen. But leave the grocery shopping to the staff—just write up your list and they will stock your fridge. A complimentary continental breakfast is brought to your suite every morning.

There is no pool on site but the health center with saunas and hot tubs on the penthouse level affords a magnificent view of the Toronto Islands. Several of the suites contain whirlpool baths.

For down time, each suite comes equipped with a VCR; videos can be rented just down the street from the hotel. In-room movies are also available. The bedroom is separated from the living area, so once the kids are asleep the adults can enjoy their movie in private.

15 Richmond St. E., Toronto, ON M5C 1N2. © **800/463-1990** or 416/368-1990. Fax 416/601-3754. www.cambridgesuiteshotel.com. 231 units. C$189–$449 (US$125–$296) suite. Children under 14 stay free in parents' room. Limited number of cribs and cots available C$20 (US$13.20). AE, DC, DISC, MC, V. Parking C$20 (US$13.20). Subway: Queen. **Amenities:** Restaurant (Continental), no kids' menu but will accommodate children; lounge; health club; Jacuzzis; saunas; 24-hour concierge; tour desk; business center; 24-hour room service; In room massage; babysitting; coin-op washers and dryers; laundry/valet service; dry cleaning; executive-level rooms. *In room:* A/C, TV w/ pay movies, VCR, fax, dataport, kitchenette, minibar, fridge, coffeemaker, hairdryer, iron, safe.

The Crowne Plaza ★★   The theater district, professional sports venues, and the Metro Toronto Convention Centre—this luxury hotel is close to it all. It is also right next door to Toronto's commuter train and cross-country train hub, Union Station. While sitting in the hotel lobby you may feel you are actually in Union Station, as a steady stream of people seek a shortcut to the convention center.

The clientele here is mainly corporate, although, depending on what the convention center is offering, there can be a mix of guests. The staff is busy but exceptionally friendly, especially the bell captains, who seem to remember each of their small guests by name.

The huge indoor pool is kept fairly cold, and although there are no pool toys or life jackets, there is a small wading pool for the little ones. Kids under 6 eat for free at this hotel, and even the fussiest eater will probably find something to like at the extensive breakfast buffet served in the Trellis Lounge on the ground floor. The waffles with strawberries and whipped cream are, in the words of my daughter, awesome.

The rooms are beautifully decorated and quite spacious. A wide range of suites is also available—they will provide you with a little more room and privacy.

225 Front St. W., Toronto, ON M5V 2X3. © **800/422-7969** or 416/597-1400. Fax 416/597-8128. www.crowne plazatoronto.com. 587 units. C$189–$289 double (US$125–$191); C$239 (US$158) and way, way up suite. Children under 18 stay free in parents' room. Crib/rollaway free. Packages available. AE, DC, DISC, MC, V. Valet parking C$25 (US$16.50). Subway: Union. **Amenities:** 2 restaurants (bistro, formal dining room, ranked as one of Toronto's top 10), kids' menu, bar; heated indoor pool with separate wading pool; health club and spa

with consultants; Jacuzzi; sauna; tour desk; car-rental desk; morning courtesy limo to downtown; complete business center; 24-hour room service; on-call physician; massage; babysitting; laundry service; 1-hour pressing; same-day dry cleaning; executive-level rooms. *In room:* A/C, TV w/ pay movies, dataport, minibar, fridge, coffeemaker, hairdryer, iron, safe, video games.

Holiday Inn on King 🔭   The Holiday Inn goes uptown. This upscale member of the family-friendly hotel chain offers all the usual amenities in an enviable location, right in the middle of the theater district. Harbourfront, Chinatown, and SkyDome are all close by.

While the lobby is ostentatious, the rooms are still standard Holiday Inn fare. The rooms are fairly small but are fine for a family of four. The suites are a far more spacious, although pricier, option. There are savings to be had with meals here, though: Kids under the age of 12 eat for free in the hotel restaurants.

Apart from its location, one of the major attractions of this hotel is its seasonal rooftop pool, which offers some great views of Lake Ontario during the summer months. The in-room amenities are on par with the high-end downtown hotels, and the staff will provide almost anything you may need during your stay—even an eyeglass repair kit my daughter found herself in need of. Video game machines are standard in the rooms, as are on-demand movies.

370 King St. W., Toronto, ON M5V 1J9. © **800/263-6364** or 416/599-4000. Fax 416/599-7394. www.hiok.com. 431 units. C$209–$229 (US$138–$151) double; C$279–$319 (US$184–$211) suite. Children under 18 stay free in parents' room. Crib/rollaway free. Packages available. AE, DC, DISC, MC, V. Parking C$18 (US$11.90). Subway: St. Andrew. **Amenities:** Restaurant (Canadian), cafe, kids' menu, lounge; seasonal outdoor pool; small exercise room; sauna; tanning beds; 24-hour concierge; tour desk; car-rental desk; secretarial services; 24-hour room service; massage by appointment; laundry/valet service; dry cleaning; executive-level rooms. *In room:* A/C; TV w/ pay movies, dataport, minibar, fridge, coffeemaker, hairdryer, iron, safe, Super Nintendo.

The Sheraton Centre Toronto Hotel 🔭🔭   For visitors who want to be in the heart of downtown, the Sheraton is the place to stay. It is connected to Toronto's famous underground PATH concourse and is mere steps away from many downtown attractions, including the Eaton Centre. Across the street from the Sheraton, the giant reflecting pool at City Hall is turned into a festive ice-skating rink each winter.

The gigantic indoor/outdoor pool is what won my children over. Even in the middle of winter, swimmers can dip underneath the plastic "windows" and swim into the courtyard, where they can enjoy their swim amid the falling snow.

Don't try to squeeze a family of more than four into one of the standard double rooms. The rooms are just big enough for two double beds, a desk, and a small table and chair. To avoid tripping over one another, you'll want to opt for adjoining rooms or even a suite instead. The view is also less than spectacular, unless you get a room on one of the uppermost floors.

V.I.K. (Very Important Kids) packages are available. These include special room deals, a supervised play area, Super Nintendo in the rooms, and free use of strollers, night-lights, and bedtime books.

Since the hotel is consistently busy, service is, while generally efficient, very impersonal.

123 Queen St. W., Toronto, ON M5H 2M9. © **800/325-3535** or 416/361-1000. Fax 416/947-4854. www.sheraton.com/centretoronto. 1,382 units. C$189–$260 (US$125–$172) double; C$350–$1,400 (US$231–$924) suite. Children under 18 stay free in parents' room. Crib free; rollaway C$30 (US$19.80). Packages available. AE, DC, DISC, MC, V. Valet parking C$32.20 (US$21.25). Subway: Osgoode. **Amenities:** 2 restaurants (casual), kids' menu, dozens of restaurants in complex; huge heated indoor/outdoor pool; health club and spa; Jacuzzi; sauna; kids' center; 24-hour concierge; shopping arcade; 24-hour room service; massage; babysitting; laundry service; same-day dry cleaning; club-level rooms. *In room:* A/C, TV w/ pay movies, fax, dataport, minibar, coffeemaker, hairdryer, iron, safe, Super Nintendo, voice mail in 4 languages.

Toronto Marriott Eaton Centre (✶   Connected to Toronto's premier shopping center, this is the perfect hotel for clothes-hungry teens and tweens. It is also located within several blocks of the city's financial and theater districts and Chinatown.

Apart from its obvious attraction for shoppers, the large rooms, as well as the availability of free cribs and cots, make this a good choice for families, although it does tend to be a little pricey. The rooms are prettily decorated in shades of gray and rose.

The moderately sized, heated indoor rooftop pool offers swimmers a fantastic view of the city. Apart from the exercise room and Jacuzzi there are few other activities offered within the hotel, but a wealth of entertainment venues, from theaters to restaurants to arcades, is located within the Eaton Centre itself.

525 Bay St., Toronto, ON M5G 2L2. © 800/228-9290 or 416/597-9200. Fax 416/597-9211. 459 units. C$159–$289 (US$105–$191) double; from C$400 (US$264) suite. Children under 18 stay free in parents' room. Crib/rollaway free. Packages available. AE, DC, DISC, MC, V. Parking C$21 (US$13.85). Subway: Dundas. **Amenities:** 3 restaurants (casual, lunch, steakhouse), kids' menu, lounge; heated indoor rooftop pool; exercise room; Jacuzzi; concierge; car-rental desk; well-equipped business center; 24-hour room service; babysitting; laundry/valet service; executive-level rooms. *In room:* A/C, TV w/ pay movies, coffeemaker, hairdryer, iron, safe.

Westin Harbour Castle (✶✶   If Toronto's numerous harborfront attractions are a main draw, this is the place to stay. In addition to its great location and excellent views of Lake Ontario (be sure to ask for a room overlooking the harbor), this hotel boasts the Westin Kids Club. This perk provides access to a small, unsupervised playroom; a free welcome bag geared to different ages; and free safety kits for rooms, a novelty among even family-friendly hotels. The pool is a good size, although there aren't many pool toys available.

The highlight for my children was the free Westin Kids Storyline. Dozens of entertaining, taped bedtime stories are available in English, French, Spanish, and German. Kids select a story and then press the corresponding buttons on the telephone to hear it.

The restaurants were renovated in early 2001 and the menus and decor have been completely overhauled. If your toddlers end up with more food on their clothes than in their mouths, don't worry. A specially priced overnight laundry service is also available for children's clothes. Another neat thing for parents with busy toddlers is the Express Meal Service. All you have to do is call ahead to any of the restaurants, and they will have your child's meal ready when you arrive. If you can't coax the kids away from the pool, you can also arrange to have your meal delivered to you poolside.

Rooms are comfortable but not overly large. Larger families might want to opt for one of the several suites of two rooms that connect via a private hallway. One room boasts a king-size bed for the adults, and the other room has two double beds. Each room has its own bathroom.

1 Harbour Sq., Toronto, ON M5J 1A6. © 800/WESTIN-1 or 416/869-1600. Fax 416/869-0573. www.westin. com. 459 units. C$149–$269 (US$98–$178) double; C$189–$309 (US$125–$204) suite. Crib/rollaway free. AE, DC, DISC, MC, V. Valet parking C$26 (US$17.15); Self-park C$15 (US$9.90). Subway: Union, then 509 streetcar to Queens Quay. **Amenities:** 3 restaurants (Italian, buffet, bistro), cafe, lounge; large indoor pool; health club; Jacuzzi; kids' center; concierge; courtesy shuttle to downtown and airport; business center; shopping arcade; salon; 24-hour room service; massage; babysitting; laundry service; dry cleaning. *In room:* A/C, TV, fax, dataport, minibar, coffeemaker, hairdryer, iron, safe, video games, kids' storyline.

MODERATE

Best Western Primrose   The aptly named Primrose sits at the corner of one of downtown Toronto's largest parks, Allan Gardens. The hotel is also within walking distance of most downtown attractions, and staff will arrange everything from tickets to sporting events and theater performances to sightseeing tours for guests.

This relatively tiny hotel was renovated in 2000 and boasts comfortable, spacious rooms that work well for families. There is a heated outdoor pool, and Allan Gardens offers plenty of space for the kids to run (don't forget that this is downtown, though—kids should be supervised). However, the main draw for this hotel is its consistently friendly and helpful staff.

111 Carlton St., Toronto, ON, M5B 2G3. © **800/268-8082** or 416/977-8000. Fax 416/977-6323. 342 units. C$89–$250 (US$59–$165) double; C$129–$399 (US$85–$263) suite. Children under 18 stay free in parents' room. Crib free; rollaway C$10 (US$6.60). AE, DC, DISC, MC, V. Parking C$20 (US$13.20). Subway: College. **Amenities:** 2 restaurants (casual); kids' menu; heated outdoor pool; modest exercise room; sauna; concierge; tour desk; small business center; room service; laundry/valet service. *In room:* A/C, TV w/ pay movies, dataport, coffeemaker, hairdryer, iron.

Comfort Suites   Built in 2000, this surprisingly affordable addition to downtown's lineup of all-suite hotels has all of the amenities of its pricier neighbors. It is also in an enviable location close to the business and financial districts and within walking distance of the theater district.

The decor is uninspired and suites are modestly sized, although most can easily accommodate an additional cot or crib. Two-room suites allow you to put the kids to bed on time and still have privacy to enjoy a movie. All suites come equipped with fridges and microwave ovens, but if you're looking for a *real* holiday, a full-service family restaurant and room service are also available.

The medium-sized indoor pool is fairly deep, but the stairs at one end offer a place for supervised small ones to sit and play in the water. In-room video games and movies supply additional entertainment for the younger set.

200 Dundas St. E., Toronto, ON M5A 4R6. © **877/316-9951** or 416/362-7700. Fax 416/362-7706. 151 units. C$119–$189 (US$79–$125) suite. Children under 18 stay free in parents' room. Crib free; rollaway C$10 (US$6.60). AE, DC, DISC, MC, V. Parking C$15 (US$9.90). Subway: Dundas. **Amenities:** Restaurant (family); lounge; heated indoor pool; small fitness center; Jacuzzi; concierge; car-rental desk; small business center; laundry service; dry cleaning. *In room:* A/C, TV w/ pay movies, dataport, fridge, microwave, coffeemaker, hairdryer; iron.

Courtyard by Marriot 🟊 *Finds*   During low season, this hotel is a steal of a deal for travelers who want to stay in the downtown area. During high season, though, rates rise substantially. The hotel is close to everything—it's within walking distance of the Eaton Centre and most downtown attractions and right on the Yonge Street subway line.

The spacious rooms contain two queen-size beds, and there is plenty of room to add an additional cot or two. The king suites are a good bet as well, offering a separate bedroom with a king-size bed and a living area with a sofa bed.

The indoor pool is small, but at a uniform depth of 1.2 meters (4 ft.) it's ideal for a game of tag. There is a small wading pool for tots. A small convenience store in the hotel can supply you with most toiletries, as well as bedtime treats for the kids.

The breakfast buffet in the restaurant is excellent and the a la carte menu has something for everyone. There are several popular fast-food outlets directly across the street from the hotel, offering quick and simple meals for families.

475 Yonge St., Toronto, ON M4Y 1X7. *C* **800/343-6787** or 416/924-0611. Fax 416/924-8692. www. marriot.com. 600 units. C$129–$199 (US$85–131) double; C$159–$350 (US$105–$231) suite. AE, DC, DISC, MC, V. Parking C$20 (US$13.20). Subway: College. **Amenities:** Restaurant (eclectic), coffee shop; small indoor pool; exercise room; Jacuzzi; limited room service; coin-op washers and dryers; dry cleaning; executive-level rooms. *In room:* A/C, TV w/ pay movies, dataport, coffeemaker, hairdryer, iron.

Delta Chelsea ★★★ *(Value)* Located just blocks from the Eaton Centre in the downtown core, Toronto's largest hotel offers resort-style facilities. And while not a budget hotel, it does have some surprisingly good deals for families, including special weekend packages. Kids can fill in their own registration cards in the kids' check-in area and receive a welcome bag that includes bubble bath, stickers, and activity packs.

Parents don't have to worry about their youngsters splashing other guests in this hotel's pool. The Delta has a pool just for families; another pool with a lounge is located on a separate floor of the hotel. Kids can spend hours discovering their creative side in the spacious, well-equipped children's creative center, located next to the family pool. The center offers supervised child care and provides parents with free use of pagers and strollers. Also on the family pool floor is the Starcade teen center, with video arcade games, a billiards table, and air hockey.

The Market Garden restaurant offers a good kids' menu. Children under 6 eat for free, and those aged 6 to 12 eat for half price.

There are a seemingly infinite variety of rooms, from large suite-style rooms that sleep six to smaller rooms that sleep four. A number of suites are also available. Rooms are not typically spacious, but they are well laid out and reservations staff can assist in finding the room style that will suit your family. Some units include kitchenettes.

33 Gerrard St. W., Toronto, ON M5G 1Z4. *C* **800/268-1133** or 416/595-1975. Fax: 416/585-4375. www.delta chelsea.com. 1,591 units. C$149–$245 (US$98–$162) double; C$169–$340 suite (US$112–$224). Children under 18 stay free in parents' room. Crib free, rollaway C$20 (US$13.20). Packages available. AE, DC, DISC, MC, V. Parking C$25 (US$16.50). Subway: College. **Amenities:** 3 restaurants (upscale Canadian, gourmet self-serve, patio grill), 3 lounges; 2 large heated indoor pools (1 for families, 1 for adults); large health club; 2 Jacuzzis; sauna; staffed kids' center; game room; billiards room; 24-hour concierge; tour desk; well-equipped business center; salon; 24-hour room service; babysitting; coin-op washers and dryers; laundry/valet service; dry cleaning; executive-level rooms. *In room:* A/C, TV w/ pay movies, fax, dataport, minibar, coffeemaker, hairdryer, iron, Super Nintendo.

Quality Hotel Toronto Downtown This is a plain Jane hotel with a good location and great rates. Constant promotions are being run, so be sure to ask about them. Both the business and financial districts are a few minutes' walk from the hotel.

The rooms are small but adequate and they contain many in-room amenities that other budget hotels often lack, such as irons, coffeemakers, and hair dryers. There is no pool and only a modest exercise room, but St. James Park across the street provides some green space for kids to run in and chase the pigeons.

The surprisingly extensive complimentary continental breakfast, served in the hotel's breakfast lounge, includes such favorites as waffles and yogurt.

111 Lombard St., Toronto, ON M5C 2T9. *C* **800/228-5151** or 416/367-5555. Fax 416/367-3470. 196 units. C$125–$199 (US$83–$131). Children under 18 stay free in parents' room. Crib free; rollaway C$15 (US$9.90). AE, DC, DISC, MC, V. Parking C$13 (US$8.60). Subway: King or Queen. **Amenities:** Cafe; modest exercise room; business services available at front desk; same-day dry cleaning. *In room:* A/C, TV w/ pay movies, coffeemaker, hairdryer, iron.

INEXPENSIVE

Days Inn Toronto Downtown   This hotel isn't as busy as it once was when Maple Leaf Gardens was still home to the Toronto Maple Leafs, but it does offer guests reasonable rates and is close to the downtown core. If professional lacrosse or independent films spark your interest, this is definitely the place to be. The Rock, Toronto's professional lacrosse team, plays next door at Maple Leaf Gardens, and the Carlton Cineplex theater screens a wide variety of indie films.

   This is definitely a no-frills hotel. It does have an indoor pool, although no pool toys or life jackets are available. The pool is shared with an attached apartment complex. The rooms were renovated in 2000 but remain uninspiring and are quite small. Cribs are available, but fire regulations prohibit the use of roll-away cots. Still, the hotel offers a great deal for budget-conscious families, and for the price of one room in other hotels you can get two adjoining rooms here.

30 Carlton St., Toronto, ON M5B 2E9. © **800/329-7466** or 416/977-6655. Fax 416/977-0502. 536 units. C$99–$159 (US$65–$105) double. Crib C$10 (US$6.60). AE, DC, DISC, MC, V. Parking C$15 (US$9.90). Subway: College. **Amenities:** Restaurant (family), kids' menu, sports bar; heated indoor pool; sauna; guest service desk; salon; laundry/valet service. *In room:* A/C, TV w/ pay movies.

Neill-Wycik College Hotel   The rooms here are typical of most college dorms—during the school year, this serves as a residence for nearby Ryerson Polytechnic University. The rooms are small and spare, containing single beds, desks, lamps, and telephones but no air-conditioning or TVs. Bathrooms are shared, as are the kitchens. The decent-sized family rooms contain four single beds, and a fifth bed can be brought in if necessary.

96 Gerrard St. E. (at Jarvis St.), 22nd Floor, Toronto, ON M5B 1G7. © **800/268-4358** or 416/977-2320. Fax 416/977-2809. www.neill-wycik.com. 309 units (none with private bathroom). C$45–$55 (US$30–$36) double; C$48–$71 (US$32–$47) family. No cribs; rollaway C$15 (US$9.90). MC, V. Parking nearby C$10 (US$6.60). Closed late Aug to early May. Subway: College. **Amenities:** Cafe (serves breakfast); shared kitchen; TV lounge; sauna; coin-op washer and dryer.

The Strathcona Hotel *(Value*   One of downtown Toronto's few great bargains, the Strathcona was extensively renovated in the last two years and still offers great rates to family and business travelers alike. If you prefer to spend your time seeing the sights in Toronto rather than being holed up in a hotel, this is a great option.

   The hotel is located in the shadow of the Royal York in the midst of Toronto's theater and shopping districts. There are no pool or exercise facilities, but guests can use the nearby Wellington Fitness Club for a small fee. Super Nintendo is available in all rooms, so there is something to keep the kids entertained. The rooms are relatively small but adequate. The suites with king-size beds, queen-size sofa beds, and fridges are an exceptionally good deal for families.

60 York St., Toronto, ON M5J 1S8. © **416/363-3321**. Fax 416/363-4679. 193 units. C$99–$129 (US$65–$85) double. AE, DC, MC, V. Parking nearby C$15 (US$9.90). Subway: Union. **Amenities:** Restaurant (eclectic), kids' menu, pub; access to Wellington Health Club for a small fee; concierge; valet service; dry cleaning. *In room:* A/C, TV w/ pay movies, dataport, coffeemaker, hairdryer, iron, Super Nintendo.

Toronto Colony Hotel   These are definitely rooms with a view. Most of the 721 rooms have an unimpeded view of the Toronto skyline, and the hotel is within walking distance of the major downtown attractions. Despite a C$18 million (US$12 million) facelift in 2000, the Toronto Colony has managed to maintain its many amenities and its reasonable rates.

The hotel has a great family policy. Kids under 17 stay for free and those under 12 eat for free in the hotel restaurants. Kids can work off their excess energy in the large, heated indoor and seasonal outdoor pool, as well as on the adjacent jogging track.

After wading through the dark lobby, with its black furnishings, dark wood, and dim lamps, it's a relief to find that the rooms are remarkably bright and dressed in cheerful colors. The room size is adequate, and most rooms can easily fit an additional crib or cot, although trying to cram in two would be a stretch. Suites are a good option if you'll require a bit more room.

89 Chestnut St., Toronto, ON M5G 1R1. © 800/387-8687 or 416/977-0707. Fax 416/977-1136. www. toronto-colony.com. 721 units. C$99–$249 (US$65–$164) double; C$380–$450 (US$251–$297) suite. Children under 17 stay free in parents' room. Crib free; rollaway C$15 (US$9.90). Packages available and rates negotiable. AE, DC, DISC, MC, V. Parking C$20 (US$13.20). Subway: Dundas or St. Patrick. **Amenities:** 3 restaurants (Continental, pizza, Chinese); kids' menu, pub; health club with jogging track, Jacuzzi; sauna; spa; concierge; tour desk; business center; salon; babysitting; coin-op washers and dryers; valet service; dry cleaning; tailor; executive-level rooms. *In room:* A/C, TV w/ pay movies, dataport, coffeemaker, hairdryer.

2 Midtown

Midtown starts above College/Carlton Street and runs north to Davenport Road between Spadina Avenue and Jarvis Street. In this slice of Toronto, families will find the Children's Own Museum, the Royal Ontario Museum, and the tony Yorkville shopping district. Downtown attractions are only a few subway stops away.

VERY EXPENSIVE

Four Seasons Hotel *✦✦✦*   The place to stay for celebrities visiting Hollywood North also caters to families. The staff boasts that you can arrive with just your baby and they will provide everything else you need. I don't doubt it for a minute.

The staff is encouraged to treat their smallest guests as very special people. The royal treatment begins at check-in, where kids get their own welcome boxes filled with everything from toys to games; miniature bathrobes and plates of cookies with their names written in chocolate await them in the room.

The rooms are graceful and spacious, as are the bathrooms, and the hotel is flexible about adding rollaway cots. The executive suite contains a king- or queen-size bed and a living room area and is roomy enough to fit in two extra cots. Everything from Super Nintendo to board games is available for your kids—just ask the concierge.

The indoor/outdoor pool is large and a fun place for kids in the summer, but during the winter it can be difficult for younger children to maneuver. The shallow end is outside, so your little ones have to enter the deep end first in colder months.

The Studio Cafe, lined with objets d'art, is a popular haunt of Toronto's business elite and thus not what you would normally think of as a family restaurant. However, for moms and dads who crave a little elegant dining, the Studio Café is most accommodating toward the younger set. There's a kids' menu, plus the chef assured me the staff will do their best to provide what your child is looking for, even if it's not on the menu.

21 Avenue Rd. (at Cumberland St.), Toronto, ON M5R 2G1. © 800/268-6282 or 416/964-0411. Fax 416/964-2301. www.fourseasons.com. 380 units. C$385–$425 (US$254–$281) double; C$570–$795 (US$376–$525) suite. Reduced weekend rates from C$285–$395 (US$188–$261) per night. Children under 17 stay free in parents' room. Crib free; extra bed in deluxe suite, 2 rollaways in executive suite free for children under 12;

Family-Friendly Midtown Accommodations

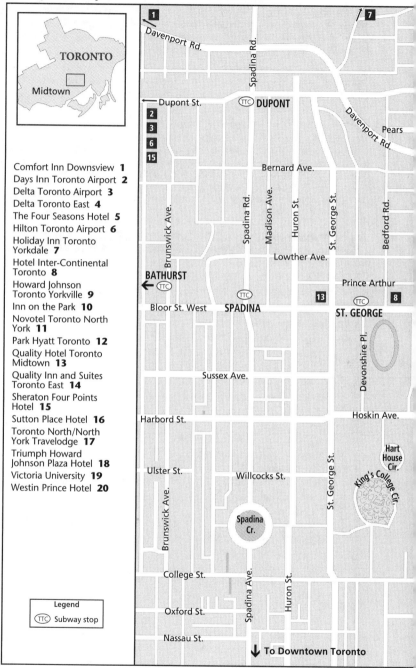

Comfort Inn Downsview **1**
Days Inn Toronto Airport **2**
Delta Toronto Airport **3**
Delta Toronto East **4**
The Four Seasons Hotel **5**
Hilton Toronto Airport **6**
Holiday Inn Toronto Yorkdale **7**
Hotel Inter-Continental Toronto **8**
Howard Johnson Toronto Yorkville **9**
Inn on the Park **10**
Novotel Toronto North York **11**
Park Hyatt Toronto **12**
Quality Hotel Toronto Midtown **13**
Quality Inn and Suites Toronto East **14**
Sheraton Four Points Hotel **15**
Sutton Place Hotel **16**
Toronto North/North York Travelodge **17**
Triumph Howard Johnson Plaza Hotel **18**
Victoria University **19**
Westin Prince Hotel **20**

Legend
TTC Subway stop

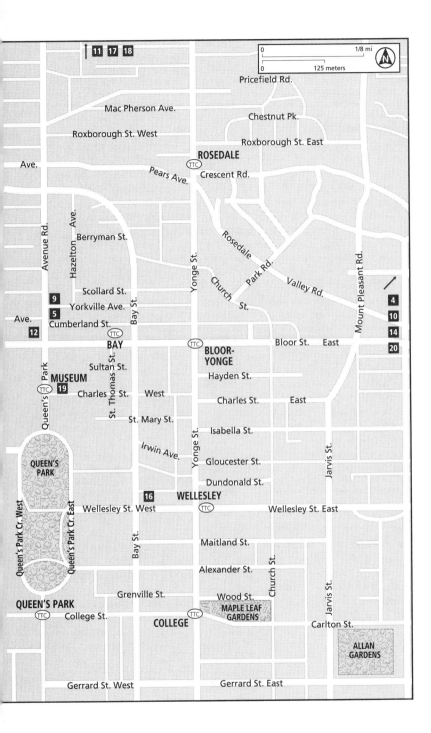

11 **17** **18**

0 | 1/8 mi
0 | 125 meters

N

Pricefield Rd.

Mac Pherson Ave.

Chestnut Pk.

Roxborough St. West

Roxborough St. East

ROSEDALE

Ave.

Pears Ave.

Crescent Rd.

Berryman St.

Avenue Rd.

Hazelton Ave.

Rosedale

Yonge St.

Church St.

Park Rd.

Valley Rd.

Mount Pleasant Rd.

4

10

Scollard St.

9

Yorkville Ave.

Bay St.

5

Ave.

Cumberland St.

14

12

TTC

BAY

TTC

BLOOR-YONGE

Bloor St.   East

20

Sultan St.

St. Thomas St.

Hayden St.

MUSEUM

TTC

19

Charles   St.

West

Charles St.

East

Queen's   Park

St. Mary St.

Irwin Ave.

Isabella St.

Yonge St.

Jarvis St.

QUEEN'S PARK

Gloucester St.

Dundonald St.

16

WELLESLEY

Queen's Park Cr. West

Queen's Park Cr. East

Wellesley St. West

TTC

Wellesley St. East

Maitland St.

Bay St.

Alexander St.

Church St.

Jarvis St.

Grenville St.

Wood St.

QUEEN'S PARK

TTC

College St.

COLLEGE

TTC

MAPLE LEAF GARDENS

Carlton St.

ALLAN GARDENS

Gerrard St. West

Gerrard St. East

rollaway C$30 (US$19.80) for ages 13 and up. AE, DC, DISC, MC, V. Overnight valet parking C$20 (US$13.20). Subway: Bay. **Amenities:** Restaurant (French), cafe, lounge with live entertainment, lobby bar and tea room; large heated indoor/outdoor pool; well-equipped health club with juice bar and massage; Jacuzzi; sauna/steam room; free bike rental; 24-hour concierge; courtesy limo downtown weekdays; 24-hour business center; secretarial services; salon; in-room massage; babysitting; laundry service; 1-hour pressing; complimentary shoeshine; same-day dry cleaning. *In room:* A/C, TV w/ pay movies, fax, dataport, minibar, hairdryer, safe, adult- and child-size bathrobes, in-room exercise equipment available, video games, portable CD players, child-size furniture, games, books.

Park Hyatt Toronto (★(★

With its recent C$60 million (US$40 million) renovation, the art deco Park Hyatt is the latest destination for well-heeled travelers. Located across the street from the Royal Ontario Museum and the Children's Own Museum, the hotel also offers some perks for families willing to splurge for a little luxury and convenience.

Rooms and suites are appointed in oak and cherry, with glass walls covering the terraces to increase floor space so that even the smallest rooms offer a generous 500 square feet. Large families with older kids can book two rooms next to each other and get the second one at half price. If you can sneak a few moments of self-indulgence, draw yourself a bath—bathrooms are equipped with plush terry-cloth robes and Aveda bath products.

Kids are issued a Camp Hyatt painter's cap and a passport, which they can have stamped and later mail in for a free backpack. There is a well-appointed fitness center and spa with an indoor lap pool, whirlpool, and sauna for adults, but children aren't permitted. If you're in need of a workout or some pampering, book the baby-sitting service for the kids, or let your older kids mind the little ones while they watch a pay movie or the Disney Channel in the room.

There are two restaurants on site: Annona, a gourmet's delight open for breakfast, lunch, dinner, and weekend brunch, and Morton's Steakhouse, open for dinner only. Both can be quite pricey, though, so you may want to browse the menus on Bloor Street or scope out the patios of Yorkville for more family-friendly prices.

4 Avenue Rd., Toronto, ON M5R 2E8. ✆ **800/233-1234** or 416/925-1234. Fax 416/924-6693. 346 units. C$225–$499 (US$149–$329) double; from C$299 (US$197) suite. Crib/rollaway free. Weekend packages available. AE, DC, DISC, MC, V. Parking C$25 (US$16.50). Subway: Museum. Small pets accepted with C$200 (US$132) deposit. **Amenities:** 2 restaurants, (International, steakhouse), kids' menu, 2 lounges; indoor lap pool and whirlpool; health club and spa; 24-hour concierge; 24-hour business center with secretarial services; 24-hour room service with kids' menu and kosher kitchen; massage; babysitting; laundry/valet service. *n-room:* A/C, TV w/ pay movies, fax, dataport, minibar, hairdryer, iron.

The Sutton Place Hotel (★(★

If you are in the mood for some serious pampering, this hotel is the place to be. A responsive, indulgent staff and all of the expected modern amenities are at your service amid the old-world elegance of tapestry-laden walls, antiques, and original artwork.

Everything from a massage to a complimentary shoeshine is available, and the staff seems determined to treat every guest like visiting royalty. Even the hotel pool, which opens onto a sundeck in the summer, has the classic appearance of a Roman bath. It has no deep end but is quite pristine, so families may find their more rambunctious youngsters seem a little out of place.

The hotel attracts a mix of business, leisure, and celebrity guests, and though it's a small hotel, it offers a variety of accommodations to suit families. All of the rooms have an excess of space, and staff can easily provide families with any items they require, from cribs to high chairs. Several of the suites contain full kitchens.

955 Bay St., Toronto, ON M5S 2A2. © 800/268-3790 or 416/924-9221. Fax 416/924-1778. www.sutton place.com. 292 units. C$189–$430 (US$125–$284) double; C$289–$460 (US$191–$304) suite. Children under 18 stay free in parents' room. Crib/rollaway free. Packages available. AE, DC, DISC, MC, V. Valet parking C$28 (US$18.50); self-parking C$20 (US$13.20). Subway: Museum or Wellesley. Pets accepted. **Amenities:** Restaurant (eclectic), lounge; heated indoor pool with sundeck; exercise/weight room; Jacuzzi; sauna; 24-hour concierge; car-rental desk; courtesy limo to financial district; elaborate business center; salon; 24-hour room service; massage; laundry/valet service; executive-level rooms. *In room:* A/C, TV w/ pay movies, kitchens in some units, minibar, fridge, coffeemaker, hairdryer, iron, safe, PlayStations.

EXPENSIVE
Hotel Inter-Continental Toronto 🏵🏵🏵
Yorkville's upscale hotels seem determined to pamper, and this one is no exception. Conveniently located on the edge of the Yorkville shopping district, the hotel is steps from several midtown museums.

Despite its formal atmosphere, the hotel genuinely welcomes family guests. The "Kids in Tow" program offers young guests aged 12 and under half-price meals, a free in-room movie, and a gift backpack that includes night-lights, outlet covers, a baseball cap, and toys. Parents receive free use of a pager, a directory of child-care providers, and a booklet that describes family-friendly activities and restaurants near the hotel.

The rooms are formal but exceptionally large. Cribs and cots can easily be added to any of the rooms and are provided free of charge. The recreation facilities here are designed more for the business traveler—the pool is a lap pool, albeit a large one, and there are no pool toys or life jackets to entertain the young ones. Teens will probably gravitate toward the state-of-the-art health club, where they can walk on the treadmill and watch MuchMusic, Canada's version of MTV.

220 Bloor St. W., Toronto, ON M5S 1T8. © 800/267-0010 or 416/960-5200. Fax 416/960-8269. www.toronto.interconti.com. 210 units. C$235–$495 (US$155–$327) double; C$525 (US$347) suite. Children under 17 stay free in parents' room. Crib/rollaway free. Packages available. AE, DC, MC, V. Valet parking C$28 (US$18.50). Subway: St. George. **Amenities:** 2 restaurants (fusion, North American), kids' menu, lounge; heated indoor lap pool; extensive health club and spa; sauna; 24-hour concierge; well-equipped business center; 24-hour room service; massage; laundry/valet service; same-day dry cleaning; executive-level rooms. *In room:* A/C, TV w/ pay movies, dataport, minibar, hairdryer, iron, safe.

MODERATE
Howard Johnson Toronto Yorkville (Value)
This former Venture Inn is a small, no-frills contrast to some of the more pricey options in fashionable Yorkville. While the hotel provides few amenities, it does offer exceptionally good deals, and its location—with Queen's Park, the Royal Ontario Museum, and the Children's Own Museum nearby—is hard to beat.

Rooms are small but well kept. Children under 19 stay for free, and a continental breakfast is included with the price of the room.

89 Avenue Rd., Toronto, ON M5R 2G3. © 800/387-3933 or 416/964-1220. Fax 416/964-1220. 69 units. C$89–$134 (US$59–$88). Children under 19 stay free in parents' room. No cribs; rollaway C$10 (US$6.60). AE, DC, DISC, MC, V. Parking C$10 (US$6.60). Subway: Bay. **Amenities:** Laundry/valet service. *In room:* A/C, TV, dataport.

Quality Hotel Toronto Midtown
Within steps of Toronto's trendy Yorkville district and a short walk from some of the city's most prominent museums, this hotel offers both location and great value for families.

Although its in-house attractions are minimal, the Quality Hotel's location is attraction enough. The Royal Ontario Museum and the fabulous Children's Own Museum are two blocks from the hotel, the Bata Shoe Museum is across the street, and downtown attractions are a 10-minute subway ride away.

Rooms are small but adequate and decorated in bland, inoffensive pastels. They are exceptionally clean and well kept and most were renovated in 2000. Staff, from the check-in desk to housekeeping, is in tune with the hotel's laid-back atmosphere. Everyone is extremely helpful and cheery.

Your room key will get you into the nearby Bally's Health Centre, a full-service fitness facility.

280 Bloor St. W., Toronto, ON M5W 1V8. ✆ **800/228-5151** or 416/968-0010. Fax 416/968-7765. 209 units. C$99–$160 (US$65–$106). Children under 18 stay free in parents' room. Crib/rollaway C$10 (US$6.60). AE, DC, DISC, MC, V. Subway: St. George. **Amenities:** Restaurant (family), cafe, kids' menu; access to nearby fitness center; secretarial services; valet service; dry cleaning. *In room:* A/C, TV w/ pay movies, dataport, coffeemaker, iron.

INEXPENSIVE

Victoria University   Directly across the street from the Children's Own and Royal Ontario museums, this university residence temporarily transforms itself into a budget hotel for the summer season.

The rooms are spare—most are furnished with a single bed, desk, and chair—but are in a lovely setting. Many are located in ivy-draped Burwash Hall, which, with its medieval-style ornament and surrounding green spaces, makes it easy to forget you're in the middle of the city. Linen, towels, and soap are provided, but bathrooms are shared. Free local calls can be made at the residence office, and laundry facilities are available in the residence. A complimentary full breakfast is provided in Burwash Hall.

140 Charles St. W., Toronto, ON M5S 1K9. ✆ **416/585-4524**. Fax 416/585-4530. http://vicu.utoronto.ca/accommodation/summer.htm. 300 units, none with bathroom. C$62 (US$41) double. Children stay free in parents' room. No cribs. Student discounts. MC, V. Parking nearby C$15 (US$9.90). Closed Sept–April. Subway: Museum. **Amenities:** Cafeteria; coin-op washer and dryer.

<hr>

3 East Toronto

Although a fair distance from downtown Toronto, this area boasts several major attractions of its own, including the Ontario Science Centre and the Toronto Zoo. A number of hotels in the area cater to the family crowd.

EXPENSIVE

Inn on the Park *⟨★⟩*   Surrounded by 600 acres of woodland in the Don Valley, this hotel is a short drive from downtown and the Toronto Zoo and within minutes of the Ontario Science Centre.

The rooms have oodles of space, and if you request a room facing southwest you will have a magnificent, unimpeded view of the city skyline from the floor-to-ceiling windows. The view is particularly awesome at night, when the stars, city lights, and occasional planes and helicopters buzzing by will vie for your attention.

The inn boasts a huge heated outdoor pool with a deck and a smaller indoor pool. A kids' activity center is open during the summer and on weekends, and there is a small playground in the hotel courtyard for the little ones. Older kids can usually find something to do in the game room or can try their hand at volleyball or shuffleboard in the summer. There are also plenty of paths in the surrounding woodlands for nature walks or jogging. The Inn on the Park shares facilities with the attached Holiday Inn.

1100 Eglinton Ave. W., Toronto, ON M3C 1H8. ✆ **800/333-3442** (US), ✆ **800/268-6282** (Canada), or 416/444-2561. Fax 416/446-3308. 269 units. C$165–$210 (US$109–$139) double; C$210–$245 (US$139–$162) suite. Children under 18 stay free in parents' room. Crib/rollaway free. Packages available. AE, DC, DISC, MC, V. Free parking. Subway: Eglinton, then no. 34 bus to Leslie St. **Amenities:** Restaurant (eclectic) kids' menu, coffee shop, lounge; heated indoor and outdoor pools; health club; Jacuzzi; sauna; kids' center; game room; 24-hour concierge; business center; shopping arcade; salon; room service; babysitting; laundry/ valet service; dry cleaning; executive-level rooms. *In room:* A/C, TV w/ pay movies, dataport, minibar, fridge, coffeemaker, hairdryer, iron, safe, video games.

Westin Prince Hotel (★(★)

A luxury resort in the city, the Westin Prince is close to the Ontario Science Centre and is a short drive from the Toronto Centre for the Performing Arts.

Active families can choose from putting greens, tennis courts, and nature walks in the surrounding parkland. The kids will be sure to go to bed pleasantly tired after splashing around in the huge heated outdoor pool, with a floating diving platform and pool toys. There is also a children's playground and a game room.

A variety of restaurants are located on site, most of which provide dining options for wee guests. The rooms are large and some offer a great view of the city or the park around the hotel.

900 York Mills Rd., Toronto, ON M3B 3H2. ℃ 800/Westin-1 or 416/444-2511. Fax 416/444-9597. www. westin.com. C$145–$200 (US$96–$132) double. Children under 18 stay free in parents' room. Crib/rollaway C$15 (US$9.90). Packages available. AE, DC, DISC, MC, V. Free parking. Subway: York Mills. **Amenities:** 3 restaurants (Japanese, Continental, grill); cafe; lounge; large heated outdoor pool; outdoor tennis court; exercise room; Jacuzzi; sauna; kids' playground; game room; concierge; business center; salon; 24-hour room service; babysitting; laundry/valet service; dry cleaning; executive-level rooms. *In room:* A/C, TV w/ pay movies, dataport, fridge, coffeemaker, hairdryer, iron.

MODERATE

Delta Toronto East (★(★ (Finds)

Yet another Toronto hotel that caters to the kiddie set, the Delta Toronto East is set apart from the hustle and bustle of the city yet still within a short drive of its attractions. It also offers some wonderful resort-style amenities to amuse your little ones after a day of sightseeing.

There are two giant water slides, one designed especially for young children and set in a huge free-form pool. The pool itself is housed in a 20,000-square-foot atrium, along with saunas, a whirlpool, a health club, and a squash court. Plenty of pool toys and life jackets are available. The well-equipped children's center hosts special children's programs during weekends, over spring break, and in the summer. Your kids might take part in a movie night or decorate cookies with the hotel chefs.

The rooms, decorated in wall-to-wall pastels, are very spacious. Cribs and cots, available at no additional charge, can stretch the sleeping capacity of a double room; another option is a suite with a pullout couch and a separate bedroom. While most of the views are uninspiring, a number of rooms have balconies overlooking the atrium and pool.

Children under 6 eat for free here and children aged 6 to 12 eat for half price, improving on the hotel's already reasonable rates.

2035 Kennedy Rd., Toronto, ON M1T 3G2. ℃ 800/663-3386 or 416/299-1500. Fax 416/299-8959. www.deltahotels.com. 368 units. C$139–$199 (US$92–$131) double; C$249–$349 (US$164–$230) suite. Children under 18 stay free in parents' room. Packages available. AE, DC, DISC, MC, V. Free parking. Subway: Kennedy, then bus no. 43 north. **Amenities:** 2 restaurants (Japanese, bistro), kids' menu; huge indoor heated pool with 2 water slides; complete health club with squash courts; Jacuzzi; saunas; kids' center and programs; game room; concierge; self-serve business center; limited room service and pizza delivery; massage; babysitting; coin-op washers and dryers; laundry service; dry cleaning; executive-level rooms. *In room:* A/C, TV w/ pay movies, dataport, coffeemaker, hairdryer, iron, video games.

Quality Inn and Suites Toronto East

Located in the Don Valley area close to the Ontario Science Centre, this chain hotel enhances its already great rates with some of the best package deals in the city.

Double rooms are moderately sized but immaculate. The small suites have a queen-size pullout sofa bed in the living room and two queen-size beds in the bedroom, which is set off by French doors. Fridges and microwaves are provided free of charge on request, making this a home away from home for guests.

Despite its budget prices, the hotel provides a surprising number of amenities, including a small indoor pool, a larger outdoor pool, saunas, and a modest exercise room. The continental breakfast is free of charge.

22 Metropolitan Blvd., Toronto, ON M1R 2T6. ✆ **800/228-5151** or 416/293-8171. Fax 416/321-7400. 200 units. C$110–$155 (US$73–$102) double; C$145–$250 (US$96–$165) suite. Children under 18 stay free in parents' room. Crib free; rollaway C$10 (US$6.60). Packages available. AE, DC, DISC, MC, V. Free parking. Subway: Warden, then no. 68 bus. **Amenities:** Restaurant (buffet); heated indoor and outdoor pools; exercise room; Jacuzzi; sauna; business services. *In room:* A/C, TV w/ pay movies, dataport, fridge and microwave available, coffeemaker.

INEXPENSIVE

Days Inn Toronto Beaches   The hot location near Toronto's Beaches district makes up for the lack of amenities at this older Toronto hotel. It is also within a 20-minute public transit ride of the downtown core.

Despite the rather rundown exterior, rooms are well kept. However, they are small, so families might want to consider two adjoining rooms—with the low rates this hotel charges, this is still an affordable option.

Although it has no pool or other entertainment, the hotel does boast a great sports bar and restaurant, Rookies Sports Cafe, with a kids' menu. There are usually as many locals in here as there are hotel guests.

1684 Queen Street E., Toronto, ON M4L 1G6. ✆ **800/329-7466** or 416/694-1177. Fax 416/694-1146. 50 units. C$49–$179 (US$32–$118) double. Children under 18 stay free in parents' room. Crib/rollaway C$10 (US$6.60). AE, DC, DISC, MC, V. Free parking. Subway: Queen, then no. 501 or 502 streetcar east. **Amenities:** Restaurant; coin-op washer and dryer. *In room:* TV w/ pay movies.

4 North Toronto

Hotels north of the city offer some great rates. Many are on the subway line and close to major highways.

EXPENSIVE

Triumph Howard Johnson Plaza Hotel 🌟   At the juncture of Keele Street and Highway 401, the Plaza is within easy driving distance of Toronto's attractions. But it's the beautifully landscaped gardens and paths that make this full-service hotel appealing—kids will love the bridge arching over the gurgling creek.

The children's activity center, seasonal kids' programs, arcade, and large heated indoor pool give kids plenty to do when you're not out sightseeing. Rooms are spacious and there is plenty of space for an extra cot or crib. Two-room suites are separated by French doors and equipped with two televisions, a dining table, and a full kitchen, which is an excellent option if your family quickly tires of restaurant food.

2737 Keele St., North York, ON M3M 2E9. ✆ **800/446-4656** or 416/636-4656. Fax 416/633-5637. www.hojo.com. 361 units. C$199–$279 (US$131–$184) double; C$279–$350 (US$184–$231) suite. Crib free; rollaway C$10 (US$6.60). Packages available. AE, DC, DISC, MC, V. Free parking. Subway: Wilson, then no. 96 bus west. **Amenities:** Restaurant (steakhouse), cafe, kids' menu, lounge; heated indoor pool; health club and spa; Jacuzzi; sauna; kids' center; game room; car-rental desk; business center; limited room service; babysitting; coin-op washers and dryers; dry cleaning; executive-level rooms. *In room:* A/C, TV w/ pay movies, dataport, fridge, coffeemaker, hairdryer, iron.

MODERATE

Holiday Inn Toronto Yorkdale   Located adjacent to Yorkdale Shopping Centre, with its trendy boutiques, restaurants, and theaters, this Holiday Inn is a short subway ride from downtown and, via Highway 401, a brief drive from Canada's Wonderland, the Ontario Science Centre, and the Toronto Zoo.

The rooms are in typical Holiday Inn style and are moderately sized. Some overlook the large heated indoor pool with its surrounding deck. In-room amenities are also standard. The hotel does offer a good deal for family travelers, though: Children under 18 stay for free, and those under 12 eat for free in the hotel restaurants.

3450 Dufferin St., Toronto, ON M6A 2V1. ✆ 800/465-4329 or 416/789-5161. Fax 416/785-6845. www.
holiday-inn.com. 374 units. C$95–$150 (US$63–$99) double. Children under 18 stay free in parents' room.
Crib free; rollaway C$10 (US$6.60). Packages available. AE, DC, DISC, MC, V. Free parking. Subway: Yorkdale.
Amenities: Restaurant (eclectic), kids' menu, lounge; large heated indoor pool; exercise room; concierge;
car-rental desk; business center; coin-op washer and dryer; dry cleaning; executive-level rooms. *In room:* TV
w/ pay movies, dataport, iron.

INEXPENSIVE

Comfort Inn Downsview   Located just off Highway 400, this hotel is an excellent launching point for forays to Canada's Wonderland. The Colossus theater, Black Creek Pioneer Village, and an IMAX theater are within a few miles of the hotel.

This is a bare-bones alternative but a good choice if you plan to spend most of your time outside the hotel seeing the sights. And the price definitely entices.

Rooms are scrupulously clean but in the usual bland Comfort Inn style. They are small but adequate for a family of four.

66 Norfinch Dr., North York, ON M3N 1X1. ✆ 800/228-5150 or 416/736-4700. Fax 416/736-4842. 144 units.
C$79–$133 (US$52–$88) double. Crib/rollaway C$10 (US$6.60). AE, DC, MC, V. Free parking. Subway: Finch,
then any Finch bus west; exit 2 stops past Jane St. **Amenities:** Restaurant (family); limited room service.
In room: A/C, TV, dataport, hair dryer.

Novotel Toronto North York   This is an excellent choice for visitors who want easy access to both downtown (via subway) and the attractions in the north and east ends of the city (via Highway 401).

The rooms are small but comfortable and exceptionally well kept. Several contain refrigerators. Cots and cribs can be brought in.

After a day of sightseeing, kids can burn off their remaining energy in the heated, oblong indoor pool.

3 Park Home Ave., Toronto, ON M2N 6L3. ✆ 800/NOVOTEL or 416/733-2929. Fax 416/733-1743. www.
accor.com. 260 units. C$109–$199 (US$72–$131). Children under 16 stay free in parents' room. Crib free;
rollaway C$15 (US$9.90). AE, DC, DISC, MC, V. Free parking. Subway: North York Centre. **Amenities:** Bistro,
kids' menu, lounge; heated indoor pool; exercise room; Jacuzzi; sauna; limited room service; laundry service;
dry cleaning. *In room:* A/C, TV w/ pay movies, dataport, fridge, coffeemaker, hairdryer, iron.

Toronto North/North York Travelodge   Another great deal north of the downtown core, this hotel offers a number of amenities and is close to Canada's Wonderland and other attractions in the north end.

The small heated indoor pool, whirlpool, and in-room video games supply entertainment for the kids, and there is a good family-style restaurant on site that provides limited room service.

Rooms are small but can accommodate an additional cot. Cribs are not available here, so if you're traveling with baby, you'll have to bring a portable crib with you.

50 Norfinch Dr., North York, ON M3N 1X1. © **888/515-6375** or 416/663-9500. Fax 416/663-8480. www.travelodge.com. 183 units. C$79–$125 (US$52–$83). Children under 18 stay free in parents' room. No cribs; rollaway $10 (US$6.60). AE, DC, MC, V. Free parking. Subway: Finch, then any Finch bus west; exit 2 stops past Jane St. **Amenities:** Restaurant (family); heated indoor swimming pool; Jacuzzi; limited room service; same-day dry cleaning; executive-level rooms. *In room:* A/C, TV w/ pay movies, dataport, coffeemaker, hairdryer, iron, video games.

5 Near the Airport

Toronto's airport is, unfortunately, quite a distance from downtown. Public transit runs from several subway stations and several private bus companies run between the airport and the downtown core. A one-way ticket on these buses costs C$12 (US$7.90); children under 12 normally ride for free. A taxi to downtown will cost approximately C$35 (US$23.10). However, if you need to be near the airport, the area has several attractions of its own, including Canada's Wonderland, the gigantic IMAX complex, and some great family hotels.

EXPENSIVE

Hilton Toronto Airport ⭐   This airport hotel is decidedly high-end but hold lots of appeal for families.

The rooms are spacious and, after a C$11 million (US$7.25 million) renovation in 1999, decorated in an oriental palette of jade green and burgundy. The two-room suites are spacious and the perfect option for families, with a sofa bed in the living room and a king-size bed in the bedroom. Reclining chairs are standard for most rooms. High chairs, bibs, and cribs can be supplied to your room, and a variety of toys and games can be signed out at the front desk. The Hilton has also recently announced the Hilton Vacation Station, which will provide young guests with a welcome gift and parents with a package listing local attractions and family-friendly dining options. Children 12 and under eat for free in the hotel restaurants.

The large outdoor pool is a delight for the kids, and plenty of pool toys and life jackets are available. Fitness buffs can catch up on the news or enjoy their favorite soap opera while working out in the exercise room. Headsets are provided for the 10 TVs mounted around the room. A squash court and saunas round out the hotel's recreational facilities.

5875 Airport Road, Mississauga, ON L4V 1N1. © **800/445-8667** or 905/677-9900. Fax 905/677-5073. www.hilton.com. 413 units. C$149–$179 (US$98–$118) double; C$169–$299 (US$112–$197) suite. Children 18 and under stay free in parents' room. Crib free. AE, DC, DISC, MC, V. Parking C$12 (US$7.90). **Amenities:** Restaurant (Buffet and a la carte), kids' menu, lounge; large heated outdoor pool; squash court; large exercise room; saunas; concierge; car-rental desk; courtesy shuttle to airport; large business center; 24-hour room service; babysitting; laundry service; dry cleaning. *In room:* A/C, TV w/ pay movies, dataport, minibar, fridge, coffeemaker, hairdryer, iron, video games.

MODERATE

Delta Toronto Airport   The huge pool encased in an octagonal solarium is the chief selling point for this hotel. The large green spaces for running and the small children's center will also appeal to family travelers.

The prices at this hotel also recommend it as a bargain for families. As in the other Delta Hotels, children under 6 eat for free and children 12 and up eat for half price. A C$2.2 million (US$1.45 million) renovation to the rooms was completed in 2000. Most are a bit small but generally adequate, and both cribs and cots can be added.

The Rusty Moose Lodge restaurant is an attraction in itself, transporting diners from the busy airport into the setting of a northern fishing lodge.

The Delta often features special package deals in association with Canada's Wonderland.

6750 Mississauga Rd., Mississauga, ON L5N 2L3. © **800/422-8238** or 905/821-1981. Fax 905/542-4036. www.deltahotels.com. 250 units. C$119–$249 (US$79–$164) double. Children 18 and under stay free in parents' room. Crib/rollaway free. Packages available. AE, DC, DISC, MC, V. Parking C$8 (US$5.30). **Amenities:** Restaurant (Canadian), kids' menu, bar and grill; large heated indoor pool; adjacent 18-hole golf course; exercise room; Jacuzzi, sauna; small children's center; concierge; car-rental desk; business center; limited room service; babysitting; coin-op washer and dryer; dry cleaning; executive-level rooms. In room: A/C, TV w/ pay movies, fax, dataport, minibar, coffeemaker, hairdryer, iron, video games.

Sheraton Four Points Hotel (★★ (Finds) With its large and secluded grounds, this hotel makes it easy to forget you are close to the airport.

Kids love everything about this hotel, from the extensive children's program and activity center to the pathways winding through the manicured garden and huge maples. On sunny days, you can order lunch at picnic tables on the garden patio. Other kid-friendly entertainment includes in-room video games and movies, a large heated indoor pool, and a game room.

Parents will love the price. Kids under 19 stay free in their parents' room. Children 12 and under eat for free in the dining room, where extensive breakfast and lunch buffets are served. Rooms in this hotel are large, but the inexpensive suites provide an even better deal for families.

5444 Dixie Rd., Mississauga, ON L4W 2L2. © **888/625-5144** (US), 800/325-3535 (Canada), or 905/624-1144. Fax 416/624-9477. 287 units. C$139–$169 (US$92–$112) double; C$202–$269 (US$133–$178) suite. Children under 19 stay free in parents' room. Crib free; rollaway C$10 (US$6.60). AE, DC, DISC, MC, V. Parking C$8 (US$5.30). **Amenities:** Restaurant (Buffet and a la carte), kids' menu; heated indoor pool; exercise room; Jacuzzi; sauna; children's center and programs; game room; salon; 24-hour room service; babysitting; laundry service; dry cleaning. In room: A/C, TV w/ pay movies, dataport, coffeemaker, hairdryer, iron, video games.

INEXPENSIVE

Days Inn Toronto Airport One of the best deals on the airport strip, this hotel is directly across from Terminal 3 and thus is a popular stopover hotel for people flying in and out of Pearson International Airport. It is also a convenient spot for families planning to visit Canada's Wonderland or Playdium Sega City.

Actively promoting its appeal to the family traveler, the Days Inn runs coloring contests and provides games and toys to its young guests. There is a good-sized indoor pool, an outdoor patio, and some green space for running. The rooms are small but well equipped and the decor is bright and cheerful. Rooms were being renovated in early 2001. The Garden Cafe restaurant offers standard options on its kids' menu.

6257 Airport Rd., Mississauga, ON L4V 1N1. © **800/387-6891** or 905/678-1400. Fax 905/678-9130. 202 units. C$99–$149 (US$65–$98) double. Children under 17 stay free in parents' room. Crib free, rollaway C$15 (US$9.90). Packages available. AE, DC, DISC, MC, V. Parking C$8 (US$5.30). **Amenities:** Restaurant (Continental), kids' menu; heated indoor pool; small exercise room; Jacuzzi; sauna; limited room service; coin-op washer and dryer; executive-level rooms. In room: A/C, TV w/ pay movies, dataport, coffeemaker, hairdryer, iron.

5

Family-Friendly Dining

With over 5,000 restaurants, Toronto is a gastronome's delight. As you would expect of one of the world's most multicultural cities, you'll find a restaurant from every country or region you can name. But there is also a surprisingly wide variety of dining styles, from family fare to hip bistros and all-day breakfasts to haute cuisine.

Toronto offers tremendous opportunities to introduce your kids to the varied cuisine of the world. A number of the city's ethnic restaurants even offer children's versions of their fare to appeal to picky taste buds. In the "Restaurants by Cuisine" listings, you'll find some of the best choices for kids.

Several districts in the city are notable for their ethnic cuisine. Try one of the trattorie in Little Italy, a Vietnamese or Chinese eatery in Chinatown, or a Greek taverna along the Danforth. Pick a restaurant to satisfy your family's whim—this is a city where you can devour Cantonese cuisine at Happy Seven at 4am, sample high tea at the Royal York Hotel at 4pm, and tuck into a home-cooked breakfast at Mars diner in the evening. Whatever you and the kids are currently craving, you're sure to find it somewhere in Toronto.

DINING OUT WITH YOUR KIDS

Although there are numerous family-style eateries in the city, I'd recommend letting your kids expand their dining horizons. If you're up to it, splurge at least once on dinner at one of the high-end eateries in the entertainment district or try one of the expensive options listed in this chapter. I've found that many of these restaurants welcome children, and even though they may lack kids' menus they are willing to meet your children's requests for something simpler. You'll want to make sure, of course, that your children are old enough to know how to behave in a formal setting and are capable of sitting relatively still for an hour or more.

If you've been indulging in passive pursuits all day or sitting still is not your child's forte, you might try a restaurant with some built-in entertainment. You can choose from the many restaurants that offer kids crayons, coloring books, and toys, or pick a spot with a great view of the harbor or street to let your children watch the world from their window. As you'll see in the following listings, several eateries also entertain kids with video games, PlayStations, jukeboxes, and TVs.

Another great option for families is eating outside at one of the many cafes and bistros that open up sidewalk or courtyard patios during the summer. Noise is generally a non-issue with patio dining—a great plus for families with small children—and messes seem less obvious and traumatizing for parents when the food is dropped outside on the patio rather than inside on the spotless floor.

If you have small children who find it impossible to sit still, you may want to avoid the obvious danger of dining along a busy street and opt instead for a quick meal at a deli or, better yet, takeout from one of the many establishments that offer takeout or delivery service. A picnic in a hotel room can be quite a treat for both kids and their tired parents. There is usually a reasonable amount of room for youngsters to blow off some steam between courses, and you don't have to worry about disturbing the wait staff or fellow diners. Toronto offers almost the same wide range of dining choices for takeout and delivery as it does for sit-down restaurants.

A NOTE ABOUT PRICES

Dining out in Toronto does not have to be an expensive venture, but be warned that the tax level is high. Meals are subject to 8% provincial sales tax (PST) and 7% goods and services tax (GST). In other words, tax and tip together can add 30% to your bill. Tips are normally left to the diners' discretion, unless there are six or more people at a table; 15% is the usual amount for good service. The price of a bottle of wine is generally quite high because of the tax on imports, but you can get around it by ordering an Ontario vintage—local wines enjoy a rising international reputation. Remember that there is a 10% tax on alcohol, whatever you are sipping.

1 Restaurants by Cuisine

AMERICAN/CANADIAN
Hard Rock Cafe (Downtown West, $$, p. 69)
Mr. GreenJeans ⍟ (Downtown East, $$, p. 75)
Planet Hollywood ⍟ (Downtown West, $$, p. 70)
Walt's Grill and Bar (Airport, $, p. 83)
Wayne Gretzky's ⍟⍟ (Downtown West, $$, p. 70)

BUFFET
Tucker's Marketplace (Airport, $, p. 82)

BURGERS
Lick's ⍟ (Downtown East, $, p. 75)

CANTONESE
Happy Seven (Downtown West, $, p. 70)

CHINESE
The Garden Gate (Downtown East, $, p. 75)

DELI
Druxy's (Uptown, $, p. 80)
Shopsy's TV Deli (Downtown West, $, p. 71)

Wrap and Roll (Midtown West, $, p. 77)

DINER
Flo's Diner ⍟ (Midtown West, $, p. 76)
Fran's (Uptown, $, p. 81)
Mars ⍟ (Downtown West, $, p. 70)

ECLECTIC
Peter Pan ⍟ (Downtown West, $$$, p. 68)
Rainforest Cafe ⍟⍟ (North Toronto, $$, p. 82)
Safari Bar and Grill (North Toronto, $$, p. 82)
The Pickle Barrel (Uptown, $, p. 81)

EUROPEAN
Mövenpick ⍟ (Downtown West, $, p. 71)

FRENCH CANADIAN
Le Papillon ⍟⍟⍟ (Downtown East, $$$, p. 74)

GREEK
The Friendly Greek (Midtown East, $$, p. 77)

ICE CREAM & TREATS
Baskin-Robbins (Midtown East, $, *p. 80*)

Greg's Ice Cream (Midtown West, $, *p. 77*)

Sicilian Ice Cream Company (Downtown West, $, *p. 74*)

ITALIAN
Alice Fazooli's! Italian Crabshack ★★ (Downtown West, $$, *p. 68*)

East Side Mario's (Downtown West, $$, *p. 69*)

Grano ★★ (Uptown, $$$, *p. 80*)

Il Fornello ★ (Midtown East, $$, *p. 77*)

Old Spaghetti Factory ★★ (Downtown East, $$, *p. 75*)

JAPANESE
Edo-ko ★ (Uptown, $$, *p. 80*)

MEDITERRANEAN
Millie's Bistro ★★★ (North Toronto, $$$, *p. 81*)

MIDDLE EASTERN
Jerusalem Restaurant ★★ (Uptown, $$, *p. 80*)

PERUVIAN
Boulevard Café ★★ (Midtown West, $$, *p. 76*)

SEAFOOD
The Fish House ★★ (Downtown West, $$, *p. 69*)

THAI
Young Thailand ★ (Downtown East, $, *p. 76*)

---

2 Downtown West

EXPENSIVE
Peter Pan ★ ECLECTIC   Twenty years after launching the Queen Street West restaurant craze, Peter Pan is still a trendsetter, offering great food with little of the attitude you can expect from other restaurants along this trendy street. The row of huge picture windows looking out onto the busy street makes this an ideal spot for people-watching.

Lineups are common during weekday lunches, when the business crowd dines out. From the mix of Italian, French, Mexican, and Caribbean flavors on the menu, the Peter Pan burger and the open-faced focaccia sandwiches are always excellent choices. There is no children's menu, but the chef will accommodate young guests with smaller, less spicy portions and corresponding prices.

373 Queen St. W. © **416/593-0917**. Reservations recommended. Main courses C$10–$20 (US$6.60–$13.20). AE, MC, V. Mon–Wed noon–midnight, Thurs–Sat noon–1am, Sun noon–11pm. Highchairs. Subway: Osgoode.

MODERATE
Alice Fazooli's! Italian Crabshack ★★ ITALIAN/CAJUN   This lively downtown restaurant mixes Italian gusto with Cajun spice. Besides an amazing array of pastas, the menu features such Cajun specialties as hush puppies (potato balls) and crawdads (crayfish). The Crabshack bread, served warm and oozing with olive oil, garlic butter, herbs, and Parmesan, is the perfect starter. On the Italian side, mushroom lovers will be unable to resist the mushroom penne— portobello, shiitake, and field mushrooms smothered in a pesto cream sauce. The Cajun seafood dishes are rated by their "bib factor," or how likely you are to end up splattered with sauce. One elbow-dripping delicacy is the combo boil—fresh seafood, corn, and potatoes simmered in a Cajun tomato broth. The children's menu includes such standbys as hamburgers, pizza, and chicken

fingers, but for more adventurous kids, all of the menu items can be prepared in child-sized portions. Deep-fried alligator, anyone?

If you're heading to the Colossus movie theater or Canada's Wonderland in Vaughan, Alice Fazooli's has another location at 20 Colossus Dr. (Hwy. 400 and Hwy. 7) (© **905/850-3565**).

294 Adelaide St. W. © **416/979-1910**. Reservations recommended. Main courses C$8.95–$17.95 (US$5.90–$11.85), kids' menu C$3–$5 (US$2–$3.30). AE, DC, MC, V. Sun–Wed 11:30am–1:00am, Thurs–Sat 11:30am–2:00am. Highchairs. Subway: St. Andrew or Osgoode.

East Side Mario's NEW YORK ITALIAN   From the peanut shells strewn across the floor to the 1960s music blaring from the speakers, Mario's makes an effort to be as laid-back as possible. Patrons will quickly find themselves responding in kind. Once the kids have finished pondering why they can't throw shells on the floor at home, they too will be delighted with this family restaurant. There's a lot to amuse them, from the kids' activity packs to the dessert menus on viewfinders.

The vegetable-laden angel hair primavera is heartwarming. From the bambino menu, the kids can choose from pastas, burgers, and pizza. The cheese cappelletti is always a favorite with our kids.

151 Front St. W. © **416/360-1917**. Main courses C$8–$13 (US$5.30–$8.60), kids' menu C$3.50 (US$2.30). AE, DC, MC, V. Highchairs, boosters. Subway: Union.

The Fish House ⓕⓕ SEAFOOD   This huge warehouse-style restaurant, with several locations around the city, is one of Toronto's top seafood restaurants. Not surprisingly, the theme is nautical and the lively oyster bar is a popular spot. Kids get to wear pirate hats while they wait, although service is generally quick.

The kids' menu is quite extensive and offers a selection of breaded fish, chicken fingers, and pasta, but my children usually go for the grilled fresh fish. On the main menu, the wide selection of seafood is flown in daily. Mahimahi, sea bass, crab, shrimp, and lobster can be ordered grilled, steamed, poached, or baked. The cedar-planked salmon, which is tied to aromatic cedar wood during baking, is a wonderful west coast–scented treat.

144 Front St. W. © **416/595-5051**. Main courses C$9–$25 (US$5.95–$16.50), kids' menu C$6 (US$3.95). AE, MC, V. Mon–Fri 11:30am–3pm and 4–11pm; Sat–Sun 4–11pm. Highchairs, boosters. Subway: Union.

The Hard Rock Cafe AMERICAN   The name says it all: A steady stream of classic rock and pop blares from the speakers, and music videos play on screens throughout the restaurant. If all this distraction isn't enough, get seats close to the window so the kids can watch when a game is on at SkyDome—the restaurant is inside the stadium.

Lil' rockers are given a coloring book menu and crayon. From the kids' menu, my gang likes the cheeseburger and the macaroni and cheese. All kids' meals come with french fries, applesauce, and a beverage. For adults, the menu offers everything from homey pot roast with roasted vegetables and garlic mashed potatoes to spicier items such as jambalaya penne pasta with andouille sausage, chicken, and vegetables topped with a Creole sauce.

There is another Hard Rock Cafe across from the Eaton Centre, at 283 Yonge St. (© **416/362-3636**).

1 Blue Jays Way (at SkyDome). © **416/341-2388**. Main courses C$9–$25 (US$5.95–$16.50); kids' menu C$7 (US$4.60). AE, DC, MC, V. Mon–Sat 11am–midnight, Sun 11am–10pm. Highchairs, boosters. Subway: Union.

Planet Hollywood (★) AMERICAN/CANADIAN   There's no need to worry about the kids making too much noise in this dining room salute to the movie industry. The movie screens scattered about the restaurant play a collage of movie clips accompanied by loud theme music.

Although the food is basic roadhouse style, the restaurant is well worth a visit for movie buffs. Kids can search for Kevin Costner's costume from *Robin Hood*, a munchkin suit from *The Wizard of Oz*, or Fred Flintstone's cave attire among the hundreds of pieces of movie memorabilia that line the walls. The children's menu contains most of the usual stuff, but our group usually goes for the ultimate decadence: chicken fingers coated in Cap'n Crunch cereal and served with fries. The menu doubles as an activity sheet and children are given crayons to help pass the time—a good idea, since short lineups are common during the dinner hour and service is slow. Adults have a wide variety of main courses to choose from—the pastas are consistently good, and the apple strudel, made from Arnold Schwarzenegger's family recipe, makes a tasty finale.

277 Front St. W. ☎ **416/596-7827.** Main courses C$8–$18 (US$5.30–$11.90); kids' menu C$5.95 (US$3.90). AE, DC, MC, V. Daily 11am–2am. Highchairs, boosters. Subway: Union.

Wayne Gretzky's (★★) CANADIAN/AMERICAN   This comfortable family-style restaurant is a hockey lover's paradise. The Great One's memorabilia decorate the walls, alongside newspaper clippings and souvenirs of other well-known stick handlers. While they wait, the kids can play one of several table hockey and hockey-themed video games. They are also given a paper hockey mask to color and take home.

The food here is surprisingly good for a theme restaurant. The grilled burger and fries are the best choice, according to my daughters, although they do occasionally try the dinosaur-shaped chicken fingers. Grilled items such as the 7 oz. aged tenderloin or the 6 oz. Great One Burger are always excellent. The latter is apparently made the way Wayne prefers it, with cheddar cheese, bacon, and plenty of onions; in a kitschy touch, the number 99 is branded onto the bun.

On warm days, diners abandon the ice rink theme for the tropical rooftop patio, complete with palm trees and a waterfall.

99 Blue Jays Way. ☎ **416/979-PUCK.** Main courses C$10–$25 (US$6.60–$16.50); kids' menu C$6 (US$3.95). AE, DC, MC, V. Mon–Wed 11:30am–1am, Thurs–Sat 11:30am–2am, Sun 11:30am–midnight. Highchairs, boosters. Subway: Union.

INEXPENSIVE

Happy Seven CANTONESE   Chinatown is jam-packed with restaurants, but this one is most often recommended by both locals and visitors. As a result, the restaurant is always busy, and staff is efficient if not effervescent.

In addition to serving consistently good food, Happy Seven boasts two separate menus. The first offers the more traditional Chinese food that North Americans have come to know—the wonton soup is wonderful. The second menu lists more exotic Cantonese fare, including pigeon and frogs' legs. My favorite dish is the stir-fried chicken with apple.

358 Spadina Ave. ☎ **416/971-9820.** Main courses C$4.50–$13 (US$2.95–$8.60). MC, V. Daily 11:30am–5am. Subway: Spadina, then any streetcar south.

Mars (★) (*Value*) DINER   The decor and menu at this Kensington Market establishment have remained virtually unchanged since the grand opening in 1951. There's little elbow room, but the long stainless steel lunch counter seats

20. While there is no children's menu, the inexpensive comfort foods here will appeal to everyone. Good choices for kids and adults alike are the huge all-day breakfasts and homemade bran muffins.

There is a newer branch at 2362 Yonge St., north of Eglinton Ave. (© 416/ 322-7111), but its kitschy diner decor doesn't compare to the real thing.

432 College St. © 416/921-6332. C$4.95–$8.95 (US$3.25–$5.90). Thurs–Sat 24 hours, Sun–Wed 7am–8:30pm. AE, MC, V. Boosters. Subway: Queen's Park, then any streetcar west.

Mövenpick *★* EUROPEAN   This Swiss restaurant chain has several locations in downtown. Operating under the names Mövenpick or Marché, each branch draws in diners with its Swiss specialties and global dishes.

With trays or baskets in hand, young diners at the Marché market-style restaurant in BCE Place not only get to pick their own ingredients but also get to watch their food being prepared at one of the many food stations. Each diner receives a ticket, which is stamped at each food station.

Food stations include everything from pastas and salads to European pastries. I usually try a stir-fry with chicken or beef and a wide selection of fresh vegetables. The hoisin sauce is fantastic, but there are others to choose from. The kids like the pizzas and the freshly cut french fries. The drawback to this restaurant is that you'll need at least one adult per child to help with carrying, or an infinite amount of patience.

The Yorkville Mövenpick maintains the European theme, but all similarity ends there. This is a sit-down restaurant. On the top floor is the Bistretto, which offers a range of European dishes, and on the bottom floor is La Pecherie, devoted primarily to seafood. The kids' menu offers great variety and includes sausages with rosti potatoes and eggs and turkey wiener schnitzel with french fries and veggies.

There are two additional Mövenpick restaurants downtown, at 42 Yonge St. (© 416/366-8986) and 165 York St. (© 416/366-5234).

Marché, 61 Bay St. (at Wellington St.). © 416/366-8986. Main courses C$4–$13 (US$2.65–$8.60). AE, MC, V. Daily 7:30am–2am. Highchairs, boosters. Subway: Union or King. Mövenpick, 133 Yorkville Ave. © 416/926-9545. Main courses C$9.25–$26 (US$6.10–$17.15), kids' menu C$4.50–$6 (US$2.95–$3.95). AE, MC, V. Sun–Tues 7:30am–midnight, Wed–Thurs 7:30am–1am, Fri–Sat 7:30am–2am. Highchairs, boosters. Subway: Bay.

Shopsy's TV Deli DELI   Looking for a way to get your kids to stay in their seats while they wait for their dinner? Shopsy's has found the answer: This deli has 40 TVs and 13 booths equipped with Sony PlayStations, joysticks, monitors, and plenty of games to choose from.

With the kids busy, the adults can take time to enjoy such classic deli fare as corned beef on rye, served with homemade Yukon Gold fries or a steaming potato latke. Comfort foods such as macaroni and cheese and chili are also popular, and the old-fashioned floats are thick and wonderful. For dessert try Wafflicious—two waffles topped with vanilla ice cream and fruit. Kids can choose from kid-sized hot dogs, hamburgers, steak, or Kraft dinner, or try something from the main menu.

Additional branches are located at 33 Yonge St. (© 416/365-3333) and 1535 Yonge St. (© 416/967-5252).

248 King St. W. (at John St.). © 416/599-5464. Breakfast C$4.95–$6.95 (US$3.25–$4.60); lunch and main courses C$6.25–$8.95 (US$4.15–$5.90). AE, DC, MC, V. Mon–Tues 8am–9pm, Wed–Sat 8am–midnight, Sun 8am–10pm. Highchairs. Subway: St. Andrew.

Family-Friendly Downtown Dining

Alice Fazooli's! Italian
Crabshack **1**
East Side Mario's **2**
Fish House **3**
Garden Gate **4**
Happy Seven **5**
The Hard Rock Cafe **6**
Le Papillon **7**
Lick's **8**
Mars **9**
Mövenpick (BCE) **10**
Mr. GreenJeans **11**
Old Spaghetti Factory **12**
Peter Pan **13**
Planet Hollywood **14**
Royal York (Fairmont)
(tea room) **15**
Shopsy's TV Deli **16**
Sicilian Ice Cream
Company **17**
Wayne Gretsky's **18**
Young Thailand **19**

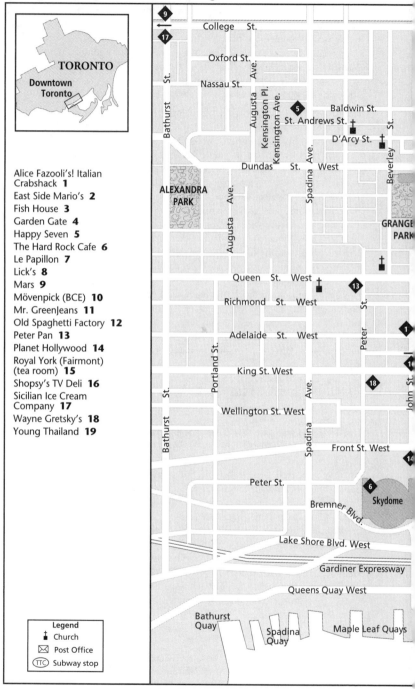

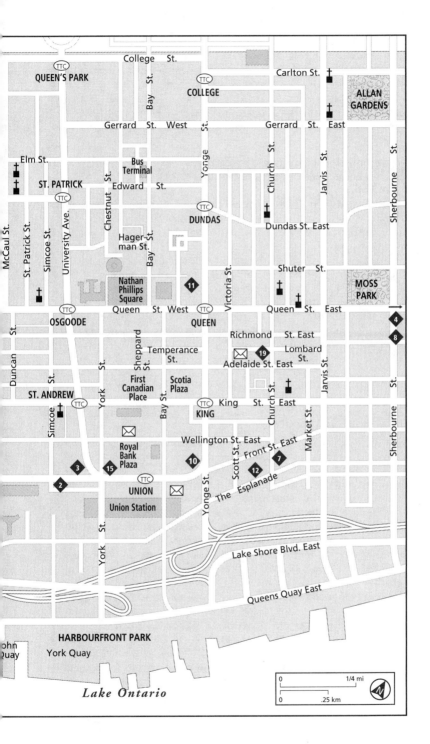

Sicilian Ice Cream Company ICE CREAM   Offering far more than just ice cream, this cafe is a bit out of the way in Little Italy but well worth the journey. In addition to the awe-inspiring selection of ice cream flavors, there are some delectable desserts, including crepes and waffles. The granita, a lemon ice, makes a refreshing summer treat.

712 College St. ℂ 416/531-7716. C$3.50–$6.95 (US$2.30–$4.60), child's scoop C$2.50 (US$1.65). No credit cards. Mon–Thurs 9am–midnight, Fri–Sat 9am–2am, Sun 11am–2am. Subway: Queen's Park, then any streetcar west.

3 Downtown East

EXPENSIVE

Le Papillon ⋆⋆⋆ *(Moments* FRENCH CANADIAN   Fine dining and an upscale children's menu make this spot unique among family-friendly restaurants. The decor is pure French countryside and the staff genuinely welcomes small guests.

From the array of Quebecois specialties on the menu, the crepes are definitely not to be missed. Crepe bergère, stuffed with apple, raisins, and lamb curry, is an interesting choice, but if crepes aren't your thing, try the feuilleté de fruits de mer, a mélange of scallops and tiger shrimp served over rice with a tarragon cream sauce. For kids, Le Papillon stays with its usual style. Young guests are offered a number of choices, ranging from apple creams to pasta and cream sauce, all at a reasonable price.

16 Church St. ℂ **416/363-0838.** Main courses C$8–$19 (US$5.30–$12.55), kids' menu C$2–$5 (US$1.30–$3.30). AE, DC, MC, V. Mon–Thurs noon–2:30pm and 5–11pm; Fri noon–2:30 pm and 5pm–midnight; Sat 11:30am–midnight; Sun brunch 11am–3pm and dinner 5–10pm. Highchairs, boosters. Subway: Union.

(Moments **Tea Parties**

All kids love tea parties. For a special treat, bring them to one of the several downtown and midtown hotels that serve afternoon or high tea. While most establishments have no special prices for children, the assorted scones and dainty sandwiches brought to the table are always plentiful enough for adults to share with the kids.

The **Royal Tea Room** at the Royal York Hotel lives up to its name—the queen has taken her afternoon tea here. A scrumptious selection of finger sandwiches and pastries is served, but the highlight is the dish of fresh seasonal berries. 100 Front St. W. ℂ **416/368-2884.** Reservations recommended. C$11.95 to $18.50 (US$7.90 to $12.20), children half price. Monday to Friday 2 to 5pm.

Tea at the **Windsor Arms** is a tribute to a bygone era. In the early 20th century, this hotel was the favorite haunt of Toronto's socialites. The setting is formal but cozy and two seatings ensure that your teatime will be relaxed and unhurried. 18 St. Thomas St. ℂ **416/971-9666.** Reservations recommended. C$20 to $32 (US$13.20 to $21.10). Daily 1:30pm and 3:30pm.

Several ritzy downtown hotels also offer afternoon teas. In Yorkville, the **Four Seasons** lobby bar is the spot for formal afternoon or high tea. Rich Devonshire cream is served with the scones, and the Irish cream coffee cake is delicious. 21 Avenue Rd. ℂ **416/964-0411.** Reservations recommended. C$24.15 (US$15.95). No children's price but kids can order a la carte. Monday to Friday 3 to 5pm, Saturday to Sunday 1 to 5:30pm.

MODERATE

Mr. GreenJeans (★) AMERICAN/CANADIAN   Famous for its burgers and buffalo chips (thinly sliced deep-fried potatoes), Mr. GreenJeans also attracts a large following for its thick 30-ounce milkshakes.

This Eaton Centre institution seats over 450 on two floors. A small patio overlooks the serene Trinity United Church, one of the few historic buildings preserved when the mall was built.

The decor is a strange mixture of beachwear, gourds, and dried herbs, and the setting provides plenty to look at, as the restaurant is consistently crowded with tourists, shoppers, and office workers from the surrounding towers. Pool tables and a video arcade will keep the kids busy while you wait.

With over 70 items on the menu there's a lot to choose from, and the portions are huge. The kids' menu includes standard items such as burgers and chicken fingers.

220 Yonge St. (in the Eaton Centre). © 416/979-1212. Main courses C$8–$19 (US$5.30–$12.55), kids' menu C$5 (US$3.30). AE, DC, MC, V. Mon–Thurs 11am–11pm, Fri 11am–midnight, Sat 11am–11:30pm, Sun 11:30am–10pm. Highchairs, boosters. Subway: Dundas.

Old Spaghetti Factory (★)(★) (Value) ITALIAN AMERICAN   Lunch at the Old Spaghetti Factory was always the highlight of school trips into the city when I was a child. It still is for many young visitors, and a peek inside will tell you why. My kids always look for a seat in the streetcar (it's the real thing), but they're also thrilled by the carousel. This huge restaurant is decorated with a lively mix of stained glass, carved wood, and Tiffany lamps. The collection of brass instruments along one wall adds to the whimsical atmosphere.

As you might have guessed, spaghetti is the highlight of the menu. The variety of sauces is infinite, ranging from traditional tomato to mushroom tarragon, and as a starter you're given delicious sourdough bread that threatens to fill you before the main courses arrive. If you can't decide on a sauce, choose the Manager's Favourite, which allows you to select two of your favorite spaghettis. Kids' meals include spaghetti with meatballs, lasagna, and chicken fingers, all of which come with a choice of minestrone soup, fruit cocktail, or salad; a beverage; and a dish of spumoni ice cream.

54 The Esplanade. © 416/864-9761. Main courses C$7.25–$15 (US$4.80–$9.90); kids' menu C$5.25–$7 (US$3.45–$4.60). AE, DC, DISC, MC, V. Mon–Thurs 11:30am–11:00pm, Fri–Sat 11:30am–midnight, Sun 11:30am–10pm. Highchairs, boosters. Subway: Union.

INEXPENSIVE

The Garden Gate (Finds) CHINESE   Don't be put off by the decrepit exterior —this place is a Beaches institution with a dedicated local clientele. Nicknamed "the Goof" when several letters on its neon sign burned out, the restaurant offers an extensive menu of North American–style Chinese, as well as a delicious all-day breakfast. The combination dinners are always a good choice, especially no. 8—a satisfying meal of beef ding, sweet and sour ribs, an egg roll, and fried rice. Most tables have jukeboxes.

2379 Queen St. E. © 416/694-3605. Main courses C$4.25–$8.50 (US$2.80–$5.60). AE, MC, V. Mon–Thurs 8am–midnight, Fri–Sat 8am–1am, Sun 8am–11pm. Subway: Main, then no. 64 bus south to Queen St. and walk east, or Queen, then any streetcar east.

Lick's (★) BURGERS   The Lick's in the Beaches area was the first one I tried and it remains a sentimental favorite of mine. There is just something about being near the beach and listening to the reggae-inspired cadence of the cooks and counter staff as they sing out the orders and team-building chants.

Kids' meals include a toy, a drink, and fries, and a choice of hamburger, hot dog, nature (veggie) burger, or safari (chicken) buddies. The burgers are a popular choice for adults, and my vegan sister claims they make one of the best veggie burgers in town. The BBQ chicken breast burger is good and comes without the breading that often coats chicken sandwiches in other fast-food restaurants.

Additional branches are located at 49 Eglinton Ave. E. (© **416/362-5425**) and 3932 Keele St. (© **416/630-6669**).

1960 Queen St. E. © **416/362-5425**. Main courses C$3–$7 (US$2–$4.60), kids' menu C$4 (US$2.65). No credit cards. Subway: Queen, then any streetcar east.

Young Thailand ⚹ THAI   The great thing about Toronto restaurants is that when one becomes popular, it usually clones itself in other parts of the city. This is the case with Young Thailand, which now has four locations across Toronto.

There are no meals specifically for children, but the main menu does offer enough variety that kids will be able to find something that interests them. There are a number of less-spicy items on the menu that would appeal to toddlers. The peanut-flavored chicken satay and the khao pad kai are mild, as are many of the soups on the menu. Toddlers eat for free and children under 12 eat for half price at the luncheon buffet.

The house specialty is Pad Thai—chicken, shrimp, and tofu combined with roasted peanuts, rice noodles, and tamarind sauce. The salads also entice; try Yam Mamuang, a satisfying blend of chicken, red onions, and green mango.

81 Church St. © **416/368-1368**. Lunch C$11–$20 (US$7.25–$13.20); dinner C$21–$30 (US$13.85–$19.80). AE, DC, MC, V. Mon–Fri 11:30am–10pm, Sat–Sun 4:30–11pm. Highchairs, boosters. Subway: King.

4 Midtown West

MODERATE

Boulevard Café ⚹⚹ (Finds) PERUVIAN   When your kids have had enough of the usual offerings of spaghetti and chicken fingers, bring them here. This is a small, sometimes crowded cafe, but the staff is consistently friendly and the children's menu has an astounding 10 items on it. The kids can choose from traditional Peruvian dishes such as empanadas and quesadillas or stick to more North American fare such as chicken brochette.

On the main menu, the fresh fish of the day, grilled in oil and garlic, and the lamb chops, marinated in wine and spices, are excellent choices.

161 Harbord St. © **416/961-7676**. Main courses C$12.95–$18.95 (US$8.55–$12.50), kids' menu C$3.75–$4.95 (US$2.50–$3.25). AE, DC, MC, V. Daily 11:30am–midnight. Highchair, booster. Subway: Bathurst, then any streetcar south.

INEXPENSIVE

Flo's Diner ⚹ (Finds) DINER   This fifties-style diner in the middle of trendy Yorkville has it all: Formica countertops, chrome stools, comfy booths, and fast and friendly service. However, the real draw for kids and adults alike is the best milkshake in Toronto, made the old-fashioned way and served in a thick glass with the leftovers brought to the table in the aluminum mixing container. Tuna melts, burgers, and fries share space on the menu with the all-day breakfast and some surprisingly excellent salad choices.

Kids are given crayons and coloring sheets and are allowed to choose their own toy prize from a tin bucket. The kids' menu offers standard diner fare such as hotdogs and hamburgers, but a new menu with healthier choices for kids will be launched soon.

70 Yorkville Ave. © **416/961-4333**. Main courses C$5–$12 (US$3.30–$7.90), kids' menu C$3–$5 (US$2–$3.30). No credit cards. Mon–Thurs 7:30am–10pm, Fri–Sat 8:30am–midnight, Sun 9am–10pm. Highchairs, boosters. Subway: Bay.

Wrap and Roll DELI   Tortilla sandwiches of every description are the mainstay of this fast-food alternative to burgers. Peanut butter with honey, jam, or bananas is a popular choice from the kids' menu. Wraps with everything from Creole chicken to prosciutto and red peppers are offered on the main menu.

There are three additional locations at 325 Queen St. W. (© **416/340-1322**), 1366 Yonge St. (© **416/921-0780**), and 450 Yonge St. (© **416/922-5339**).

192 Bloor St. W. © **416/323-3212**. Wraps C$5.50–$6.50 (US$3.65–$4.30), kids' menu C$3 (US$2). AE, MC, V. Mon–Wed 8:30am–9pm, Thurs–Sat 8:30am–11pm, Sun 11am–9pm. Highchairs, boosters. Subway: Museum.

Greg's Ice Cream ICE CREAM   Some of the most delectable among the many flavors of natural ice cream made and sold here include roasted marshmallow and vanilla chocolate. The more adventurous might want to try a scoop of green tea or stout ice cream.

200 Bloor St. W. © **416/961-4734**. C$2–$4.85 (US$1.30–$3.20), kids' scoop C$2 (US$1.30). No credit cards. Daily 12–9pm; summer, daily 12pm–12am. Subway: St. George.

5 Midtown East

MODERATE

The Friendly Greek GREEK   This Greektown restaurant stays true to its name, offering classic Greek cuisine in a relaxed, friendly atmosphere. Now a chain with 12 additional locations, this restaurant is decorated in a style reminiscent of the Greek islands, complete with a stone floor and a large, open kitchen.

Pork and chicken souvlaki are the mainstays of the kid's menu, but burgers and chicken fingers are also available. For adults, the pork souvlaki accompanied by lemon-roasted potatoes and steamed vegetables is a treat.

Additional branches can be found at 2245 Yonge St. (© **416/483-8588**) and 525 Bloor St. W. (© **416/530-4511**).

551 Danforth Ave. © **416/469-8422.**. Main courses C$8.95–$11.95 (US$5.90–$7.90), kids' menu C$3.25–$4.35 (US$2.15–$2.85). AE, DC, MC, V. Sun–Thurs 11am–1am, Fri–Sat 11am–4am. Highchairs, boosters Subway: Pape.

Il Fornello ITALIAN   This little bit of Italy in the middle of Greektown is decidedly family-friendly, from the extensive children's menu to the attentive, sociable staff.

The pastas include a rich penne with chicken and cream sauce. The grilled chicken salad with walnuts and orange-flavored dressing makes a nice change from pasta or pizza, but it may be hard to resist the wood oven–baked pizzas, which are among the best in the city. The kids' menu includes a wide variety of pizzas, one of the most popular of which is the Hawaiian. An alternative menu offers wheat-free, gluten-free, dairy-free, and yeast-free items.

Il Fornello has additional locations at 1968 Queen St. E. (© **416/691-8377**), 55 Eglinton Ave. E. (© **416/486-3660**), 35 Elm St. (© **416/598-1766**) and 214 King St. W. (© **416/599-0312**).

576 Danforth Ave. © **416/466-2931**. Main courses C$9.50–$21.95 (US$6.25–$14.50), kids' menu C$4.95 (US$3.25). AE, DC, MC, V. Mon–Thurs 11:30am–10pm, Fri 11:30–11pm, Sat–Sun 11am–11pm. Highchairs, boosters. Subway: Pape.

Family-Friendly Midtown Dining

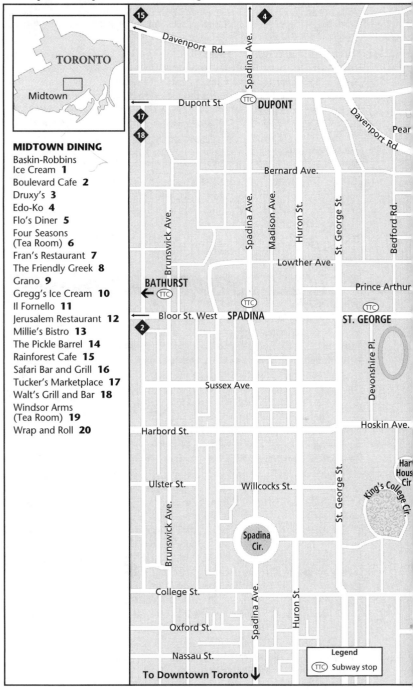

TORONTO

Midtown

MIDTOWN DINING

Baskin-Robbins
Ice Cream **1**
Boulevard Cafe **2**
Druxy's **3**
Edo-Ko **4**
Flo's Diner **5**
Four Seasons
(Tea Room) **6**
Fran's Restaurant **7**
The Friendly Greek **8**
Grano **9**
Gregg's Ice Cream **10**
Il Fornello **11**
Jerusalem Restaurant **12**
Millie's Bistro **13**
The Pickle Barrel **14**
Rainforest Cafe **15**
Safari Bar and Grill **16**
Tucker's Marketplace **17**
Walt's Grill and Bar **18**
Windsor Arms
(Tea Room) **19**
Wrap and Roll **20**

Davenport Rd.

Spadina Ave.

Dupont St. (TTC) **DUPONT**

Davenport Rd.

Pear

Bernard Ave.

Brunswick Ave.

Spadina Ave.

Madison Ave.

Huron St.

St. George St.

Bedford Rd.

Lowther Ave.

BATHURST
← (TTC)

Prince Arthur

Bloor St. West **SPADINA** (TTC)

ST. GEORGE (TTC)

Devonshire Pl.

Sussex Ave.

Harbord St.

Hoskin Ave.

Har
Hous
Cir

Ulster St.

Willcocks St.

St. George St.

King's College Cir.

Brunswick Ave.

Spadina
Cir.

College St.

Spadina Ave.

Huron St.

Oxford St.

Nassau St.

To Downtown Toronto ↓

Legend
(TTC) Subway stop

INEXPENSIVE

Baskin-Robbins ICE CREAM   When I was in high school I was so addicted to the German chocolate cake ice cream here that a friend brought me a 5-gallon tub of it. They no longer sell German chocolate cake, but this chain does have 31 changing flavors of decadent ice cream. The ice cream cakes are perfect for birthdays or for bringing back to your hotel as a treat at the end of a long summer day.

536 Church St. ✆ **416/925-3131.** C$2–$3/scoop (US$1.30–$2), child scoop C$1.50 (US$1). No credit cards. 11am–midnight. Subway: Wellesley. Many locations citywide.

6 Uptown

EXPENSIVE

Grano ✶✶ ITALIAN   Even from the outside Grano looks like it belongs on a quiet Roman side street rather than on Toronto's busiest thoroughfare. Inside, the faux plaster walls, warm tile, and opera playing in the background complete the illusion. The courtyard patio, with its kitschy fountain, is especially popular with families. Scaled-down dishes from the main menu are available for young guests, or they can choose from the more than 40 antipasti selections in the glass display case. The bread is baked fresh on the premises and the white chocolate raspberry flan will satisfy even the sweetest tooth.

2035 Yonge St. ✆ **416/440-1986.** Main courses C$20–$30 (US$13.20–$19.80). AE, DC, MC, V. Mon–Fri 9:30am–11pm, Sat 9am–11pm. Highchairs, boosters. Subway: Davisville, then walk north on Yonge St.

MODERATE

Edo-ko ✶ JAPANESE   There are two versions of this kid-friendly restaurant, Edo and the much larger Edo-ko. The children's bento box, which includes a tempura rice burger or yakitori, sushi, salad, and fruit, is a fun way to introduce your children to Japanese cuisine. At C$9.95 (US$6.55), it's a little on the pricey side, though. Another option is to select from the generous portions on the main menu, which includes an extensive selection of sushi and even more adventurous items such as barbecued eel.

Edo-ko, 431 Spadina Rd. ✆ **416/482-8973.** Main courses C$12–$24.95 (US$7.90–$16.45), kids' menu $9.95 (US$6.55). AE, MC, V. Tues–Sun 12pm–1am. Subway: St. Clair West, then no. 33 bus north. **Edo**, 484 Eglinton Ave. W. ✆ **416/322-2033.** Subway: Eglinton, then any bus west.

Jerusalem Restaurant ✶✶ MIDDLE EASTERN   This calm, intimate restaurant offers classic children's fare with a Middle Eastern twist. Burgers and chicken breasts are served in pitas, and shish tawoo, skewed chicken, is a popular choice for little tykes. The main menu is spare, but everything from the falafel to the lamb and chicken shish kebob is consistently excellent.

The restaurant is small and tables are placed close together, but the decor is warm. Budding artists will love the detailed, colorful murals of Middle Eastern scenes covering the walls.

955 Eglinton Ave. W. ✆ **416/783-6494.** Reservations recommended for dinner. Main courses C$10.95–$15.95 (US$7.20–$10.50), kids' menu C$5.95 (US$3.95). AE, MC, V. Mon–Sat noon–11pm, Sun noon–10pm. Highchairs, boosters. Subway: Eglinton, then any bus west.

INEXPENSIVE

Druxy's DELI   With 32 locations across Toronto, Druxy's serves classic deli fare including made-to-order sandwiches on your choice of bread. Several locations, such as the one at the Royal Ontario Museum, feature a small salad bar.

The food is consistently good and fresh, and despite frequent lineups the counter service is speedy.

Additional convenient locations are at 29 Queen St. E. (℃ **416/367-3904**); 1 Front St. W. (℃ **416/304-0000**); 218 Yonge St., in the Eaton Centre food court (℃ **416/979-9747**); 101 Queen's Park Cres., in the ROM front entrance (℃ **416/586-5563**); and 1200 Eglinton Ave. E. (℃ **416/385-9500**).

1 Eglinton Ave. E. ℃ **416/481-5363**. C$4.95–$6.95 (US$3.25–$4.60). No credit cards. Mon–Sat 7am–3pm. Highchairs, boosters. Subway: Eglinton.

Fran's *(Value)* DINER   With its streetcar exterior and neon sign, Fran's is a classic forties-style diner. Slide into a faux-leather booth or grab a chrome counter seat, and order up some classic diner fare.

While the menu includes some surprisingly sophisticated items, the all-day breakfast is filling, if not fancy, and the grilled beef and bacon or veggie burger is still the best choice. The kids' menu includes burgers, macaroni and cheese, and grilled cheese sandwiches, but my gang usually goes for the pancakes with chocolate chips. The word is that Fran's also makes a superb Shirley Temple. The menu is actually a coloring page, and kids are given crayons to draw what they see outside the window. The resulting artwork is then proudly displayed around the restaurant.

Fran's has two other locations at 21 St. Clair Ave. W. (℃ **416/925-6337**) and 20 College St. (℃ **416/923-9867**), but they are somewhat lacking in atmosphere.

45 Eglinton Ave. E. ℃ **416/481-1112**. Main courses C$6–$12 (US$3.95–$7.90), kids' menu C$3–$4 (US$2–$2.65). AE, MC, V. Highchairs, boosters. Subway: Eglinton.

The Pickle Barrel ECLECTIC   This family-friendly eatery has a number of branches scattered across Toronto. Most offer a similar menu, but the Bloombury Pickle Barrel has an all-you-can-eat buffet.

Kids will get a kick out of the pickle people and other pickle-inspired works of art, and the menu doubles as a coloring sheet. Favorites from the lengthy children's menu include the corned beef sandwich with fries and the wings and fries. For adults, the barbecue meals are especially tasty—try the chicken, baby back ribs, or rib steak, or go for a hearty meal of liver and onions with a side of latkes.

2300 Yonge St., in the Yonge-Eglinton Centre. ℃ **416/485-1244**. Main courses C$9–$15 (US$5.95–$9.90), kids' menu C$4–$5 (US$2.65–$3.30). AE, DC, DISC, MC, V. Sun–Mon 8am–11pm, Tues–Fri 8am–midnight, Sat 8am–1am. Highchairs, boosters. Subway: Eglinton.

7 North Toronto

EXPENSIVE

Millie's Bistro ★★★ *(Finds)* MEDITERRANEAN   The menu at this upscale bistro takes its cue primarily from the southern Mediterranean cuisine of Turkey and North Africa, with some interesting choices from France and Spain to add to the mix.

The selection of Turkish flatbreads and tapas are second to none in Toronto. Since each one is as wonderful as the next, ask your server to arrange a selection on a tray so everyone at the table can share.

The rooms are narrow and somewhat crowded but very sunny. The solarium is a favorite spot with my kids. Young diners will find many appealing dishes on the adult menu, but they can also select such items as grilled cheese sandwiches, chicken fingers, pizza, and organic french fries from the limited children's menu.

Coloring books and crayons are provided at the table and menu prices are geared to kids' ages.

1980 Avenue Rd. ✆ **416/481-1247.** Reservations recommended. Main courses C$11.95–$24.85 (US$7.90–$16.40), kids' menu C$1 (US66¢) per year of age to a maximum of C$7 (US$4.60). AE, MC, V. Daily 11:30am–11pm. Highchairs, boosters. Subway: York Mills, then walk west to Avenue Rd.

MODERATE

Rainforest Cafe ⟨★★ ⟨Moments⟩ ECLECTIC   This is my girls' hands-down favorite, and I have to admit, even jaded adults will be thrilled by this jungle-themed restaurant in Yorkdale Shopping Centre.

Diners enter the restaurant through an aquarium archway populated by a variety of colorful fish. The moving, lifelike elephants, apes, and snakes will wow the kids, and just wait until the thunderstorm comes. The restaurant darkens, lights flash, and the distant roar of thunder echoes about the restaurant. Don't miss the hippo bathing in a lagoon on the way out.

The menu appeals to adults and children alike. On the main menu, the China Island chicken salad with crispy noodles, bok choy, sesame seeds, chicken, and veggies is light yet satisfying. From the kids' menu, younger kids might opt for pasta or burgers, while older kids may prefer chicken linguini or fish and chips. Kids' meals include a drink, and they can keep the rainforest-themed cup as a souvenir.

3401 Dufferin St. (in Yorkdale Shopping Centre). ✆ **416/780-4080.** Reservations recommended. Main courses C$9–$19 (US$5.95–$12.55), kids' menu C$6.50–$7.50 (US$4.30–$4.95). AE, DC, MC, V. Mon–Thurs 11am–10pm, Fri–Sat 11am–11pm, Sun 11am–9pm. Highchairs, boosters. Subway: Yorkdale.

Safari Bar and Grill ECLECTIC   In the summer, the patio at this north-end restaurant is as full of strollers as it is people. The restaurant begins to fill up by 7pm so try to arrive before then.

The most popular items on the menu are the stone oven–baked pizza and pizzadillas—tortillas with pizza toppings. The green pizzadilla, topped with basil puree, grilled chicken, red pepper, and goat cheese, is wonderful. The kids' menu is pricey but boasts a generous selection of burgers, pizza, pasta, and wings.

1749 Avenue Rd. ✆ **416/787-6584.** Main courses C$8–$12 (US$5.30–$7.90), kids' menu C$6.95 (US$4.60). AE, DC, MC, V. Daily 11:30am–2am. Highchairs, boosters. Subway: Eglinton, then no. 5 bus north to Fairlawn Ave.

8 Near the Airport

INEXPENSIVE

Tucker's Marketplace BUFFET   This market-style buffet is a great place to bring your finicky eaters. Choose from a wide variety of food stations with selections that run the gamut from thick, succulent steaks to pasta and stir-fries. Avoid the salad bar, though, which is large but disappointing.

This is an affordable option for parents, especially since kids under 5 eat for free Monday through Thursday and during Sunday brunch. Kids are given coloring books, crayons, and occasionally balloons when they arrive. The waiters, who are friendly but exceptionally slow, will serve your beverages. The fruit smoothies, available in both adult and child sizes, are wonderful concoctions of ice cream blended with strawberries, blueberries, or cherries. Kids get to keep their spill-proof cups.

15 Carlson Court (off Airport Rd.). ℂ **416/675-8818.** Fri–Sun buffet C$18 (US$11.90), Mon–Thurs buffet C$15 (US$9.90), kids under 12, half price. Kids under 5 eat for free Mon–Thurs and Sun brunch; half price other times. AE, DC, MC, V. Mon–Thurs 11:30am–2pm and 5–9pm; Fri 11:30am–2pm and 5–10pm; Sat 4:30–10pm; Sun 10:30am–2pm and 4:30–9pm. Highchairs, boosters.

Walt's Grill and Bar AMERICAN/CANADIAN   Despite the name, the emphasis here is definitely more bar than grill—even Jell-O is served in a shot glass. However, if you can get past the peanut shell–strewn floor, the food is homey and good and the menu is extensive.

Pizza, pogos, and burgers dominate the inexpensive kid's menu, and as an added bonus they eat free for free on Fridays. The main menu features standard roadhouse-style fare such as fajitas and pasta. The meatloaf is particularly good and served with potatoes smothered in mushroom gravy and vegetables.

5 Carlson Court. ℂ **416/213-9258.** Reservations not accepted. Main courses C$8.95–$13.40 (US$5.90–$8.85), kids' menu C$3.95–$4.25 (US$2.60–$2.80). AE, MC, V. Sun–Wed 11am–1am, Thurs–Sat 11am–2am. Highchairs, boosters.

Dining In

In this city of many cultures you can have almost any type of cuisine delivered directly to your hotel room door. Here are some good options when you're too exhausted from sightseeing to go out to eat but want to avoid the expense of room service.

You can order from the menus of over 30 ethnic restaurants through **Super Waiter** (ℂ **416/782-7877**, fax 416/782-8289, or check the restaurant menus online at www.superwaiter.ca). The standard delivery charge is C$4.95 (US$3.25), and delivery time is usually 45 minutes. Lunch is delivered Monday to Friday 11am to 2pm and dinner daily 4:30pm to 9:30pm.

A similar service is available from **Restaurant on the Go** (ℂ **416/932-3999**; www.foodroute.com). This company delivers a wide range of cuisine from over 60 restaurants in the Toronto area for a delivery charge of C$4.95 (US$3.25).

The following downtown and midtown restaurants also will deliver:

- **Amato Pizza.** ℂ **416/977-8989.** C$12.65 to $19.55 (US$8.35 to 12.90). AE, V, MC. Monday to Saturday 10am to 2am, Sunday 11am to midnight.
- **B.B. Ques.** ℂ **416/323-3663.** Main courses C$4.95 to $18.95 (US$3.25 to $12.50). AE, MC, V. Daily noon to 11:30pm.
- **Edo-Ko.** ℂ **416/482-8973.** Main courses C$12 to $24.95 (US$7.90 to $16.45); kids' menu $9.95 (US$6.55). AE, MC, V. Tuesday to Sunday noon to 1am.
- **Lee Garden.** ℂ **416/593-9524.** Dinner for 4 C$39.95 (US$26.35). AE, MC, V. Friday to Saturday 4pm to 1am, Sunday 4pm to midnight.
- **Mr. Sub.** ℂ **416/736-8888.** C$3.75 to $8.75 (US$2.50 to $5.80). AE, MC; V. Daily 11am to midnight.

6

What Kids Like to See & Do

With over 21 million visitors each year, Toronto has built up a strong worldwide reputation as a cultural and business center. It's not surprising, then, that the city offers a wealth of attractions for adults. What is surprising is that Toronto also provides so much for its young visitors.

Toronto seems to have a little bit of everything. After exploring the high-tech science center, step into the 19th century at Riverdale Farm, located on the edge of a wood with a view of the city skyline. Explore the miles of shops and restaurants in the massive Eaton Centre complex and the underground concourse, then soak up some sunshine while strolling the boardwalk at Harbourfront. Take a short bus ride to Canada's largest amusement park, then find your land legs in the vast wilderness of the conservation area next door.

Make sure your schedule fits in both big-venue and more intimate attractions. Alongside the Disney productions and other children's plays frequently staged at the major theaters, Toronto is home to the highly respected Young People's Theatre. YPT produces a number of stage plays each year, just for kids. Many of the city's cultural institutions, including the Toronto Symphony and the Canadian Opera Company, sponsor their own junior programs with young performers.

Also be sure to mix both the indoors and the outdoors into your itinerary. Toronto is very much an urban center, but its founders had the foresight to preserve much of the area's forests, marshes, and green spaces. More than 17% of urban Toronto is green space, and it's impossible to walk far in the city without coming across at least one park, garden, or playground.

There are busy spots in the city—Yonge Street is perpetually crowded, especially in the summer—but for the most part the pace is relaxed. Aside from the CN Tower and Paramount Canada's Wonderland, few of the major venues have lineups. Adopt this same relaxed pace as you explore the city—make a plan, but don't worry about abandoning it if you come across something else that sparks your child's interest. Try to balance the passive with the active. Take in a museum and then take a hike through High Park. Allow the kids some free, unscheduled time to run and play at one of the more than 800 playgrounds in the city.

Getting there can be half the fun in this city. Park your car and take public transit—it's a far less stressful and time-consuming way to explore Toronto. Kids love subway rides, and Toronto's subway system will take you to most attractions in the downtown and midtown areas; connecting buses will take you anywhere else. The kids will enjoy the ferry ride if you decide to visit the Toronto Islands. GO Transit, the city's commuter train and bus system, will take you to the most far-flung attractions, such as Paramount Canada's Wonderland, and kids love to ride the upper decks of these fast trains.

Many of Toronto's cultural venues offer free or almost free admission at specific times during the week—check out "Free (or Almost Free) Things to Do in Toronto," later in this ch There are also many free con , craft workshops, and educational events taking place across the city during weekends and holidays, and almost daily during the summer months.

SUGGESTED ITINERARIES BY AGE GROUP

For Toddlers

If you have 1 day   Greet the animals at the **Toronto Zoo.** Bring a hat and sunscreen, and, if you're really organized, a picnic lunch, although there are plenty of places to eat on-site. Check the zookeepers' schedules to see when the elephants will be taking their bath and anything else that might be of interest, and plan your day around those activities. Be sure to visit the animals in the petting zoo, and when the kids have had enough walking, take them on a train ride through the zoo grounds.

If you have 2 days   Spend the next morning exploring the **Children's Own Museum.** Try to give the kids enough time to make the craft of the day and perform in at least one stage play before you leave. If you still have time, check out Franklin's World at the **Royal Ontario Museum.** Then grab a quick takeout lunch at **Druxy's Deli** and head over to **Riverdale Farm** to meet the farm animals and climb on the tractors before returning to your hotel for a quick swim and an early bedtime.

If you have 3 days   Have an early breakfast, shop for some picnic supplies in **St. Lawrence Market,** and catch the ferry to the **Toronto Islands.** Head to the amusement park at **Centreville** first, before it gets too busy, then take the kids to see the animals at **Far Enough**

Farm. Stop for a leisurely picnic lunch at one of the many picnic tables, preferably one near the playground so once your kids have finished eating, they can play while you bask in the sun. Visit the beach at Hanlan's Point and then head back to the ferry whenever the kids are ready to call it a day. Don't worry if they're not ready before the last ferry leaves—a water taxi also services the island.

If you have 4 days   The next morning, pack some sun hats and sunscreen and take everyone to **Ontario Place** for the day. Take a few minutes to explore the complex before you decide what you want to do, but opt for the important rides first, before the crowds arrive. Save the splash pool until later in the day, when the heat will make you happy for once to have the kids splashing water at you. Grab a quick bite at one of the eateries in Ontario Place. Let the kids drench one another in the water park and get their faces painted, then head back to your hotel for an early dinner.

For Ages 5 to 7

If you have 1 day   Spend the day at the waterfront. Take in the games, rides, and water park at **Ontario Place.** You'll find many places to grab some lunch there as well. Let the kids get a removable tattoo on the way out. Head back to the hotel for a quick dinner and then an evening out at the **Young**

People's Theatre or at a Disney production in the theater district.

If you have 2 days Spend the following morning playing in the **Children's Own Museum,** and afterward take everyone to a Yorkville restaurant for lunch. Make a brief stop to look in the shops and then climb the rock in **Yorkville Park** before heading to the **Royal Ontario Museum.** Once you're at the ROM, don't miss the Discovery Centre and the Bat Cave. Pick up some takeout on Bloor Street and enjoy dinner and a movie back at your hotel room.

If you have 3 days Spend the third morning at the **Toronto Zoo,** exploring the African pavilion and riding the train. Check out the zookeepers' schedules and take in a show or two. Grab a quick lunch and then head to the **Ontario Science Centre** for the afternoon or, if your kids can wait, have lunch in the great cafeteria at the science center. When the kids have finished exploring—or when closing time is called—head back to the hotel and check out one of the kid-friendly restaurants in chapter 5, "Family-Friendly Dining."

If you have 4 days Spend the next day exploring the **Toronto Islands.** Begin in **Centreville**—before the lineups start. Then take your picnic lunch to a table near the playground and enjoy some quiet time. Take a walk to the **Gibraltar Point lighthouse** or rent some bikes and cycle over. Give the kids some time to watch the swans and ducks and perhaps play in the sand at **Hanlan's Point** before catching the ferry back to the mainland.

For Ages 8 to 10

If you have 1 day Check out the rides and other attractions at **Paramount Canada's Wonderland.**

Be prepared to spend the day here—it's not the kind of place you go to spend only a few hours. Get up early and be the first at the park—the lineups normally don't build up until 11am or so. Another option is to get up early and explore **Kensington Market** with the kids, pick up a quick breakfast in the market, and then drive north to Paramount Canada's Wonderland. This will get you into the park much later, but you can always stay into the evening when the crowds begin to thin out.

If you have 2 days Spend the next morning at the **Ontario Science Centre,** then take a leisurely lunch in the cafeteria before packing the gang up for an afternoon at **Playdium.** Try to get the kids out of Playdium before the after-work crowd begins to arrive at 5pm. Take the kids out for dinner and then to a show in the theater district or a concert or game at SkyDome or Air Canada Centre.

If you have 3 days The next morning, do a mall crawl at the **Eaton Centre** or visit some music or electronics shops. Treat the kids to lunch at a cafe inside the mall, then head down to **Harbourfront** for the afternoon. Let the kids spend the evening at the pool or treat them to a movie.

If you have 4 days Get everyone up early for a jaunt to **Kensington Market**—they may complain loudly about being up so early, but the vivid sights, sounds, and smells will soon wake them up. Then, head over to the **Royal Ontario Museum** to explore some of the exhibits. When the kids have had enough of doing the museum thing, take them down to **Ontario Place** to cool off and enjoy some rides. Have your dinner there or order takeout when you return to your hotel.

For Preteens

If you have 1 day   Follow the same Day 1 itinerary as for the 8- to 10-year-olds.

If you have 2 days   Follow the same Day 2 itinerary as for the 8- to 10-year-olds but, depending on your kids' interests, consider substituting the science center with the **Art Gallery of Ontario, the Design Exchange,** or the **Hockey Hall of Fame.** If you have history

buffs in your family, switch **Playdium** to the morning and then take the kids to **Black Creek Pioneer Village** for the afternoon.

If you have 3 days   Follow the same Day 3 itinerary as for the 8- to 10-year-olds, but allow more time to explore the **Harbourfront** galleries and activities.

If you have 4 days   Follow the same itinerary as for the 8- to 10-year-olds, but also check out the **Bata Shoe Museum.**

1 Kids' Top 10 Attractions

There are so many attractions in Toronto that I had a hard time narrowing down this list. I finally went with both the most popular attractions and those that appeal to the widest range of ages.

Centreville Amusement Park ⊛   **Ages 2 and up.** A large part of the fun of this amusement park is the ferry ride from downtown to **Centre Island.** Be sure to take the Centre Island Ferry—if you take the ferry to Hanlan's Point you'll face a 3.5-kilometer (2.17 mile) walk to the park, and the Ward's Island Ferry is primarily for island residents.

Reminiscent of a Victorian town, this park is designed for the youngest of kids, so those 9 and older may find it a bit tame. The train is one of the highlights of the park; be prepared to cover your ears as it passes through a long tunnel and the kids try to outscream one another. Other highlights include swan boats, antique cars on rails that the kids can drive, and the requisite log flume ride. A small petting zoo and Far Enough Farm are also part of the fun.

I strongly suggest you pack both a picnic lunch and a bathing suit. Food can be bought on the island, but there are plenty of picnic tables and this is one of Toronto's most scenic picnic spots, with many playgrounds and pathways for walking (and running). The bathing suits will allow the kids to play in the wading pool and enjoy some of the beaches following your day at the park.

Toddlers to age 4   Centreville will hold the most appeal for kids in this age group. The animal farm, the train, and the Ferris wheel are the best places to take toddlers.

Ages 5 to 7   Log flume rides and roller coasters usually go over well with kids this age, and Centreville boasts one of each. The water playground is also a good choice.

Ages 8 to 10   This group is a little tougher to please, as most of the rides on the island are fairly sedate. They'll enjoy the log flume ride and the bumper boats, and the carousel has a genteel appeal that some kids this age will appreciate.

Preteens   These kids will be happiest spending their time seeing and being seen on one of the nearby beaches. Keep in mind that half of Hanlan's Beach is clothing optional, so if you're uncomfortable with nude beaches, keep your kids on the clothing-required side. Preteens will also enjoy the miniature golf course.

What Kids Like to See & Do Downtown

TOP FAMILY ATTRACTIONS
Centreville Amusement Park **1**
CN Tower **2**
Harbourfront Centre **3**
Ontario Place **4**
Playdium **5**

MUSEUMS AND GALLERIES
Art Gallery of Ontario/
Grange House **6 / 6A**
Redpath Sugar Museum **7**
Toronto Police Museum **8**
Toronto's First Post Office **9**

LOCAL HISTORY
Campbell House **10**
Enoch Turner School House **11**
Fort York **12**
HMCS Haida
[near Ontario Place] **13**
Mackenzie House **14**
Montgomery's Inn **15**

SCIENCE AND NATURE/ OUTDOOR SPACES/ MARKETS
Allan Gardens **16**
Kensington Market **17**
St. Lawrence Market **18**

SPECIAL INTERESTS
Canada Sports Hall of Fame **19**
Canadian Broadcasting
Corporation Museum **20**
Canadian Motorsports Hall
of Fame & Museum **21**
Hockey Hall of Fame **22**

Legend

✝ Church
✉ Post Office
(TTC) Subway stop

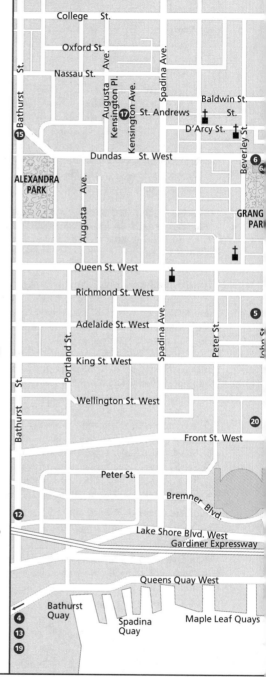

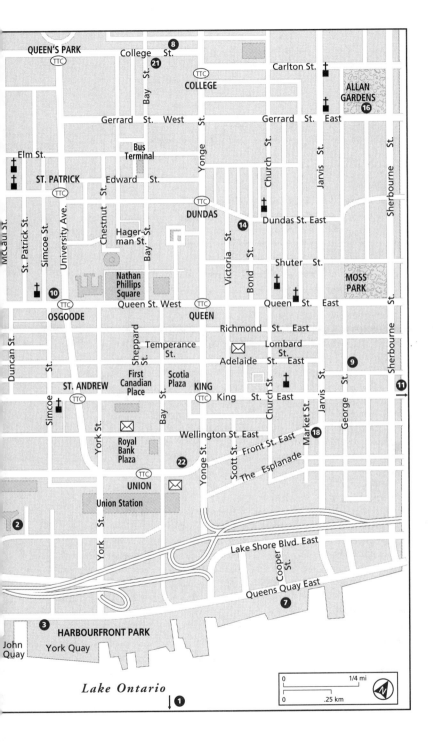

Where to Eat   There are several snack bars and restaurants on the island, but this is also the perfect venue for a picnic lunch. There are plenty of picnic tables and parkland for spreading out a picnic blanket.

Centre Island, Toronto Islands, Lake Ontario. © **416/203-0405.** All-day ride pass C$18.65 (US$12.30), C$13.05 (US$8.60) children 122cm (4 ft.) and under. Ferry return fare C$5 (US$3.30) adults, C$2 (US$1.30) children 2–12, free for children 2 and under. Victoria Day–end of June Sun–Thurs 10:30am–5pm, Fri–Sat 10:30am–7pm; July–Aug daily 10:30am–8pm; first 3 weeks in May and last 4 weeks in Sept Sat–Sun 10:30–7pm. Subway: Union, then no. 509 streetcar to Queens Quay. Catch the Toronto Islands Ferry at the terminal on Queens Quay W. at the foot of Bay St. Cars are not allowed on the ferry.

Fun Fact

One-quarter of Canada's population lives within 160 kilometers (100 miles) of Toronto; more than 60% of the population of the United States is within a one-hour flight of Toronto.

Children's Own Museum ⭑⭑⭑   **Ages 8 and under.** This museum has been a hit with my family since it first opened in early 1998. "Museum" is a bit of a misnomer, though, as this attraction is dedicated more to imaginary play than anything else.

When you first arrive, take a few minutes to tour around and find out what's there. If you don't, the kids will probably be so enamored of the first station they encounter they'll miss everything else.

The museum is organized as a neighborhood with a market, construction site, house, alley, garden, theater, art workshop, and shops. Even though most of the museum is geared toward children age 6 and under, my 8- and 9-year-olds are always just as thrilled by a visit. They've spent hours in the theater donning costumes and makeup and staging a play on the museum stage with the help of a volunteer coordinator, who does a remarkable job of organizing a bunch of kids of varying ages and personalities into a great show. The rest of us watch the production from benches out front.

My 6-year-old is most thrilled by running her own shoe store, and my 2-year-old spends most of her time in the house, vacuuming and making dinner from the food supplies, which include plenty of vegan options. My crafty 5-year-old has made everything from green goop to finger-painted houses in the art workshop.

The museum frequently hosts special events, including story hours, craft workshops, and parenting sessions. The staff is knowledgeable and involved, particularly the volunteers staffing the art and theater stations. Other staff members roam the museum looking for unattached children and identifying their caregivers, while one stands guard at the door to make sure that no little ones leave without their parents.

Toddlers to age 4   Your kids will find their own special places quickly enough, but the house, treehouse, and construction center are always popular stops for kids this age. If you're looking for a few moments of quiet time with your toddler, seek out the hidden reading room, with its overstuffed pillows and large selection of books.

Ages 5 to 7   The arts and crafts center, stores, and theater are the best places in the museum for this age group.

Ages 8 to 10   Though these kid are on the cusp of being too old for this museum, they are still enthralled with the wonderful costumes and makeup and the chance to perform on the museum's stage.

Preteens   Unless they have younger siblings or are considering a career in early childhood education, this is probably not the place to take your preteens.

Where to Eat   There are no dining facilities within the Children's Own Museum. Your best bet is to try **Druxy's Deli** next door at the Royal Ontario Museum or walk to nearby Bloor Street or Yorkville. Bloor Street houses an assortment of fast-food outlets, and Yorkville is home to several good kid-friendly restaurants.

90 Queens Park (next to the Royal Ontario Museum). © **416/542-1492**. Admission C$4.65 (US$3.05). Tues 10am–8pm, Wed–Sat 10am–5pm, Sun noon–5pm. Subway: Museum.

CN Tower *☆*   **Ages 5 and up.** This Toronto landmark provides an amazing view, but at a price that can be prohibitive for many families. Still, it may be worth the expense for the kids to be able to say they were at the top of the world's tallest freestanding structure.

Waiting in line to take the elevators to the observation deck can be an entertaining experience, as various videos, quiz games, and touch screens explain the history and significance of the tower. Once you make it through the lineup, you'll reach the top in just under a minute in the glass-fronted elevators, which travel at a whopping 22kmph (15 mph). The guides will ask the kids to come to the front to give them the best view. You'll then transfer to SkyPod elevators, which will take you up an additional 33 floors to the observation deck, with its telescopes, arcade, and food vendors. One floor below the observation level, my girls had a ball walking and dancing on the glass floor while their nervous mother stuck to the more solid sides. We also took a brief walk on the outside observation deck—those faint of heart, beware! We then splurged on an extra elevator ride to the **Space Deck**—the world's highest public observation deck—at a cost of C$4 (US$2.65). This extra can easily be skipped, as the observation and glass-floor levels definitely provide a better view.

The CN Tower complex also houses two simulator rides that are great favorites with the kids; both feature airplane rides, one of which could more accurately be called a rocket ride. An **IMAX theater** shows a film of a journey across Canada.

Toddlers to age 4   This venue is largely wasted on kids this age, who are just as thrilled with looking out the window of their hotel room. Thankfully, kids 3 and under get in for free, so it may still be worth a visit.

Ages 5 to 7   The high point for this show-no-fear age group will be the glass-bottomed observation deck. You should also check out the interactive touch screens scattered throughout the concourse as you walk toward the elevators. Kids get a huge kick out of placing the CN Tower in unlikely spots such as mountains or oceans. The IMAX movie is good but small ones have a hard time sitting through it.

Ages 8 to 10   Even though they have a better understanding of their own mortality, these kids are also thrilled with the glass-bottomed deck, as well as the outside deck. They'll like the speed of the elevators that take you up the tower, and you'll probably have trouble dragging them away from the arcade on the observation deck. Have them check out Hop, Skip and Jump on the touch screens in the concourse on the way to the elevators. This is a wacky look at some of the ways people have gone up and down the CN Tower. Included are a man who scaled the tower without a net, and others who have tumbled down the almost 2,000 stairs (on purpose) or leapt off the top on hang gliders and bungee cords.

Preteens   These kids are young enough to be awed by the sites offered on the observation decks and old enough to appreciate the work involved in building the tower. The glass observation decks and the arcade will probably be a good draw. They'll also enjoy the IMAX film and the concourse videos that show the tower being built.

Where to Eat   There are snack bars and a restaurant on the observation deck, but be warned—they tend to be expensive. **360 Restaurant at the Tower** (𝄢 **416/362-5411**) offers fine dining at the top of the tower, but it's not really suitable for children.

301 Front St. W. 𝄢 **416/360-8500.** www.cntower.ca. Lookout, glass floor, and SkyPod C$22.50 (US$14.85) adults, C$17.50 (US$11.55) children 4–12, free for children 3 and under. Rides C$7.50 (US$4.95). Combination tickets available starting at C$17.50 (US$11.55). May–Sept daily 8am–11pm; Oct–Apr daily 9am–10pm. Subway: Union, then walk west on Front St. to the Skywalk.

(**Fun Fact**   **CN Tower Trivia**

1. How did Ashrita Furman get to the top of the world's longest metal staircase (1,967 steps) at the CN Tower in 1960?
2. In 1979, what did Norman Alexander and Joe Squire carry up the tower steps in just over 7½ hours?
3. In 1990, how did stuntman Roger Brown get down the tower steps?
4. What did 17-year-old Patrick Bailie drop from the tower in 1979 to earn himself a place in the *Guinness Book of World Records*?
5. The higher you climb, the colder it gets. How many degrees cooler is the air at the 360 Restaurant level than on the ground?
6. On average, how many times a year does lightning strike the tower?
7. How many loonies (Canadian dollar coins) would you have to stack in order to equal the height of the CN Tower?
8. How much does the tower weigh?
9. How are birds prevented from colliding with the tower during the annual fall and spring migrations?
10. How tall is the tower?

ANSWERS: 1. He hopped on a pogo stick. 2. A grand piano. 3. He tumbled (on purpose). 4. An egg. 5. 10°C (18°F). 6. 3 times. 7. 283,205 loonies, or 54,222 CDs. 8. 140,208,000 kilograms (130,000 tons). 9. Tower staff turn off all nonemergency lights to avoid attracting the birds. 10. 553.33 meters (1,815 ft., 5 in.).

Harbourfront Centre (★ (Value   **All ages.** Salvaged from the abandoned warehouses and decrepit factories that once hugged the Lake Ontario water-front, Harbourfront is a government-owned nonprofit arts center and urban park. It is also the most picturesque spot in downtown Toronto. Here, Torontoians come to stroll with the kids along the boardwalk, enjoy a picnic, or spend a sunny afternoon on the lake in a rented sailboat.

Harbourfront is a novelty among big entertainment complexes—admission to the center is free, and many of its entertainment programs are free or almost free. Each year more than 4,000 events take place at Harbourfont, many geared toward children. The **Harbourfront Reading Series** and the **International Festival of Authors** both feature readings by well-known children's authors. The summer-long **Rhythms of the World** festival series, which starts in July, features multi-ethnic music and arts, film, food, dance, and hands-on workshops. In the popular **HarbourKids Creative Workshops,** kids can learn to create their own crafts and artworks (see chapter 7, "For the Active Family"). The **Harbourfront Cushion Concerts**, with musical performances and storytelling, and the **Milk International Children's Festival of the Arts,** with productions and workshops from around the world, also are big draws for kids (see chapter 8, "Entertainment for the Whole Family").

Harbourfront is designed as a series of adjoining quays, beginning with **Queens Quay** at the foot of York Street and to the west of the Westin Harbour Castle Hotel. Ferries to the Toronto Islands depart from this quay, and in the refurbished warehouse you'll find the **Premiere Dance Theatre** and two floors of shops and restaurants. Also at Queens Quay is the **du Maurier Theatre Centre,** home of the World Stage theater festival, with many children's productions among its adult offerings, and the **Power Plant,** a contemporary art gallery.

West at **York Quay Centre,** kids are fascinated by the **Craft Studio,** where they can watch the craftspeople create glass, ceramics, textiles, and jewelry. Below the Lakeside Eats terrace is a pond where young sailors can stay dry sailing remote-controlled laser sailboats; in the winter, the pond becomes a skating rink. At the **Nautical Centre,** your family can rent a canoe or kayak—just watch that the kids don't steer you too close to the fountain! Powerboats and sailboats can also be rented on Lake Ontario.

Toddlers to age 4   There are two wonderful playgrounds for toddlers at Harbourfront, and, of course, all kids like to watch the big boats sail by. Kids this age are welcome to take part in the Harbourkids Creative Workshops, but 3 and unders might find the crafts a little challenging—you'll have to help!

Ages 5 to 7   Catch the Harbourfront Cushion Concerts and drop by the Harbourkids Creative Workshops. These free activities are just the thing for this active and inquisitive age group.

Ages 8 to 10   These kids will enjoy the Harbourkids Creative Workshops too, although they'll find the Cushion Concerts a little beneath them. Definitely let them take a turn driving one of the remote-control sailboats on the pond.

Preteens   Kids this age often have surprisingly eclectic tastes in music and art. They'll probably enjoy the galleries as well as the frequent dance and music exhibitions at Harbourfront. Check the Harbourfront schedule for details.

Where to Eat   There are several restaurants within the Harbourfront complex, but the best choice for kids is **Lakeside Eats.** This casual, cafeteria-style restaurant has plenty of reasonably priced options for everyone. In warm weather you can eat on the terrace and watch the sailboats on the lake.

Queens Quay W. ✆ **416/973-3000** (special events information) or 416/973-4000 (box office). www. harbourfront.on.ca. Free admission, but varying prices for some special events. Subway: Union, then no. 509 or no.510 streetcar.

What Kids Like to See & Do Midtown

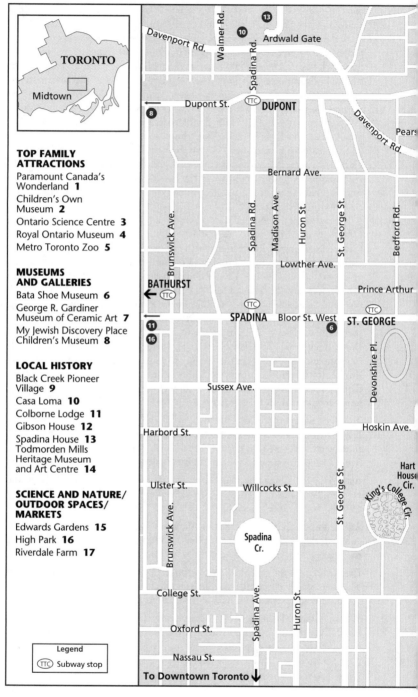

TORONTO

Midtown

TOP FAMILY ATTRACTIONS
Paramount Canada's Wonderland **1**
Children's Own Museum **2**
Ontario Science Centre **3**
Royal Ontario Museum **4**
Metro Toronto Zoo **5**

MUSEUMS AND GALLERIES
Bata Shoe Museum **6**
George R. Gardiner Museum of Ceramic Art **7**
My Jewish Discovery Place Children's Museum **8**

LOCAL HISTORY
Black Creek Pioneer Village **9**
Casa Loma **10**
Colborne Lodge **11**
Gibson House **12**
Spadina House **13**
Todmorden Mills Heritage Museum and Art Centre **14**

SCIENCE AND NATURE/ OUTDOOR SPACES/ MARKETS
Edwards Gardens **15**
High Park **16**
Riverdale Farm **17**

Legend
TTC Subway stop

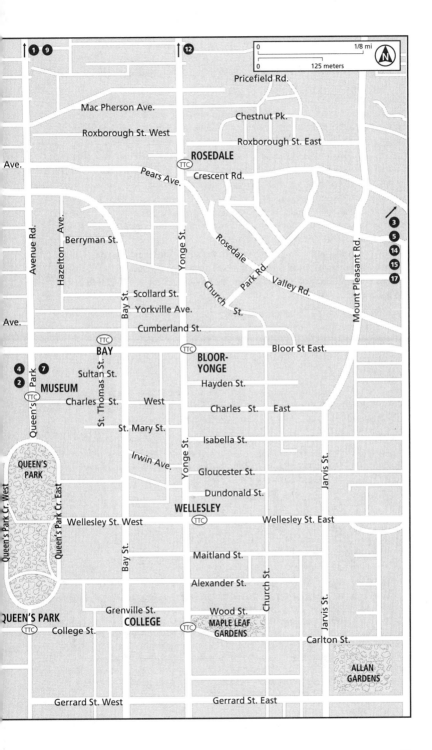

Ontario Place *★★*   **Ages 2 and up.** This futuristic-looking park, with its giant white pods and interconnecting bridges, is a big draw for everyone, but your smallest ones will find it especially exciting. Be warned, though—this can be an extremely busy spot on a hot summer's day.

The **Children's Village,** an area set aside for those 12 and under, has a multitude of interactive games and entertainment. Here, toddlers can roam the foam forest, slip down the super slide, and romp in the ball crawl. For kids both young and old, the bumper boats, Megamaze, and Mars Simulator Ride are a big hit. The Wilderness Adventure Ride is a wild and woolly raft ride through canyons and past several animated characters, culminating in a 12-meter (40 ft.) drop—though the adults may be terrified, even the littlest kids love it. If you're planning to try it, bring along bathing suits or raincoats to avoid getting soaked.

Ontario Place also hosts some amazing shows and festivals. The **Festival Stage** is the best venue here for kids' entertainment. Past performances have featured the children's cartoon characters Little Bear, Rupert Bear, Babar, King of the Elephants, and Elliot Moose. The **Molson Amphitheatre** seats 16,000 under a copper canopy and on the grass and attracts top entertainers. The complex also includes a year-round **IMAX theater** and the **HMCS Haida Naval Museum** (see below).

Toddlers to age 4   The ball crawl and the foam forest are big favorites for this age group. Check out the other rides and play areas in the Children's Village.

Ages 5 to 7   My kids in this age group love to drive, so they gravitate toward the bumper boats and go-carts. The water park also draws more than its share of kids from this age group.

Ages 8 to 10   These kids enjoy the Mars Simulator Ride and getting drenched in the Wilderness Adventure Ride. The Rush River Raft Ride takes groups of kids on a wild tube ride down a 262-meter (873 ft.) water slide.

Preteens   Older kids will enjoy taking out a paddle boat and putting in the miniature golf course. There are three thrill zones in the park with a wide range of video and virtual reality games. Picasso Painters offers black henna body painting, hair wraps, and tattoos (don't worry, they're temporary).

Where to Eat   Ontario Place has lots of fast-food outlets, but for a truly Canadian experience, try some beaver tails at one of several outlets within the park. This deep-fried pastry can be served as a dessert or as a meal with cheese and tomato sauce. There are also **Pizza Pizza, Mr. Sub,** and fresh fruit and juice stands throughout the park.

If you prefer a sit-down meal, your best bet would be **Marina Grill,** a family-style restaurant in the Marina Basin operated by the restaurant chain J.J. Muggs.

955 Lakeshore Blvd. W. ② **416/314-9811** or 416/314-9900 (recorded information). www.ontarioplace.com. Play-all-day pass (includes admission, rides, and IMAX screenings) C$15 (US$9.90) ages 55 and older, C$24.50 (US$16.15) adults and children 106cm (41.34 in.) and taller, C$11 (US$7.25) children 4 and up under 106cm (41.34 in.), free for children 3 and under, after 5pm C$10 (US$6.60) ages 4 and up, free for children 3 and under. Grounds admission only (allows access to Children's Village and the shows) C$10 (US$6.60) ages 4 and up, free for children 3 and under; after 5pm all ages free. Pay-as-you-play tickets C$6 (US$3.95) ages 4 and up; Water park requires two tickets for adults ages 54 and under. IMAX tickets C$6 (US$3.95). Mid-May–Labour Day daily 10am–dusk, special events and dining facilities excepted. Subway: Union, then no. 509 streetcar west, or Bathurst, then any streetcar south.

Ontario Science Centre *★*   **Ages 2 and up.** While the exhibits are plentiful and interactive, it's the shows that keep the kids coming back. It's almost impossible to see the entire science center in one visit, so study the map handed out at the entrance and make your plan of attack. At the electricity demonstration, kids can lay their hands on a Van De Graff generator and watch each other's hair stand on end. Or, they can step on a scale while water fills a beaker beside them, showing them how much water their bodies contain. In the sports room, they can take a simulated bobsled ride.

Kids ages 7 and older will probably get the most out of the exhibits, but there are a few places that appeal to the younger set. Little kids will love exploring the tropical rain forest, with its humid air, palm trees, and tree house, and the spaceship in the space exhibit. All kids will want to return to the **Science Arcade,** with its interactive sound and visual activities such as electronic keyboards and the Chinese percussion room.

Toddlers to age 4   If you're pressed for time, skip the Timescape, Communication, Matter, Energy, and Change and Technology exhibits and head straight to the science arcade and the simulated rain forest. These are the exhibits that most entranced my youngest children. They will also find some of the exhibits in the various sections interesting.

Ages 5 to 7   Don't miss the interactive demonstrations, especially the one on electricity. These kids will also enjoy the tornado in the living earth room and the highly interactive sports room.

Ages 8 to 10   The information highway exhibit is an excellent destination for this group. They can explore the inner workings of a computer and try out all the latest CD-ROMs.

Preteens   Mindworks is a cool spot, with its demonstrations of how the mind works. Truth/Vérité is a wonderful exhibit that challenges kids to question known "truths" and identify their own biases.

Where to Eat   There are two restaurants at the science center. The downstairs cafeteria is probably the best and fastest choice for kids, but the buffet restaurant on the top floor is a nice spot as well.

770 Don Mills Rd. (at Eglinton Ave. E.). © **888/696-1110** or 416/696-3127. www.osc.on.ca. Admission C$12 (US$7.90) adults, C$7 (US$4.60) children 13–17, C$6 (US$3.95) children 5–12. Omnimax tickets C$10 (US$6.60) adults, C$6 (US$3.95) children 13–17, C$5.50 (US$3.65) children 5–12. Combination tickets available starting at C$9 (US$5.95). Parking C$7 (US$4.60); free after 5pm. Daily 10am–5pm. Omnimax hours extend into the evening and vary. Subway: Eglinton, then no. 34 bus to Don Mills Rd., or Pape, then no. 25 bus to St. Dennis Dr. By car: From downtown, take the Don Valley Pkwy. north to Don Mills Rd. exit, then Don Mills Rd. north. From Hwy. 401, take the Don Valley Pkwy. south to Wynford Dr.

Paramount Canada's Wonderland ⭑⭑   **Ages 3 and up; best value for kids ages 7 and up.** Cartoon characters, live shows, and exciting rides draw the summertime crowds to Canada's largest theme park. The park is owned by Paramount, so characters include such Saturday morning favorites as Scooby Doo and the Flintstones. The shows are splashy and short enough to keep little ones amused, and the sea lion show, puppet show, and Scooby Doo Mystery Show are always a big hit.

However, it's really the rides the kids come for. **Kidsville** and **Hanna-Barbera Land,** the two areas set aside for children's rides, offer more than 20 rides. The most popular are the Taxi Jam roller coaster in Kidsville and the Ghoster Coaster in Hanna-Barbera Land. For younger or less daring kids, there is a beautiful antique carousel in the World Exposition of 1890 pavilion and a vast playground at the **Candy Factory** that many kids will be content to spend the whole day exploring. This brings me to the major drawback of this and other amusement parks: The smallest kids (under 112cm, or 44 in.) are prohibited from many of the rides. If your family includes both older kids and toddlers, you should be able to find enough activities to amuse the youngest ones, but if all your kids are under 3, it's probably not worth bringing them here. Young families will make better use of their money at attractions such as Ontario Place or Centreville.

Lineups can get quite intense, especially in the afternoons, so try to come as early as possible or stay later in the evening. Definitely check each ride before you wait in line to make sure your kids are tall enough. It can be heartbreaking to be told the kids are too small for a roller coaster or other ride after waiting for 15 minutes.

On hot summer days the park can also be a great place for kids to cool off. There are numerous thrill rides, including water slides and several exhilarating white-water rafting rides. Smaller kids are content with the thrills offered at the **Pumphouse**—a collection of scaled-down slides, tunnels, and, of course, rotating water guns, spouts, and other water gadgets.

Toddlers to age 4   Kids this age will probably be as thrilled with the playground at Candy Land as they would be with any of the rides in Kiddie Land or Hanna-Barbera Land—you may want to save your money and take them to one of the free playgrounds within the city. The shows are excellent, though, and there are several that appeal to this crowd.

Ages 5 to 7   Hanna-Barbera Land and Kiddie Land are the top spots in the park for this age group. Unfortunately, most kids this age are too short for the huge roller coasters you can see from the highway, but these areas have several roller coasters just for this age group. Kids this age also love water, so be sure to drop by the Pumphouse.

Ages 8 to 10   The thrill rides are the big draw for this age group—the faster and scarier, the better. Take them on the Black Hole, a four-story water plunge in complete darkness. There is also a wealth of roller coasters for this group. The Vortex, a suspended roller coaster that travels 90kmph (55 mph) and the Mighty Canadian Minebuster, Canada's largest and longest wooden roller coaster, are both big draws.

Preteens   The Seventh Portal, a virtual reality ride, is a huge hit with kids this age. Many leave the ride only to get right back in line to try it again. The Seventh Portal is a 3D action adventure that makes you feel like you've landed in the middle of a cartoon, with heart-stopping graphics and characters hurtling at you from the screen.

Where to Eat   There are plenty of fast-food outlets on-site. My family has a passion for Italian, so we usually head for **Mrs. Vanelli's** or **Pizza Pizza.** The **Southside Grill** has good burgers but is generally packed, especially during the lunch and dinner hours, so you might want to eat either early or late to avoid lineups. The quick and easy solution is to grab a hot dog or pizza slice from one of the many small kiosks. You can also bring your own picnic hamper into the park, but be forewarned: Your car may be parked quite a distance from the front gates.

9580 Jane St., Vaughan. ℂ **905/832-7000** or 905/832-8131. www.canadaswonderland.com. Play-all-day pass (includes park admission and most rides) C$44.99 (US$29.70) ages 7–59, C$22.49 (US$14.85) ages 3–6 and ages 60 and older, free for children under 3. June 1–21 Mon–Fri 10am–8pm, Sat–Sun 10am–10pm; June 22–Labour Day daily 10am–10pm; late May and early Sept to early Oct Sat–Sun 10am–8pm. Closed mid-Oct–mid-May. Subway: Yorkdale or York Mills, then Wonderland Express GO Bus. By car: Take Hwy. 400 north, exit at Rutherford Rd., and follow the signs.

Playdium ⭐   **Ages 7 and up.** When they first walked into this shrine to video games and virtual reality, my daughters were overwhelmed. However, after a few minutes of staring in awe at the multitude of offerings, they were ready to jump right in—with both feet. Their first choice: a virtual reality roller coaster. I watched as the girls were seated, belted, and then enclosed in a steel box, and then waited confidently for the panic button to come on. It didn't. They emerged several minutes later and promptly went back inside for another turn. Their other favorites included a Jurassic Park video game (not for the squeamish) and a line of racing cars where they could compete against each other and other visitors.

This arcade is a great spot for those ages 7 and over, although there are a few games to interest 5- and 6-year-olds and a tiny section for the 4 and under set. For the most part, though, younger kids will lack the dexterity to get much out of the games at Playdium.

This multilevel complex is open concept, allowing players to see the offerings on all three levels. The **Speed Zone** on the ground floor includes both the virtual roller coaster and the Cliff Hanger, where older kids and adults can engage in some wall climbing (they have a version for the small fry as well), tightrope walking, and bungee jumping. The **Target Zone,** with a variety of video games, and the **Contact Zone,** featuring virtual combat games, are on the second level. In the **Music Zone** recording booths, also on the second floor, kids can accompany their favorite group on the drums. The third floor is given over to the **Sports Zone,** where you can go virtual fishing, compete against the kids in a virtual Indy, or try your hand at tossing a football or basketball. There are guides on every floor to assist with problems and help you get your game started. They're quick with advice and know their games well.

The best time to visit is during the day and possibly early evening. Playdium is quiet on weekdays during the school year, so this is a great time to go if you dislike crowds. The business crowd often comes here to relax (or perhaps to vent) after work and there are several licensed bars in the complex, so it's probably not the best place to bring kids late at night or on Friday evenings.

Toddlers to age 4   The selection of games for little ones is limited. These kids would probably be far more thrilled with Ontario Place, Centreville, or the Children's Own Museum.

Ages 5 to 7   Kids on the lower end of this age group will probably lack the dexterity to manipulate many of the games, but there is still a lot to entertain them. Take them to the music section in the back or let them race against you and other kids in the virtual Indy.

Ages 8 to 10   The virtual reality rides thrill this age group. They'll want to head straight to the physically challenging Speed Zone on the first floor, where they can ride on virtual roller coasters and tackle the rock-climbing wall in the center of the building.

Preteens   With its music, bright lights, and state-of-the-art video and virtual reality games, this place is pure heaven to this age group. Make sure this is the last place you take them in the day or you might have trouble convincing them to go anywhere else.

Where to Eat   There is a snack bar on the premises. The two restaurants are licensed and are not good places to bring the kids. You'll find plenty of better options on Richmond Street.

126 John St. ✆ **416/260-1400**. www.playdium.com. Pay-as-you-play game card available in a variety of denominations, ranging from C50¢–$5 (US35¢–$3.30); 1 hour of unlimited play C$17.95 (US$11.85). Sun–Thurs 10am–midnight, Fri 10am–4am, Sat 10am–2am. Subway: Osgoode, then 2 blocks west.

Royal Ontario Museum

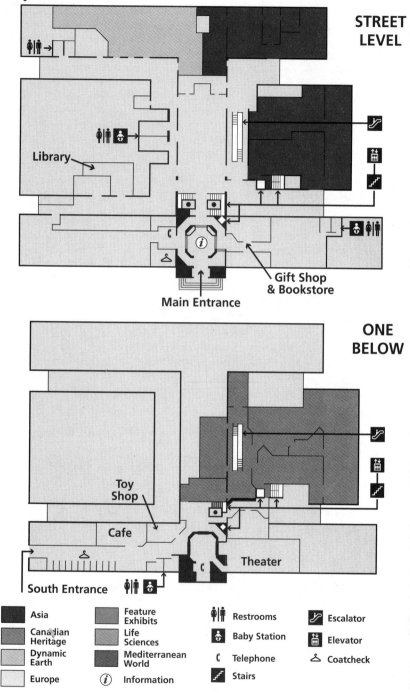

STREET LEVEL

Library

Gift Shop
& Bookstore

Main Entrance

ONE BELOW

Toy
Shop

Cafe

Theater

South Entrance

	Asia		Feature Exhibits		Restrooms		Escalator
	Canadian Heritage		Life Sciences		Baby Station		Elevator
	Dynamic Earth		Mediterranean World		Telephone		Coatcheck
	Europe	*(i)*	Information		Stairs		

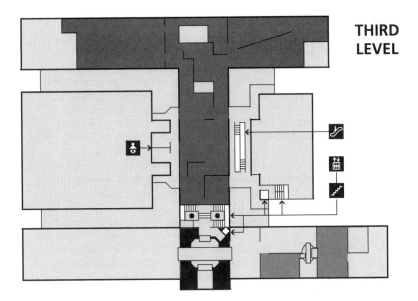

THIRD LEVEL

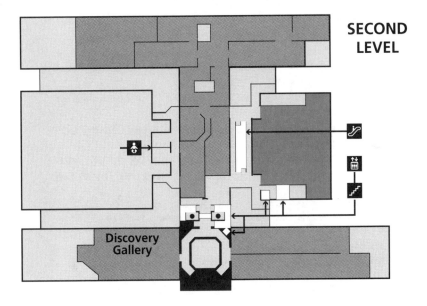

SECOND LEVEL

Discovery Gallery

Royal Ontario Museum (★★★   **All ages.** The stately ROM, Canada's largest museum, houses an impressive collection of more than 6 million artifacts and frequent traveling exhibits. Everything from Egyptian mummies to earth sciences can be explored in the many galleries here.

For kids, the **Discovery Gallery** offers hands-on learning. My girls had a ball digging for dinosaur bones, trying on heavy suits of armor, and writing their names in Egyptian hieroglyphics. Next door, my youngest children had fun exploring the house, pond, and meadow in **Franklin's World,** staging their own puppet show, and exploring the animal fur and other objects in the hands-on activity drawers.

Within the museum proper, the hands-down favorite with my kids was the **Bat Cave.** I lost count of the number of times they went through the darkened tunnel. They also enjoyed the dinosaur exhibit, the **Hands-on Biodiversity Gallery,** with its living-display touch tables and discovery boxes, and the unique toy shop in the basement.

You'll need to allow yourself a full afternoon to explore the museum, although you could easily spend the entire day here (and if you have the time, I suggest you do). If you're pressed for time, start on the third floor with the Mediterranean and European displays, then visit the second floor for the **Life Sciences** and **Discovery galleries.** The basement and street-level exhibits offer more for adults than children, and your younger ones may start dragging their feet here. There is a lot of walking involved, even with a short visit, so bring a stroller for small children or rent one at the coat check.

Toddlers to age 4   Franklin's World is probably the best bet for kids this age, although they will also like the animals in the Life Sciences Gallery.

Ages 5 to 7   These kids will enjoy both Franklin's World and the more advanced Discovery World next door. The creepy crawlies in the Life Sciences Gallery also go over well with this age group.

Ages 8 to 10   Discovery World, the Bat Cave, and the dinosaur exhibit are good spots to take these kids.

Preteens   The Egyptian exhibit is a surprising hit with preteens. You'll also not want to miss the astronomy exhibits.

Where to Eat   There are several dining options at the ROM, including a formal dining room on the third floor, but the best bet for kids is the **Druxy's Deli** inside the front entrance.

101 Queens Park Cres. © **416/586-8000** (recorded information) or 416/586-5549 (switchboard). www.rom.on.ca. Admission C$15 (US$9.90) adults, C$8 (US$5.30) children 5–14, free for children 5 and under. Sun–Thurs 10am–6pm, Fri 10am–9:30pm, Sat 10am–6pm. Subway: Museum.

Toronto Zoo (★★   **All ages.** Because all kids love animals, the zoo is always a safe choice for families whose kids range widely in age. Our two-year-old had as much fun chasing the geese while we ate our picnic lunch as she did looking at the zoo animals, but for her older sisters, the more exotic the animal, the better.

More than 5,000 animals roam the Toronto Zoo's 287 hectares (710 acres). The zoo is divided by geographical region—African Savanna, Eurasia, the Americas, and the Canadian Domain—so if you have limited time you can target the animals your kids most want to see.

As you enter the zoo, be sure to check the zookeepers' schedule, which gives feeding times and the location of special shows, including the ever-popular elephant bath. Try to visit pavilions when the zookeepers are there—they're always happy to answer your kids' questions.

Toronto Zoo

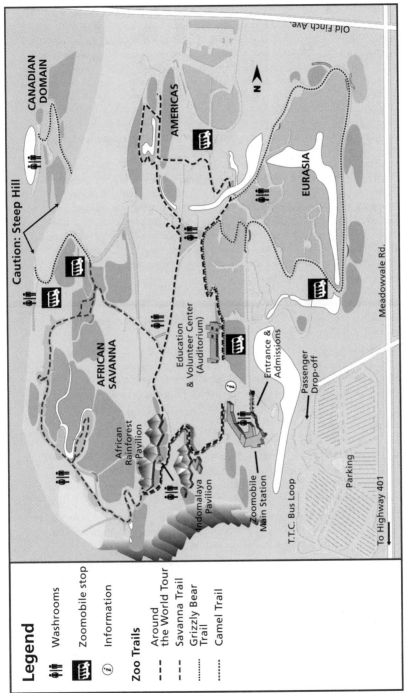

Legend

- 🚻 Washrooms
- 🚌 Zoomobile stop
- ⓘ Information

Zoo Trails

- – – – Around the World Tour
- – – Savanna Trail
- .... Grizzly Bear Trail
- —–—– Camel Trail

Caution: Steep Hill

CANADIAN DOMAIN

AMERICAS

EURASIA

AFRICAN SAVANNA

African Rainforest Pavilion

Indomalaya Pavilion

Education & Volunteer Center (Auditorium)

Zoomobile Main Station

Entrance & Admissions

Passenger Drop-off

T.T.C. Bus Loop

Parking

To Highway 401

Old Finch Ave.

Meadowvale Rd.

N

While the kids will head for the large and loudest inhabitants of the zoo first, try to squeeze in a visit the **Butterfly Garden.** More accurately termed a meadow than a garden, this area is planted with species that attract many colorful species of butterflies. Of special interest to kids is the larval food plant bed where butterflies lay their eggs and the young are hatched.

All of my girls enjoyed **Kesho Park,** in part because it houses African favorites such as white lions and elephants, but also because of its layout. Designed to resemble an African national park, it encompasses a bush camp, watering holes, and interactive features such as a termite mound the kids can peer into, elephant tusks they can touch and hold, and a large baobab tree they can walk through.

Many of the animals are housed in outdoor paddocks in natural settings, much to the delight of my older children. All can be seen via the 9.5 kilometers (6 miles) of trails that traverse the grounds. That's a lot of walking. If you have little ones, you might want to rent a wagon or stroller at the front gate. You can also give kids a break from walking by hitching a ride on the trackless **Zoomobile,** which takes passengers on a 45-minute ride around the grounds; you can get on and off at several stations if you see something that demands a closer look. In the summer, we find the Zoomobile a welcome respite from the sun, even for a few minutes at a time.

Much of the outdoor zoo is open to the sun and offers very little shade, so sun hats and a lot of suntan lotion are a must. You can take a break from the sun in one of the interesting indoor pavilions. Look for the touch tables and other interactive displays inside these pavilions.

Toddlers to age 4   Children in this age group tend to be thrilled by the smaller animals they can get close to. Often, the animals in the more open pavilions, such as the African and Australian pavilions, are much too difficult to spot. The Zoomobile is always a big hit, as are the monkey houses.

Ages 5 to 7   This is the lion, tiger, and bear set, at least in my family. They also tend to go for the larger and more exotic animals. The less technical zookeeper shows such as the elephant show have great appeal for this group.

Ages 8 to 10   My 8- and 9-year-olds both read, and they like nothing better than to explain some startling fact about an animal to their younger, awestruck sisters. The Komodo dragon is a consistent favorite, as are the gorillas. Don't miss some of the zookeeper shows.

Preteens   This group is most impressed with the open African pavilion, so starting there is a good idea. They also enjoy the zookeeper presentations, although you can probably skip the Zoomobile.

Where to Eat   There are several fast-food outlets within the zoo itself, including **Harvey's, Mr. Sub,** and **Pizza Pizza,** but we usually pack our own picnic lunch to enjoy inside the zoo grounds.

361A Old Finch Ave. ✆ **416/392-5900.** Admission C$15 (US$9.90) ages 15–64, C$11 (US$7.25) ages 65 and older, C$9 (US$5.95) children 4–14, free for children 3 and under. Wild Rides (Zoomobile, camel, pony) C$3–$3.50 (US$2–$2.30) per rider. Parking C$6 (US$3.95); stroller rental C$8 (US$5.30), C$5 (US$3.30) refundable; wagon rental C$10 (US$6.60), C$5 (US$3.30) refundable. Jan 1–Mar 9 9:30am–4:30pm (last admission at 3:30pm); Mar 10–May 18 9am–6pm (last admission at 5pm); May 19–Sept 3 9am–7pm (last admission at 6:30pm); Sept 4–Oct 28 9am–6pm (last admission at 5pm); Oct 29–Dec 31 9:30am–4:30pm (last admission at 3:30pm). Subway: Sheppard, then no. 85B or no. 85D bus, or Kennedy, then no. 86A bus. By car: Take Hwy. 401 east to Meadowvale Rd., take Exit 389, and follow the signs.

2 Museums & Galleries

Toronto is home to many original museums and galleries. Besides the big venues such as the Art Gallery of Ontario and the Royal Ontario Museum, there is a also a rich collection of museums dedicated to such diverse subjects as ceramics, textiles, sugar, and even shoes.

Free (or Almost Free) Things to Do in Toronto

As the cultural center of Canada, Toronto is determined to make sure that everyone, especially children, has access to the city's cultural attractions. Many of the city's museums and galleries offer free or pay-by-donation admission on certain days, and many theaters set aside pay-what-you-can tickets.

During the summer, take in some free concerts at Harbourfront, in the Beaches, or at Nathan Phillips Square. But don't limit yourself to major venues when hunting down bargains. Take the kids for a swim in one of more than a dozen outdoor municipal pools, or hike though one of the city's endless parks and ravines. In the winter, skate on one of the many outdoor ice rinks in the city, enjoy the multicultural sounds of the street musicians in the subway or underground shopping concourse, or cross-country ski through a woodland or park.

Here is just a sampling of some of the free (or almost free) things you can do in Toronto:

- Visit the **Art Gallery of Ontario** any time and pay what you can.
- Explore the **Bata Shoe Museum**. It's free to all on the first Tuesday of each month.
- Visit the **Canada Sports Hall of Fame**—it's always free.
- Play at the **Children's Own Museum** on Friday afternoons and pay what you can.
- During **Kids Night Out Toronto,** held throughout the month of February, take your kids to the theater for free, although adults will pay normal ticket prices. More than 30 of the entertainment district's top theaters participate in this unique program.
- Check out the Chinese porcelain at the **George R. Gardiner Museum of Ceramic Art**. It's free on the first Tuesday of each month.
- Pet the animals at the **Riverdale Farm**—it's always free.
- Visit the Bat Cave at the **Royal Ontario Museum**. Admission is free one hour before closing every day, and it's pay what you can between 4:30 and 9:30pm on Fridays.
- Solve a crime at the **Toronto Police Museum**. Admission is free but donations are accepted.
- Write a letter with a quill and have it canceled with a stamp that reads 1830 at **Toronto's First Post Office**. Admission is free, and it will cost you only C$1 (US65¢) to mail a letter.
- Take in a show at the **Young People's Theatre**. A limited number of pay-what-you-can seats are set aside for all performances.

Art Gallery of Ontario ⭐ **Ages 4 and up.** One problem with going to galleries is it tends to demand quiet contemplation, something kids are seldom very good at. A visit to the AGO, however, can be both interactive and fun.

The first stop during your visit should be at the **Gallery Shop,** where for C50¢ (US30¢) you can pick up an interactive activity guide called *High Art: The Official Activity Book for Kids,* which features puzzles, games, and creative activities, all based on the gallery displays. For instance, one activity provides an image of only the head of a Henry Moore sculpture, and kids are asked to sketch in the body. Another activity asks kids to compare a Peter Broygal painting of a dinner with a picture in the booklet and then find the 10 imposters at the dinner.

Don't miss **Off the Wall!** the AGO's hands-on creative arts center for kids. Open Saturdays and Sundays from 1 to 5pm, this drop-in center allows young visitors to create their own high art through such activities as dressing up as a painting, taking an imaginary sketching trip to Algonquin Park, or creating drawings on small slides that are projected into giant works of art.

317 Dundas St. W. (between McCaul and Beverley sts.). © 416/977-0414. www.ago.on.ca. Pay what you can; extra fee for special exhibits. Tues and Thurs–Fri 11am–6pm, Wed 11am–8:30pm, Sat–Sun 10am–5:30pm. Subway: St. Patrick.

Bata Shoe Museum **Ages 5 and up.** Imelda Marcos wannabes aside, there is much to be learned about human history by looking at the shoes we've worn. This museum was created from the private collection of Sonja Bata of the Bata Shoe family. Fans of the Spice Girls will appreciate Ginger Spice's white platforms, while monarchists can take a peak at Queen Victoria's ballroom slippers. Some of the more eclectic shoes in the 10,000-piece collection include French chestnut-crushing boots and human hair slippers made for Australian Aboriginal executioners. There are also changing exhibits, which have featured everything from a display on Chinese foot binding to an entire gallery devoted to sports shoes. Allow about 1½ hours to see all four floors.

327 Bloor St. W. (at St. George St.). © 416/979-7799. www.batashoemuseum.ca. Admission C$6 (US$3.95) adults, C$2 (US$1.30) children, family pass C$12 (US$7.90). Tues–Wed and Fri–Sat 10am–5pm, Thurs 10am–8pm, Sun noon–5pm. Subway: St. George.

🅒 Rainy Day Activities

Besides its infinite outdoor activities, Toronto has plenty of options for rainy day fun. Here are a few suggestions:

- Explore the PATH—Toronto's underground shopping concourse that connects numerous office towers in the city.
- Spend a day exploring the nooks and crannies of the Royal Ontario Museum.
- Let your kids' imaginations run wild at the Children's Own Museum.
- Take a walk through the conservatories at Allan Gardens.
- Shop at the Eaton Centre or Yorkdale Shopping Centre.
- Experiment at the Ontario Science Centre.

George R. Gardiner Museum of Ceramic Art   Ages 8 and up. This collection includes pre-Columbian figures, 18th-century European porcelain figurines, and a 200-piece collection of Chinese ceramics from the Ming and Quing dynasties. Special children's programming is offered occasionally—call for details.

111 Queens Park (at Bloor St.). ℭ **416/586-8080**. Admission C$10 (US$6.60) adults, C$6 (US$3.95) children 5–12, free for children under 5. Mon, Wed, and Fri 10am–6pm, Tues and Thurs 10am–8pm, Sat–Sun 10am–5pm.. Subway: Museum.

McMichael Canadian Art Collection   Ages 5 and over. This gallery just outside the city is home to more than 2,000 works of art by Tom Thomson and the Group of Seven, Canada's most famous group of painters, as well as other notable Canadian artists. Much of the work is inspired by Canada's rugged wilderness and provides an interesting way to show the kids the rich landscapes of Canada. While the magnificent art is draw enough, the **Drop-In Studio,** held on Sundays from 1 to 4pm, offers a bonus for young visitors. Programs vary from making sock puppets to molding a landscape from plasticine or painting a still life to take home. Special family days and art lessons are frequently scheduled throughout the year.

10365 Islington Ave., Kleinburg. ℭ **905/893-1121**. www.mcmichael.on.ca. Admission C$9 (US$5.95) adults, C$5 (US$3.30) students, free for children under 5. Parking C$5 (US$3.30). May–Oct weekdays 10am–4pm, Sat 11am–4pm, Sun 11am–5pm; Nov–Apr Tues–Sat 10am–4pm, Sun 10am–5pm. Subway: Islington, then no. 37 bus north to Steeles Ave. At Steeles and Islington aves., take the Vaughan no. 3 bus north on Islington Ave. By car: From Hwy. 401, take Hwy. 400 north to Major Mackenzie Dr. Take Major Mackenzie Dr. west and turn north onto Islington Ave.

Museum of Contemporary Canadian Art   Ages 8 and up. Young artists will enjoy browsing this eclectic museum located in the **Toronto Centre for the Arts,** with changing exhibits ranging from painting to photography and sculpture. If you're catching a performance at the arts center, make time to visit the museum before the performance or during the intermission.

Toronto Centre for the Arts, 5040 Yonge St., North York. ℭ **416/395-0067**. www.mocca.toronto.on.ca. Free admission. Tues–Sun noon–5pm. Subway: North York Centre.

My Jewish Discovery Place Children's Museum ⭐ (Finds) **All ages.** This small but delightful hands-on museum is designed to spark children's imaginations and teach them a little about Jewish history and religion and Judaism today. It scores on both points. At the reproduction of the Wailing Wall, children are encouraged to write or draw pictures of their prayers to God and leave them between the cracks in the bricks. There is a miniature synagogue, a trunk filled with Noah's Ark costumes, a play kitchen where kids can create a traditional Sabbath dinner, and a wonderful craft area, as well as several other interactive play centers.

Bathurst Jewish Centre, 4588 Bathurst St. (north of Sheppard Ave.). ℭ **416/636-1880** ext. 456. www.bjc.on.ca. Admission C$2 (US$1.30). Mon–Thurs 10am–5pm, Sun 11am–4pm. Subway: Sheppard, then any Sheppard bus west.

The Pier Waterfront Museum   Ages 3 and up. This highly interactive museum, housed in a 1930s shipping warehouse, always makes a great impression with kids. Hands-on activities allow kids to explore a shipwreck or navigate a boat through a series of canals. There is also an interesting exhibit on the history of shipbuilding.

245 Queens Quay W. ℭ **416/338-PIER**. Admission C$5 (US$3.30) adults, C$4 (US$2.65) children, C$15 (US$9.90) families. Early Mar–June 30 daily 10am–4pm, July 1–Labour Day daily 10am–6pm, Labour Day–Oct 31 daily 10am–4 pm, closed Nov–early Mar. Subway: Union, then no. 510 streetcar west.

C Ethnic Museums

In keeping with Toronto's multicultural character, a number of museums reflect the history of various ethnic groups. Here are just a few:

- **Beth Tzedec Reuben and Helene Dennis Museum** The history of Jewish religion and culture is the focus of this museum. More than 1,000 artifacts emphasize the Jewish ritual at home and in the synagogue. 1700 Bathurst St. (*C* **416/781-3511**, ext. 32).

- **Holocaust Education and Memorial Centre of Toronto** This museum serves as a memorial to the more than 6 million victims of the Holocaust. Guided tours are available. 4600 Bathurst St. (*C* **416/631-5689**).

- **Taras H. Shevechenko Museum** Ukranian decorative arts and a history of Ukranian immigration to Canada are the focus of this interesting museum. 1614 Bloor St. W. (*C* **416/534-8662**).

Redpath Sugar Museum **Ages 5 and up.** This is definitely the sweetest museum in the city. The history of sugar, beginning with its discovery in India in 500 B.C., is portrayed in this small but engaging museum. Operated by the Redpath Sugar Company, it offers artifacts such as a 100-year-old sugar cone and explains things your kids have always wanted to know—like why brown sugar is brown.

95 Queens Quay E. *C* **416/366-3561**. Free admission. Mon–Fri 10am–noon and daily 1–3pm. Call ahead, as work on the refinery site can occasionally disrupt the museum schedule. Subway: Union, then no. 509 streetcar to Queens Quay.

Fun Fact Why Is Toronto Known as Hogtown?

One explanation is that in the early 19th century, while Montreal was considered an elegant and sophisticated city with a multitude of amusing diversions, Toronto was simply a place for conducting business—possibly in one of the city's many pork-packing plants. (How things have changed!)

Another suggestion is that jealous citizens of other parts of the province gave Toronto this title in reference to the wealth and greed of a good proportion of its citizenry.

Toronto Police Museum **Ages 8 and up.** This unique museum chronicles the evolution of the Toronto Police Department. Historical displays include a vintage Harley Davidson motorcycle and a 1914 paddy wagon. In the interactive exhibits, kids examine clues such as fingerprints, eyewitness reports, and even a sun-bleached skull and then attempt to solve the crimes. A theater also runs a selection of videos, the most popular being the 911 emergency story. Older kids will enjoy the true-life crimes section, which details the exploits of nine real-life Toronto criminals, including the Dirty Tricks Gang, whose members conducted at least 10 armed robberies in the late 1940s. A word of caution, though: Some of the materials in this section are quite graphic, even for older children.

Toronto's Best View

David Dunlap Observatory   Ages 7 and up. This observatory is home to the largest optical telescope in Canada. Tours are offered to the public on weekends from April to September, but you can also call ahead and ask to join one of the school tours held on Thursday mornings during the school year. Depending on the time of year and the weather, you and the kids may get an amazing view of the moon, Mars, Jupiter, Saturn, double stars, star clusters, or galaxies.

123 Hillsview Dr., Richmond Hill. © 905/884-2112. Admission C$5 (US$3.30) adults, C$3 (US$2) children and seniors. Apr–June and Sept Sat evenings only; July–Aug Fri–Sat evenings only. Times vary so call ahead.

40 College St. (1 block west of Yonge St.). © 416/808-7020. www.torontopolice.on.ca. Free, but donations accepted. Daily 9am–9pm. Subway: College.

Toronto's First Post Office 🌟 (Finds)   **Ages 6 and up.** If you're having a hard time convincing your kids to write thank-you notes to relatives, take them here and let them write their letters the way children did in the 1830s—with a quill pen and sealing wax. For C$1 (US65¢), the kids' letters will be stamped with a replica of an 1830s stamp and posted. This national historic site houses many artifacts tracing both the history of the Canadian Postal Service and the historic town of York, now known as Toronto. One of the museum's prize possessions is a topographical model of the city as it looked in 1837—have the kids try to figure out where the Eaton Centre and CN Tower would be. The gift shop offers beautiful handmade notepaper, quills, and ink.

260 Adelaide St. E. © 416/865-1833. Admission free. Mon–Fri 9am–4pm, Sat–Sun 10am–4pm. Subway: King, then 1 block north.

(Fun Fact What Languages Are Spoken in Toronto?

French and English are Canada's two official languages, but English, Cantonese, and Italian are the languages most often spoken in Toronto. Toronto's citizens speak in more than 100 languages and dialects.

---

3 Local History

Toronto is rich in local history. Since the French built the first trading post here in 1720, it has been the site of several major invasions, one by the British and one by the Americans. With its natural harbor, rivers, and fertile farmland, Toronto is the industrial heart of the province of Ontario. Much of this history has been preserved in the restored private residences, forts, villages, farms, and industrial mills and factories.

During the winter holidays these historic homes are often decorated as they would have been for Christmas in the past. Many historical sites provide special crafts and activities for kids during this season, as well as during spring break and summer holidays.

Heritage Toronto, 205 Yonge St. (℅ **416/392-6827**), offers guided walking tours of some of Toronto's heritage sites, as does the **Royal Ontario Museum,** 101 Queens Park Cres. (℅ **416/586-8600**).

Black Creek Pioneer Village Ages 4 and up. A restored Victorian

village is the setting for a trip back in time. Kids love peering in the houses, watching the servants work, and playing with the toys of a century ago. They're also given a chance to learn from the tinsmith, blacksmith, and local doctor, whose servant will explain the good doctor's cures. There are more than 35 houses, schools, and shops to explore. The post office, with its generous supply of rock candy, and the horse and buggy ride topped the list of my girls' favorite experiences there. We even took home a souvenir photo of all of us dressed in period costume and about to take off in a bright Victorian balloon.

Of the several restaurants on-site, the cafeteria-style deli on the bottom floor of the entrance/administration building is probably the best and fastest choice for kids.

1000 Murray Ross Pkwy. (at Steeles Ave. and Jane St.), Downsview. ℅ **416-736-1733.** Admission C$9 (US$5.95) adults, C$5 (US$3.30) children 5–14, free for children under 5. May–June weekdays 9:30am–4pm, weekends and holidays 10am–5pm; July–Sept daily 10am–5pm; Oct–Dec weekdays 9:30am–4pm, weekends and holidays 10am–4:30pm. Closed Jan–Apr and Dec 25. Subway: Jane, then no. 35B bus north. By car: Take Hwy. 400 north, exit at Steeles Ave., and drive east to Jane St.

Campbell House Ages 5 and up. Costumed guides take visitors on guided

tours of this restored Georgian-style home, built in 1922 by the sixth chief justice of Upper Canada, Sir William Campbell. In 1972 a group of Toronto-area lawyers bought the house and moved it from its original location on Duke Street (now Adelaide Street) to its present site near Osgoode Hall, the home of the Law Society of Upper Canada. This tour, as well as those of other historic homes, provides a brief but excellent introduction to a slice of Toronto's history.

160 Queen St. W. (at University Ave.). ℅ **416/597-0227.** Admission C$4.50 (US$2.95) adults, C$2 (US$1.30) children 12 and under, C$10 (US$6.60) families. Mon–Fri 9:30am–4:30pm, Sat–Sun noon–4:30pm. Subway: Osgoode.

Casa Loma Ages 3 and up. Secret passageways, opulent suites, and a 244-

meter (800 ft.) tunnel are the highlights of this castle home, built by Toronto financier Sir Henry Pellat in 1911. This is not a true castle in the European sense, but it does boast two towers (one Norman, one Scottish), and quite frankly the kids don't care about authenticity. They are thrilled to find the secret staircases in Sir Henry's office that led to his private suite above and the wine cellar below or to climb the numerous stairs to the tower battlements. A tunnel, which is made of concrete and so can be quite cold even in summer, leads to the luxurious stables outfitted with mahogany stalls and Spanish tile floors.

The castle hosts a number of special events in the elegant conservatory and the Great Hall, with its 18-meter (60 ft.) ceilings. We've watched everything from pirate shows to magicians there. While kids will probably tire quickly of touring the rooms, even they can appreciate their opulence. A large room on the third floor is often the setting for special craft workshops and displays. My kids' favorite activity was building their own castles from thousands of Lego blocks.

Tours are self-guided. There is a small cafeteria in the castle basement close to the tunnel entrance. There are seldom enough parking spaces, but they do tend to free up quickly.

1 Austin Terrace. ℅ **416/923-1171.** www.casaloma.org. Admission C$10 (US$6.60) adults, C$6.50 (US$4.30) children 14–17, C$6 (US$3.95) children 4–13, free for children under 4. Parking C$2.50 (US$1.65) per hour to a maximum of C$7 (US$4.60). Daily 9:30am–5pm (last entry at 4pm). Subway: Dupont, then walk 2 blocks north.

(*Fun Fact* **Calling Casa Loma**

When it was a private home, Casa Loma had 59 telephones, with the castle's switchboard operator handling more calls than did the entire city of Toronto!

Colborne Lodge   Ages 5 and up. When visiting High Park, take a few minutes to tour this Regency-style cottage, built in the 1830s by Toronto architect John George Howard and Jemima Howard, the original owners of the country estate that is now High Park. Guided tours are available on weekends and special events are often scheduled, such as Victorian egg decorating during the Easter holiday.

High Park. ✆ **416/392-6916**. Admission C$3.50 (US$2.30) adults, C$2.75 (US$1.80) seniors and children 13 and up, C$2.50 (US$1.65) children under 13. Tues–Sun noon–5pm. Call ahead—hours may vary. Subway: High Park.

Enoch Turner School House (*Moments*   **School age.** If your kids think school is tough today, give them a taste of what it was like 150 years ago. This one-room schoolhouse was built in 1848 for poor Irish immigrants living in the city. In this living history museum, the resident schoolteacher instructs kids in writing on slate boards and gives deportment lessons. The curriculum is at a grade-3 level.

106 Trinity St. (at King St.). ✆ **416/863-0010**. Free admission. By appointment only. Subway: King, then any streetcar east.

Fort York   Ages 5 and up. Although the original garrison was built in 1783, most of the structures at this historic site date from 1813, when the fort was rebuilt after invading Americans burned it down. For many years the fort was the center of Toronto's economic and social world, with merchants and innkeepers setting up shop just outside its gates.

Today, the fort has been restored to how it would have appeared at the time of the War of 1812. Costumed guides give tours of the dozen or so buildings and provide demonstrations of country dancing, musket practice, and period music. They also host drill classes. Demonstrations are held on the hour and tours are given every half hour.

Garrison Rd. (off Fleet St. between Bathurst St. and Strachan Ave.). ✆ **416/392-6907**. Admission C$5 (US$3.30) adults, C$3 (US$2) children. June–Oct Mon–Wed and Fri 10am–5pm, Thurs 10am–7pm, Sat–Sun noon–5pm; Nov–May Tues–Fri 10am–5pm, Sat–Sun noon–5pm. Subway: Bathurst, then any streetcar south.

(*Fun Fact* **The Charred House?**

During the War of 1812 (which lasted until 1815), the Americans invaded and blew up Fort York. In retaliation, a group of Canadians traveled to the American president's residence and torched it. The Americans later whitewashed the house to hide the charred wood—hence the name, the White House.

Gibson House Museum   Ages 5 and up. Costumed guides answer questions and perform typical household chores of the 1850s. This house was originally the home of David and Elizabeth Gibson and their seven children. David

Gibson was a land surveyor, local politician, and farmer. He was involved in the Rebellion of 1837. The bookstore has a collection of adult and children's books on life in the 19th century.

5172 Yonge St. ℂ 416/395-7432. Admission C$2.75 (US$1.80) adults, C$1.75 (US$1.15) children. Tues–Fri 9:30am–4:30pm, Sat–Sun and holidays noon–5pm. Subway: North York Centre.

Grange House   Ages 5 and up. Built in 1817, the Grange was Toronto's first brick home. Costumed guides offer a tour that older kids will find especially interesting, and everyone can sample some 19th-century treats from the home's kitchen.

The Art Gallery of Ontario, 317 Dundas St. W. ℂ 416/979-6648. Admission free with pay-what-you-can admission to the Art Gallery of Ontario. Tues and Thurs–Fri 11am–6pm, Wed 11am–8:30pm, Sat–Sun 10am–5:30pm. Subway: St. Patrick.

HMCS Haida   Ages 5 and up. This fully restored 1930s destroyer saw action in World War II and Korea and then served with the NATO fleet in the Atlantic. Retired in 1963, it is now anchored in the harbor off Ontario Place and serves as a maritime and military museum.

Tours of this massive warship give kids a glimpse of what life at sea is like, including the crowded bunks and hammocks and galley food. Kids will be awestruck by the intimidating deck guns.

955 Lakeshore Blvd. W. ℂ 416/314-9811 or 416/314-9900 for recorded information. www.ontario place.on.ca. Admission free with Ontario Place admission. Subway: Bathurst, then any streetcar south.

Mackenzie House   Ages 6 and up. William Lyon Mackenzie, Toronto's first mayor and leader of the 1837 Upper Canada Rebellion, once owned this home. The house has been restored to 1850s style, with a print shop, similar to the one Mackenzie once owned, as part of the attraction. Costumed guides give tours and explain aspects of 19th-century life.

82 Bond St. ℂ 416/392-6915. Free admission. May–Sept 1 Tues–Sun noon–5pm; Sept 2–Dec Tues–Sun noon–4pm; Jan–Apr Sat–Sun noon–5pm. Subway: Dundas.

Montgomery's Inn (Value   **Ages 4 and up.** Costumed staff at this restored 1830s inn go about their business much as the servants would have in the early part of the 19th century. The tour takes about 1½ hours and may be a bit long for small children, but it is highly interactive, especially in the inn's fully operational kitchen, where visitors are encouraged to help cook the traditional meals. Try to get here for an authentic 1850s afternoon tea, served Tuesday to Sunday from 2 to 4:30pm. There is also a charming gift shop that sells reproductions of early 19th-century toys.

4707 Dundas St. W. ℂ 416/394-8113. Admission C$3 (US$2) adults, C$2 (US$1.30) children 5–12, free for children under 5. Afternoon tea C$3 (US$2) adults, C$1 (US65¢) children. Tues–Thurs 1–4:30pm, Sat–Sun 1–5pm, closed Mon. Subway: Islington, then no. 37 bus.

Spadina House   Ages 6 and up. Located next door to Casa Loma, this home was built by Toronto businessman and financier John Austin in 1866 and was the home of four successive generations of Austins until it was bought by the City of Toronto. Tours of the building are offered on the quarter-hour, and 5 acres of gardens are among the most elaborate in the city.

285 Spadina Rd. ℂ 416/392-6910. Admission C$5 (US$3.30) adults, C$3.25 (US$2.15) seniors and children 12 and up, C$3 (US$2) children under 12. Tues–Fri noon–4pm, Sat–Sun noon–5pm. Subway: Dupont.

Todmorden Mills Heritage Museum and Art Centre   Ages 6 and up. This area was first settled in the 1790s and was home to some of Toronto's earliest industries, including grist and lumber mills and a brewery. Today the museum provides a record of the city's industrial past. Kids can visit historic millers' homes, the Brewery Gallery, the Paper Mill Gallery and Theatre, and the relocated Don train station. The East Side Players stage regular theatrical productions here during the summer months, and the Don Valley Art Club offers art lessons. Special events, classes, and workshops for kids are offered throughout the season. Call ahead to see if something is being offered while you're in town.

67 Pottery Rd. ℂ **416/396-2819.** Admission C$3 (US$2) adults, C$1.50 (US$1) children 5–12, free for children under 5. May 1–Sept 28 Tues–Fri 11am–4:30pm, Sat–Sun noon–5pm. Subway: Broadview, then take any bus north to Pottery Rd. and walk down the hill.

4 Nature Centers

Chudleigh Farm *(Moments* **All ages.** The best time to come to this apple farm is in the fall, when you and the kids can pick your own apples and pumpkins, but there are plenty of activities in other seasons. A tractor/wagon ride will take you to the apple orchards and pumpkin patch, and the kids can explore an innovative straw maze, small play area, and petting zoo. There is also a bakery on site.

9528 Hwy. 25, Milton. ℂ **905/826-1252.** www.chudleighs.com. Admission C$3 (US$2) per person, which is credited toward a purchase. July–Oct 9am–7pm; Nov–June Fri–Sun 10am–5pm. By car: Take Hwy. 401 west to Hwy. 25, Exit 320. Go about 3km (1.8 miles) north on Hwy 25.

Cullen Gardens & Miniature Village *(* *(Finds* **All ages.** What began as a greenhouse business has evolved into a fantasyland of miniature villages, play places, and live entertainment.

The girls and I were enchanted. A pathway meanders past more than 180 half-scale homes, shops, and businesses along Main Street, and several of the buildings are recognizable Toronto area landmarks. The village is brought to life by vivid sights and sounds and animated mannequins—a fireman with real smoke billowing around him douses a fire, the church bells ring, and a toilet whooshes as it's flushed in the replica campground.

The miniature city residents escape to the country via a highway with cars zipping past and a train that meanders through the complex. Cottage country is dotted with cottages around a small lake, and there's even a ferry to take the tiny residents across the lake. A miniature fairground completes the scene.

Admission to the grounds also includes a pioneer wagon ride and a visit to Lynde House, where the girls were entranced by two turn-of-the-century animated mannequins engaging in a game of hide and seek. Water slides and a wading pool are also part of the complex playground.

Special events are planned throughout the year, but if you have the chance, visit during the Christmas season, when the entire village and gardens are decorated and lit with cheery Christmas lights.

There are several options for eating, but I recommend picking up some hot dogs and french fries at the outdoor snack bar and dining on one of the many picnic tables. While the kids are busy eating, you can admire the breathtaking gardens you've been too busy to look at so far. Don't let the kids miss looking at the dinosaurs and other animals carved from hedges scattered throughout the gardens.

Taunton Rd., Whitby. ℂ **905/686-1600.** www.cullengardens.com. Admission C$12 (US$7.90) adults, C$5 (US$3.30) children 3–12, free for children 2 and under. Summer daily 9am–8pm; spring and fall daily 10am–6pm; closed early Jan–mid-Apr. By car: Take Hwy. 401 to Exit 410, Whitby. Travel north on Hwy. 12 to Taunton Rd. Drive west on Taunton Rd. for about 1km (0.6 miles).

⌐nough Farm **Ages 1 to 9.** This tiny farm is a short walk from Centreville on Centre Island. Kids can feed and pet the ducks, geese, cows, and pigs. While almost all kids love barnyard animals, this farm is a special treat for your smallest family members.

Centreville, Toronto Islands. © 416/393-8195. Free admission. Ferry return fare C$5 (US$3.30) adults, C$2 (US$1.30) children 2–12, free for children 2 and under. Open dawn–dusk. Directions: Catch the Toronto Islands Ferry at the terminal on Queens Quay West, at the foot of Bay St. No cars are allowed on the ferry.

Riverdale Farm ★★★ (Value) **Ages 1 to 9.** Visit the early 19th century at this wonderful working farm in the heart of Toronto. Numerous animals call this farm home, including Clydesdales, cows, goats, pigs, donkeys, geese, ducks, and chickens. There are also gardens to explore and demonstrations by the costumed staff of farming chores typical of the time, including milking, cream separating, butter churning, egg collecting, sheepshearing, wool spinning and dying, and floral and herb gardening. Be sure to check out the antique wagons in the barn, the butterfly garden, and the apple orchard.

201 Winchester St. © 416/392-6794. Free admission. Daily 9am–5pm. Subway: Castle Frank, then no. 65 bus to Parliament St.

5 Outdoor Spaces

There is no shortage of green space in Toronto, but the real thrill for Torontonians and visitors alike is what the city has accomplished with that green space. Nature trails through wooded ravines, formal gardens and conservatories, playgrounds for kids, and even working farms are all to be found within the city limits.

Allan Gardens **Ages 2 and up.** The outdoor gardens are beautiful in the spring and summer, but kids are most interested in the conservatories. In this series of five buildings, pathways meander through tropical palms and flowers and past waterfalls, Koy fishponds, and a paddle wheel. This is a wonderful spot to take the kids to wind down after a day of sightseeing.

14 Horticultural Ave. (between Jarvis and Sherbourne sts.). © 416/392-7288. Free admission. Mon–Fri 9am–4pm, Sat–Sun 10am–5pm. Subway: College, then any streetcar east.

Edwards Gardens **All ages.** This formal garden spread over 35 acres in the Don Valley area is a wonderful place for a quiet family stroll. Kids will like the quaint bridges spanning the creek that winds through the property. Of special interest to kids is the **Teaching Garden,** where various programs teach kids how to care for the environment. In the fall and spring the garden is booked with school groups, but in the summer plenty of programs are offered for the public. Activities at the garden are always hands-on and include hikes, gardening, and arts and crafts. The teaching garden is at the west end of Edwards Gardens, beside the Red Garden House and Alphabet Garden. It's open from early April to late October; public programs are offered in July and August at various prices—call © 416/397-1355 for details.

Lawrence Ave. E. and Leslie St. © 416/397-1340. Free admission. Daily dawn–dusk. Subway: Lawrence, then any bus east.

High Park ★★ (Moments) **All ages.** This is Toronto's own Central Park, but it's much safer. Many would argue that this 400-acre park is the city's best—it certainly qualifies as the park with the most amenities. In addition to plenty of green space, sports fields, and tennis courts, the park has a small zoo, a playground, a pool, and even its own train. The train runs from spring to autumn and will pick you up and drop you off at any one of seven stations.

The High Park Adventure Playground is the place my kids run to first and where we always wind up our visit. This 930-square-meter (10,000-sq.-ft.) playground is shaped like a castle. A separate area for toddlers is enclosed within a fence. At Grenadier Pond, a 15-minute train ride from the playground, the kids can chase the Canada geese in the summer and skate on the pond in the winter. The zoo is home to bison, goats, llamas, and sheep and there is also a duck pond, another favorite with kids.

Young naturalists will appreciate the many hidden gardens on the property. Take them to Hillside Gardens, which has a wealth of streams and pools and the usual creatures that delight young children, and don't miss the giant maple leaf flowerbed beside Grenadier Pond. The park also sponsors a drop-in gardening program in its children's garden, located in the south end of the park on Colborne Lodge Drive. Targeted to kids aged 6 to 12, the children's garden is open on Thursdays from 10am to noon and on alternate Sunday afternoons through July and August. Topics and activities include everything from butterfly gardens to First Nations history and storytelling and composting, and kids are always encouraged to pitch in and help with the vegetable and flower gardening.

On a hot day you can wrap up your visit by cooling down at the large outdoor pool or wading pool at the Bloor Street entrance.

Historic **Colborne Lodge** is also located on the park grounds, and every summer the Canadian Stage Company holds the **Dream in High Park,** an outdoor Shakespearean production.

Bloor and Keele sts., south to the Gardiner Expressway. Free admission. Daily dawn–dusk. Subway: High Park.

6 Markets

With its ethnically diverse population, Toronto is virtually guaranteed to have eclectic and fascinating markets. Kensington and St. Lawrence markets are two of the best known.

Kensington Market ✦ (Finds) **Ages 5 and up.** The best time to shop at Kensington Market is as early as possible. In the early morning hours, the vendors unload their wares and pile the crab, squid, salted fish, cheeses, and freshly baked bread onto their street tables and in their storefront windows.

The market had its beginnings in the 1900s, when it was primarily a Jewish area and vendors set up stalls in front of their homes. Today, Kensington Market offers goods from more than 30 cultures. A walk through this international bazaar is an essential part of Toronto's multicultural experience. Amid the constant buzz of dozens of languages, you can select from exotic fruits and spices, barrels of beans and grains, and bolts of fabric and lace. The crates of live chickens, rabbits, and pigeons fascinate kids. A word of warning, though—they are not being sold as pets!

While many visitors are there just to look, it's a good place to go for cut-rate new and vintage clothing. Public transit is probably your best bet for getting there, as the streets within the market are narrow and crowded and parking spots are hard to come by.

Bounded by Dundas St., Spadina Ave., Baldwin St., and Augusta Ave. No central phone. Most stores open Mon–Sat. Subway: St. Patrick, then Dundas streetcar west to Spadina Ave., or Spadina, then any streetcar south to Dundas St.

St. Lawrence Market   **Ages 5 and up.** Since 1803, the St. Lawrence Market has been supplying Torontonians with fresh foodstuffs. The south end of the market currently houses more than 50 vendors of fresh meats, vegetables, and fruits. Early on Saturday mornings, a farmer's market is held in the north end of the market. Experienced shoppers know to arrive early, but there is still plenty to look at in the main building later in the day. On Sundays, the north end of the market opens its doors to more than 80 antique vendors.

The Market Gallery in the south end displays the City of Toronto's vast collection of artifacts, art, photographs, and memorabilia. Kids may find this gallery a bit dry, but admission is free and it's worth a quick peek.

92 Front St. E. ✆ **416/392-7219.** www.stlawrencemarket.com. Tues–Thurs 9am–7pm, Fri 8am–8pm, Sat 5am–5pm; antique market Sun 5am–5pm. Subway: Union.

7 For Kids with Special Interests

Canada Sports Hall of Fame   **Ages 6 and up.** The interactive and informative exhibits in this museum celebrate many of Canada's greatest athletes. The Red Foster Theatre screens several interesting short movies, including the *Terry Fox Story* and *Great Moments in Canadian Sport.*

Exhibition Place. ✆ **416/260-6789.** Free admission. Mon–Fri 10am–4:30pm. Subway: Bathurst, then any streetcar south.

Canadian Broadcasting Corporation (CBC) Museum   **Ages 3 and up, tours ages 8 and up.** Canada's public broadcaster has been on the air for more than 60 years, and this museum is dedicated to preserving that history. Highlights include a spot where youngsters can record themselves telling a story, as well as a treasure trove of video and audio clips, some dating from the 1950s. The back of the museum contains a puppetry display and puppet theater equipped with video monitors so young puppeteers can stay hidden from their audience. Tours of the CBC studios feature a walk through some of the sets and a close-up look at some of the props. The tour is probably best suited to children ages 8 and over.

Room 1J202, 250 Front Street W. ✆ **416/205-5574.** www.cbc.ca/museum. Free admission. Tours C$7 (US$4.60) adults, C$5 (US$3.30) seniors and children. Mon–Fri 9am–5pm, Sat 12–4pm. Subway: Union.

Canadian Motorsports Hall of Fame and Museum   **Ages 7 and up.** If your kids are into speed, this museum is for them. Exhibits cover all motor sports— from stock cars to Indy cars—and include many cars belonging to former racing giants such as Jacques Villaneuve. In addition to the dozen vehicle exhibits, there are many smaller displays of driving gear, trophies, and racing memorabilia.

777 Bay St. (in College Park mall). ✆ **416/597-2643.** www.canadianautomotivecollection.ca. Free admission. Mon–Fri 10am–4:30pm. Subway: College.

Design Exchange *Finds*   **Ages 7 and up.** Budding fashion and graphic designers, engineers, and architects will be inspired by this museum dedicated to design. The only museum of its kind in North America, the Design Exchange has two exhibition galleries. Admission to the ground floor is free and exhibits change frequently. The upper gallery has a small admission fee and changing exhibits have included Japanese graphic art, Canadian furniture, and Finnish industrial design. Lectures and guided tours are available—call ahead.

234 Bay St. ✆ **416/216-2160.** www.designexchange.org or www.dxnet.net. Admission C$5 (US$3.30) adults, C$3.50 (US$2.30) students. Mon–Fri 10am–6pm, Sat–Sun noon–5pm. Subway: Union, then walk north along Bay St.

Hockey Hall of Fame *★★*   **Ages 4 and up.** Even non–hockey fans are thrilled by this highly interactive salute to Canada's most popular sport. In virtual reality games, players can take shots on famous goalies like Jacques Plante or play goalie against their choice of NHL greats. Table hockey games (including one from the 1920s) and video games are scattered throughout the building. Also popular are the stations where infrared lasers record the speed and accuracy of the player's shots. The highlight for my kids, though, was the broadcast booth, where they could call a game with the use of TelePrompTers and then have the video and audio clip played back to them. Space is at a premium here, and the museum uses it well. The broadcast booth, for instance, is located high above the rest of the action and is accessed by a metal staircase.

A ton of hockey memorabilia is housed here, including retired jerseys and sticks and other equipment belonging to hockey's stars. The Great One himself, Wayne Gretzky, has an entire exhibit devoted to his career. Kids can also walk through a replica of the Toronto Maple Leafs' dressing room and the Great Hall, where the NHL trophies are housed, including the coveted Stanley Cup. There is an interesting exhibit in the back dedicated to life in the 1950s when professional hockey had its beginnings. It failed to capture the kids' interest, but the adults enjoyed it.

BCE Place, 30 Yonge St. (at Front St.). © 416/360-7765. www.hhof.com. Admission C$12 (US$7.90) adults, C$8 (US$5.30) children 4–18, free for children under 4. Late June–Labour Day Mon–Sat 9:30am–6pm, Sun 10am–6pm; Sept–mid-June Mon–Fri 10am–5pm, Sat 9:30am–6pm, Sun 10:30am–5pm. Subway: Union.

Martin House Museum of Doll Artistry & Store *(Value*   **Ages 2 and up.** A delight for doll lovers of all ages, this museum features a rare and exquisite doll collection by master doll artists of the 19th and 20th centuries. Themes for exhibits include ethnic, character, and storybook dolls. The gift store offers Canada's largest selection of dolls, teddy bears, dollhouses, and miniatures.

46 Centre St., Thornhill. © 905/881-0426. Free admission. Mon–Sat 10am–5:30pm. Subway: Finch, then either Richmond Hill C bus or Brampton no. 77 bus. By car: Drive north on the Don Valley Pkwy. to Steeles Ave. and then take Steeles Ave. to Yonge St. Go north on Yonge St. about 1.5km (1 mile) and turn west onto Centre St.

Museum for Textiles   **Ages 7 and up.** This museum houses a diverse collection of everything from Turkish rugs to Chinese children's hats and traditional Nigerian clothing to medieval tapestries. In a collection that numbers more than 8,000 pieces, the history of the world is traced through our use of textiles. Aspiring seamstresses and designers will find lots to look at, but all kids will find something fascinating in this unique museum.

55 Centre Ave. © 416/599-5321. www.museumfortextiles.on.ca. Admission C$5 (US$3.30) adults, free for children 12 and under. Tues and Thurs–Fri 11am–5pm, Wed 11am–8pm, Sat–Sun noon–5pm. Subway: St. Patrick.

MZTV   **Ages 5 and up.** "Television is not a problem to be managed, but an instrument to be played," said Moses Znaimer, Canadian television mogul and founder of MZTV, the museum dedicated to the history of North American television. Located east of the CHUM/CITY building, this museum opened in the summer of 2001 and houses televisions from 1928 to 1985, as well as such TV memorabilia as remote controls and TV guides. The museum can be visited by tour only, offered on the hour.

277 Queen St. W. Tickets must be purchased at the City Store in the City TV Complex. © 416/599-7339. www.mztv.com. Admission C$5 (US$3.30) adults, C$4 (US$2.65) seniors and students. Call to check children's prices. Mon–Sat 10am–6pm. Subway: Osgoode.

Osgoode Hall   Ages 9 and up. Kids interested in the law and the court system will enjoy a tour through this elegant 160-year-old building. It currently serves as the home of the Law Society of Upper Canada; the Ontario Court of Appeals also maintains several courtrooms that are open to the public.

130 Queen St. W. ℂ **416/947-3300.** Free admission. Mon–Fri 9am–6pm; free tours July–Aug Mon–Fri 1:15pm. Subway: Osgoode.

Stock Market Place   Ages 8 and up. The Richie Riches in your family will appreciate this up-close look at how empires are built and lost at the Toronto Stock Market. The real trading floor is closed to visitors, but former floor traders act as guides to the museum and are quick to answer questions and make suggestions.

Although visitors will benefit from a basic knowledge of stocks and money, the interactive exhibits ensure that everyone can have fun here. The Learning Playground is an interactive area that features a media wall with real-time television. Sorry, there are no cartoons—the TVs are tuned to reports on stock market performance. One computer simulator allows the kids to run a public company, and another lets them research and make pretend investments and then track their progress. The History of Money is a fascinating exhibit. Another exhibit traces the history of stock exchanges from ancient bartering systems to ticker tape and modern computerized systems.

The Exchange Tower, 130 King St. W. ℂ **800/729-5556** or 416/947-4676. www.tse.com. Admission C$5 (US$3.30) adults, C$3 (US$2) children. Mon–Fri 10am–5pm; May–Oct Mon–Sat 10am–5pm. Subway: King.

Thomas Fisher Rare Books Library   Ages 8 and up. Junior bibliophiles are fascinated by this collection of early writing artifacts, which includes a 1789 B.C. Babylonian cuneiform tablet from Ur, Egyptian papyrus fragments, and medieval illuminated manuscripts. The library displays more than 350 themed special collections on a rotating basis.

120 St. George St., University of Toronto. ℂ **416/978-1667.** Free admission. Mon–Fri 9am–5pm. Subway: St. George.

Military Museums

A number of museums are dedicated to Canadian military history and life in the armed forces, including the following:

- **48th Highlanders Museum,** 75 Simcoe St. (at King St. W.) (ℂ **416/596-1382**).
- **Queen's Own Rifles of Canada Regimental Museum,** Casa Loma, 1 Austin Terrace (ℂ **416/923-1171**). Free with admission to Casa Loma.
- **Royal Canadian Military Institute,** 426 University Ave. (ℂ **416/597-0286**).
- **Toronto Aerospace Museum (TAM),** at the former site of the Canadian Forces Base, Downsview Park, 65 Carl Hall Rd. (ℂ **416/638-6078**).

---

8 Kid-Friendly Tours

This is the best way to get to know the city. If you have a few days, you can take a tour on the first day and then choose your activities based on what you've seen. Be selective, though—some tours are more suitable for kids than others. Don't take any bus tour that's longer than an hour, unless it has frequent stops or allows on-off privileges. For walking and cycling tours, ask about distance as well as terrain. The last thing you want to be doing on a hot day is carrying your toddler on your shoulders.

Great Lakes Schooner Company **Ages 5 and up.** For a real treat, take the kids on a two-hour tour of the Toronto Harbour and Islands on a fully restored tall ship. The tour aboard the three-masted schooner *Kaiyama* is not narrated, but this actually turns out to be a good thing. The kids can explore the ship and view the sights as they choose. A large dining room dominates the space below deck, and above deck there are benches and plenty of open space. The licensed bar also sells snack foods for perpetually hungry little ones.

249 Queens Quay W., Suite 111. ℂ 416/203-2322. www.greatlakesschooner.com. Tickets C$18.95 (US$12.50) adults, C$10.95 (US$7.20) children. Call ahead for departure and boarding times, which vary.

National Helicopters **Ages 5 and up.** If your kids have always wanted to ride in a helicopter, now might be the time to indulge them. This tour company offers two package tours. The first is a tour of the city that lasts about eight minutes; the second is a two-hour tour of the Niagara Region, including Niagara Falls and a stop for a tour and lunch at the Niagara vineyards. You can also plan your own itinerary at a similar cost or take the much more expensive option of chartering one of the company's two helicopters. The city tour departs from the Docks entertainment complex at Harbourfront, the Toronto Island Airport, or Ontario Place. The Niagara tour departs from the Docks.

11339 Albion Vaughan Rd., Kleinburg. ℂ 416/361-1100. www.nationalhelicopters.com. City tour C$40–$50 (US$26.40–$33) per person; Niagara tour C$200 (US$132) per person (price does not include lunch); charter of 6-seater C$850 (US$561) per hour and 4-seater C$700 (US$462) per hour. June–Labour Day daily 11am–8pm.

Old Towne Tours (★(★   **Ages 5 and up.** This tour company is the best choice for young families for several reasons. Even kids who aren't thrilled with sightseeing will have fun riding in a double-decker bus or a pseudo trolley car. If you have to make frequent stops to accommodate a restless child or a toddler who is potty training, or if you want a closer look at some of the historic sites you're driving past, you can hop off the tour at any time and then catch the next bus or trolley—they're usually 15 to 30 minutes apart.

This narrated tour of the downtown area takes in 18 city landmarks, including the Hockey Hall of Fame, Casa Loma, the Royal Ontario Museum, and Ontario Place, and offers a hop on/hop off service whenever you want to take in any of the sights. It would be almost impossible to explore all the attractions on one tour, but it's a good way to get your bearings in the city. You may want to take in a few of the minor venues on the tour and set aside other days for the major attractions such as Ontario Place.

Tours leave Nicholby's Sports and Souvenirs (123 Front St. W.) every hour at 25 minutes past the hour. Tickets are available from the tour bus operators, at most hotel concierge desks, and at all Nicholby's stores.

123 Front St. W. Tours depart from Nicholby's. Subway: Union. ℂ 416/798-2424. Tickets C$25 (US$16.50) adults, C$12 (US$7.90) children. Oct 16–May 15 9am–5pm, May 16–Oct 15 9am–6pm.

Taste of Toronto (Taste of the World) **Ages 5 and up walking tours, ages 7 and up biking tours.** This company offers lively walking and biking tours of the Toronto area that will introduce you to Toronto's local color and history. With unique offerings ranging from haunted houses to Chinese culinary delights and Toronto Islands mysteries, this is one of the few tours that attracts both local families and visitors. All of the tours set a leisurely pace that is perfect for kids, with time built in to stop, sit on benches, and admire interesting details such as the gargoyles in Yorkville or creatures on the islands.

One of the biggest favorites with kids is the walking tour of haunted Yorkville, with a stop at University College, where a murdered stonemason was once entombed and where *Dracula* was recently filmed. Another walking tour samples some of Chinatown's many delightful shops, with highlights including a cleaver demonstration, a dim sum lunch, and lessons in Chinese etiquette.

If you prefer to ride, several bike tours are offered, including one to the Toronto Islands. The total distance is about 10 kilometers (6 miles), with plenty of stops to view the sights, snap pictures, and listen to stories. The kids love the lighthouse ghost stories. Bikes and (mandatory) helmets are supplied.

P.O. Box 659, Stn. P, Toronto, ON M5S 2Y4. © **416/923-6813**. Fax 416/925-0554. www.TorontoWalks Bikes.com. Walking tours C$15–$35 (US$9.90–$23.10) adults, C$13–$30 (US$8.60–$19.80) seniors and youths, C$9–$22 (US$5.95–$14.50) children under 12. Bike tours (including helmet and bike) C$45 (US$29.70) adults, C$40 (US$26.40) seniors and youths, C$30 (US$19.80) children under 12. Call or visit the website to book tours.

Toronto Hippo Tours (★   **All ages.** If your kids groan every time you hop on a tour bus, take them on this one and listen to their gasps of surprise and delight when the tour bus drives straight into Toronto Harbour. These tours are a huge hit with kids of all ages, not because of the content but because of the mode of transportation. Families are taken on tours of the downtown and the harbor on an "amphibus"—think amphibian. These specially constructed bright yellow buses are designed to travel on both land and water.

The content of the tours is fairly standard and includes uninterrupted, narrated tours of downtown landmarks such as the Eaton Centre, Hummingbird Centre, Hockey Hall of Fame, and, of course, the waterfront.

Tours depart from the base of the CN Tower, south side; the 9am tour departs from the Delta Chelsea Hotel, with a pickup at 9:15am from the Sheraton Centre Hotel.

31A Parliament St. © **877/635-5510** or 416/703-4476. www.torontohippotours.com. Tickets C$35 (US$23.10) adults, C$23 (US$15.20) children 4–17, free for children under 3; family rate (2 adults/ 2 children) C$100 (US$66), plus C$15 (US$9.90) for each additional child. May–June 9am–5pm, tours depart every 2 hours; July–Oct 9am–7pm, tours depart every hour.

For the Active Family

1 Places to Run & Walk

Toronto has endless green spaces where kids can run and play, both downtown and in outlying areas. Below, I've listed some of my kids' favorite parks and playgrounds.

NATURE WALKS

A walk through almost any of the city-owned parks will bring your kids into close contact with nature. No matter where you go, make sure that you and the kids wear comfortable shoes and don't go too far—remember, you'll have to walk back! The good news is that parks within the city usually have washrooms and benches for resting along each trail.

Try a hike around the gardens, streams, and ponds of **High Park,** south of Bloor Street in the west end of the city, or along the Thomas H. Thomson Nature Trail in **Sunnybrook Park,** at Eglinton Avenue and Leslie Street in North York. For information on these and other parks and ravines, the City of Toronto publishes a series of guides called *Discovery Walks.* Call the **Parks Department** at ℭ **416/392-8186,** or visit their website at www.city.toronto.on.ca.

Kortright Centre for Conservation ⍟ The best time to visit this conservation area is in the spring, when it hosts its most kid-friendly activities. From the end of February to the second week of April, the Maple Syrup Festival is celebrated. Kids can learn about both modern and pioneer methods of making maple syrup by peering into the buckets hanging from the park's maple trees and helping the costumed pioneers stir the huge iron kettles of sap. Kids (and adults, too) are encouraged to taste the sweet sap and the maple syrup, and pancakes are served with homemade syrup at the center's cafeteria.

Another popular spring event is the Pond Life workshop. Kids, nets in hand, are led to several ponds and given magnifying glasses for a close-up view of some of the park's slimiest inhabitants and their habitats. Another great event is the annual Kite Festival, where kids can attend a kite-making workshop. Even the filtration building is fascinating—it contains a display of the park's ecosystem, where kids can get view tree roots and plant life and learn how wastewater is treated so that it can be reused.

The park itself is worth visiting any time of the year. It boasts three aquariums containing many of the fish native to the area and 16 kilometers (10 miles) of trails that wind their way through forest, meadow, rivers, and marshland. Some of the park's permanent residents include deer, fox, coyotes, rabbits, wild turkeys, and pheasants. On summer weekends, regularly scheduled guided tours are offered, and during the winter, several trails are kept open for cross-country skiing.

Outdoor Activities

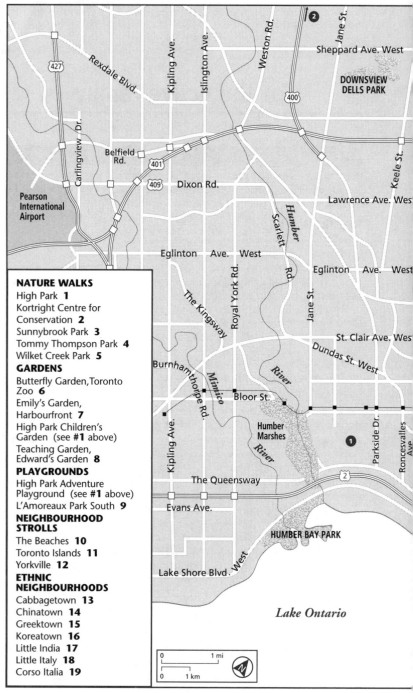

NATURE WALKS
High Park **1**
Kortright Centre for
Conservation **2**
Sunnybrook Park **3**
Tommy Thompson Park **4**
Wilket Creek Park **5**

GARDENS
Butterfly Garden, Toronto
Zoo **6**
Emily's Garden,
Harbourfront **7**
High Park Children's
Garden (see **#1** above)
Teaching Garden,
Edward's Garden **8**

PLAYGROUNDS
High Park Adventure
Playground (see **#1** above)
L'Amoreaux Park South **9**

**NEIGHBOURHOOD
STROLLS**
The Beaches **10**
Toronto Islands **11**
Yorkville **12**

**ETHNIC
NEIGHBOURHOODS**
Cabbagetown **13**
Chinatown **14**
Greektown **15**
Koreatown **16**
Little India **17**
Little Italy **18**
Corso Italia **19**

Pearson
International
Airport

DOWNSVIEW
DELLS PARK

Sheppard Ave. West
Rexdale Blvd.
Kipling Ave.
Islington Ave.
Weston Rd.
Jane St.
Carlingview Dr.
Belfield Rd.
Dixon Rd.
Lawrence Ave. Wes
Keele St.
Scarlett Rd.
Humber
Eglinton Ave. West
Royal York Rd.
The Kingsway
Jane St.
Eglinton Ave. West
St. Clair Ave. Wes
Dundas St. West
Burnhamthorpe Rd.
Mimico
River
Bloor St.
Humber
Marshes
River
Parkside Dr.
Roncesvalles Ave
The Queensway
Kipling Ave.
Evans Ave.
HUMBER BAY PARK
Lake Shore Blvd. West
Lake Ontario

0   1 mi
0   1 km

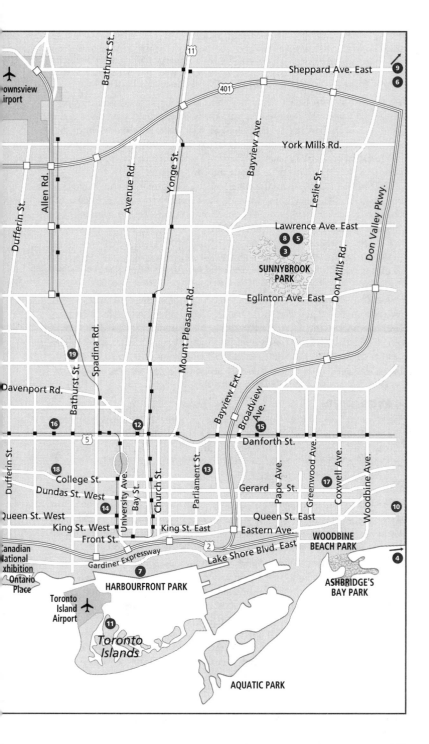

9550 Pine Valley Dr. ℂ **905/832-2289.** www.kortright.org. Admission C$6 (US$3.95) adults, C$4 (US$2.65) children. May be additional charges for special events. Daily 10am–4pm. Guided program available weekends only 11:30am–1pm and 2:30pm. Subway: Islington, then no. 37 bus north to Steeles Ave. Take the Vaughan no. 3 bus north on Islington Ave. to Rutherford Rd. By car: From Hwy. 401, take Hwy. 400 north to Major Mackenzie Dr. Drive 2km west on Major Mackenzie Dr., then 1km south on Pine Valley Dr.

Tommy Thompson Park   Also referred to as the Leslie Street Spit, this park was created when sand was dredged from the bottom of Lake Ontario to create a new port in the harbor. The main draw for kids is the multitude of birds that now nest here. It is home to the world's largest colony of ring-billed seagulls, as well as ducks, geese, terns, and snowy egrets. During nesting season you may be lucky enough to spot giant blue herons and cormorants.

Make sure the kids look for the telltale wildlife tracks that are abundant along the paths. Rabbits, beavers, and raccoons are frequently spotted, as is the occasional fox or coyote. Snakes are also common, but don't worry—none are venomous. The roadway is paved but closed to cars, making it a perfect spot to cycle, skate, or push a stroller along.

South end of Leslie St. ℂ **416/661-6600.** Free admission and parking. Free shuttle bus to the spit from the park gates operates early May–early Oct. Apr–Oct 9am–6pm, Nov–Mar 9am–4:30pm. Subway: Queen, then any streetcar east to Leslie St. Transfer to no. 83 bus south to park gates at Commissioners St.

Wilket Creek Park   If you're toting babies or toddlers, this park boasts a wide, paved nature trail that is perfect for strollers. The trail meanders along the Don River past flocks of ducks, over several bridges, and under a grove of huge maple trees. It's only about five minutes from the Ontario Science Centre, so it's a good place to take the kids for a little fresh air before heading back to your hotel.

Enter through Edwards Gardens, corner of Lawrence and Leslie sts. ℂ **416/392-8186.** Free admission. Daily dawn–dusk. Subway: Lawrence, then any bus east to Leslie St.

PLAYGROUNDS

L'Amoreaux Park South *(Finds*   After a hot day at the zoo, this park is a perfect place to stop and cool off. The play structures are colorful and imaginative and there is a great hill for rolling and running. However, the park's major attraction is the Kidstown Water Playground. For only C$1 (US65¢) per child, this water park is a wonderful bargain. Highlights include a water-spurting bicycle, a water slide, and water guns so the kids can spray you and each other. There is also an interesting tubular corridor that sprays water from every direction at those who try to navigate through it. The wading pool is just the right size and depth for toddlers.

3159 Birchmount Rd., Scarborough. Admission C$1 (US65¢) children. Daily mid-June–Labour Day Mon–Fri 10am–5pm. Subway: Warden, then no. 17 bus north to McNichol Ave. (north of Finch Ave.).

High Park Adventure Playground *(★*   It took more than 3,000 volunteers just over six days to build this enormous playground in Toronto's High Park. The play structure features dozens of nooks and crannies to hide in, most drawn from the imaginations of more than 1,000 local school children who submitted their ideas to the park's planning committee. The miniature village is the highlight of the playground, which also offers slides, swings, and a treehouse lookout tower. After the kids have played themselves out (they may need more than a little urging) take them to the High Park wading pool or to the park's free zoo (see chapter 6, "What Kids Like to See & Do"). High Park is also the setting for **Dream in High Park**—the Canadian Stage Company's outdoor Shakespearean production (see chapter 8, "Entertainment for the Whole Family").

High Park, Parkside Dr. entrance (south of Bloor St. at High Park Blvd.). Free admission. Daily dawn–dusk. Subway: Keele.

2 Neighborhood Strolls

For some low-key activity, take your kids for an afternoon or all-day stroll. You can start anywhere in the city and find some interesting architecture, a spot for lunch, and a park or two to run in. You'll find a few of the most kid-friendly places to stroll below.

THE BEACHES ★★★ (Moments)

It's hard to believe you're still in Canada's largest metropolis when you're walking along the boardwalks of the Beaches, an area that runs along Queen Street East from Woodbine Avenue to Victoria Park Avenue. The neighborhood has the liveliness of a southern US resort town combined with the hominess of small-town Ontario. It's warm, relaxed and, since many of Toronto's young families call this area home, very child-oriented.

You can easily spend an entire day exploring this area, and I suggest you allow at least a few hours to fully experience it. On a sunny day, the best place to start is on **the beach** itself. Stroll the boardwalk, take some time to let the kids build a sandcastle, and enjoy the sounds of the musicians who frequently play in the parks.

Queen Street East is the next stop in the Beaches. Eclectic shops sell everything from beach toys to Harry Potter memorabilia. You can get the kids a quick haircut at one of the kids-only salons, or indulge in a few pounds of sweets at one of the candy shops. There are also the requisite beachfront ice cream shops to cool the kids off after a day at play.

When it's time to stop for lunch, sample one of the many wonderful cafes along Queen Street or grab some takeout from **Lick's** (1960 Queen St. E.) and head to the picnic tables at **Kew Beach Gardens,** where you'll be surrounded by beautiful gardens and shaded by towering trees.

To enjoy some additional shade, take a walk through the nearby **Glen Stewart Ravine.** With its gray squirrels and foxes, it is a paradise for budding naturalists. The ravine provides a remarkable contrast to lively Queen Street and the busy beaches. Heavily forested, it is usually several degrees cooler, and once you're on the trails you'll be amazed at how the sounds of the city immediately disappear.

The Beaches is a very busy spot on the weekends, so if you're averse to crowds you should try to visit during the week.

THE TORONTO ISLANDS (Moments)

You know you've found a kid-friendly venue when the first sign you see reads, PLEASE WALK ON THE GRASS! Cars are not allowed on the islands, making this a perfect destination for a family picnic or a day of cycling.

Native peoples originally used the islands as a base for fishing the once-rich waters of Lake Ontario. The first Europeans settled here in the 1830s for much the same reason, but by the 1920s the area had become the summer playground of Toronto's wealthy elite. In the 1950s the newly formed municipal government of Toronto decided to turn the islands into a large park, but the permanent residents of Algonquin and Ward's islands refused to cooperate, and many still maintain homes there.

There are more than a dozen Toronto islands, but the most popular for visitors are Centre and Ward's islands, each of which has a distinctive personality. On **Centre Island,** you'll find picnic areas, gardens and, of course, **Centreville,** an amusement park and petting zoo. **Hanlan's Point** offers a great beach (as well as a nude beach) and the **Gibraltar Point Lighthouse,** where kids can hear some scary ghost stories. **Ward's Island** boasts a beautiful boardwalk and masses of wildflowers, as well as the quaint cottages of the island's permanent residents. Swans and ducks nest in the numerous ponds and inlets throughout the islands, so even if you skip the amusement park there is still plenty to entertain the kids.

(Fun Fact Island Trivia

The **Toronto Islands** were originally a series of sandbars joined to the mainland by a long peninsula. In the early 1800s Toronto's citizens would don their summer finery and head across the peninsula in their carriages. Some of the wealthier citizens maintained summer homes on the sandbars. Eventually, storms and constant erosion separated the sandbars from the mainland, and a magnificent storm in 1858 finally severed the islands permanently.

Babe Ruth hit his first home run as a professional baseball player here during a game at Hanlan's Point Stadium on September 15, 1914, before he joined the major leagues. A downtown bar claims to have the ball he hit, but popular lore maintains that the ball lies at the bottom of Lake Ontario.

Gibraltar Point Lighthouse, built in 1808, is the oldest structure in Toronto still in its original location. The lighthouse guided ships into Toronto Harbour for more than 150 years until it was replaced in the 1950s by an automated version.

YORKVILLE

Located just north of Bloor Street, between Bay Street and Avenue Road, this tony neighborhood is a wonderful spot to take a leisurely stroll with the kids. Because it's a compact area, no lengthy walking is required.

The area has undergone several transformations through the years. At one time it was the center of Toronto's hippie culture, but today it is home to charming cafes, exclusive shops, and some of the most distinctive gift stores in the city.

Compared to the busy thoroughfares surrounding this area, the streets within Yorkville are remarkably narrow and calm. Pedestrians fill the wide sidewalks and frequently spill out onto the road. The roads are still very much open to traffic, though, and Toronto drivers being what they are, it's best to keep your little ones close by.

Stroll down **Cumberland Street** and check out the funky gift store **Ice** and candy store **Retro Fun.** Take a peek into **Lush,** if only for the pure sensory experience of inhaling the fragrance of the hundreds of lotions and soaps sold here, and maybe pick up a bath bomb or two for the kids to use back at the hotel.

Wander along Yorkville Avenue and be sure to turn north when you reach the sign for **Hazelton Lanes.** This village-like shopping center houses many of Toronto's most exclusive and expensive shops. When it's time for a rest, there are many wonderful cafes in Yorkville as well as kid-friendly **Flo's Diner** and a designer ice cream store called **Greg's,** at 200 Bloor Street West. Try to choose one of the cafes with an outdoor patio—people-watching in Yorkville can provide great entertainment for the kids while they wait for their lunch.

You can also take a break in tiny **Yorkville Park.** The themed garden beds that represent marshlands, orchards, and herb gardens are too stylized to excite the kids, but the mammoth piece of the Canadian Shield draws them like a magnet. The Village Rock, as it is known, weighs 715 tonnes (650 tons) and is thought to be over 1 billion years old. Residents were alternately awed and outraged when it was revealed the city had paid more than C$500,000 (US$330,000) to have the rock moved here from its original site near Gravenhurst, Ontario. But kids love to climb on this expensive landscaping fixture, and you can relax on the comfortable bistro-style chairs and listen to the rainfall patter of the curtain fountain that adjoins the rock.

The **Children's Own Museum, Royal Ontario Museum,** and **Bata Shoe Museum** are all within a few blocks of Yorkville, so you can make a day of visiting this area. Yorkville itself, however, can be easily be explored in an hour or two.

DOWNTOWN

Downtown is not a great place to stroll with toddlers, but your older kids will likely find it pretty stimulating. Try to extend your stroll through the Eaton Centre, particularly if you have teenagers. Yonge Street is colorful but very busy and a little on the seedy side, especially between Dundas and College streets.

If you have younger children, take a walk through **Nathan Phillips Square** or **St. James Park,** next to glorious St. James Cathedral. With its cafes and cathedrals, the area around Church and Front streets is a lovely place to stroll.

To the west, **Queen Street West** is a popular spot for people-watching, but again, older kids will be the most appreciative audience. A walk through this trendy area would probably be wasted on younger children, who would rather be visiting zoo animals or chasing seagulls.

TORONTO'S ETHNIC NEIGHBORHOODS

Cabbagetown This largely residential neighborhood takes its name from disparaging comments made about the Irish immigrants who settled here in the early 19th century and, it is said, grew cabbages on their front lawns. Cabbagetown slid into neglect and disrepair until it was revitalized by renovation fever in the 1970s. Today, houses that were bought in the 1970s for C$25,000 (US$16,500) regularly sell for more than C$500,000 (US$330,000). For the kids, the largest draw here is probably **Riverdale Farm,** a working farm that replicates rural life in the 19th century.

Chinatown Toronto actually has five separate Chinatowns, but the most visible and best known is in the area branching out from Dundas Street and Spadina Avenue—you can't miss the gilt dragons that adorn the street corners and the middle of the street. Your kids will be in a constant state of distraction in this vibrant, noisy section of the city. In market stalls cluttering the sidewalks, merchants sell jellyfish, crabs, glazed ducks, chickens (often with the heads still attached), exotic fruits, and teas. The restaurants in this area eschew the more familar North American–style Chinese food in favor of Szechwan, Hunansese, Mandarin, and Cantonese cuisine.

While this is a wonderful spot for a stroll it also offers some interesting shopping. Chinese silk, porcelain, and even electronics are often good buys here.

Greektown Most of Toronto's Greek residents no longer live in the area, but it still serves as a cultural and social hub. There are a vast number of traditional Greek restaurants on this strip of the Danforth between Broadview and Pape avenues. Many are modest tavernas, while others rate among the top restaurants in the city. The area is also crowded with lively outdoor patios. You'll find a number of great shops to pop into as you explore the neighborhood; be sure to point out the bilingual (English and Greek) signs to the kids as you walk along. During the **Taste of the Danforth Festival,** held in August, visitors can sample traditional Greek cuisine, as well as flavors from around the world, and join in a celebration of Greek culture. The festival always promises to be busy, as Toronto is home to the second-largest population of Greeks outside of Greece (the largest is in New York).

Koreatown In a few short blocks along Bloor Street West between Bathurst and Christie streets lies an area that was the first Korean settlement in the city of Toronto. Today, it is primarily a business district with an assortment of acupuncturists, herbalists, Korean restaurants, karaoke bars, and tiny retail shops selling made-in-Korea merchandise.

Little India Little India stretches for four blocks west of Coxwell Avenue on Gerrard Street East. The name is a bit of a misnomer, however, as the area is more accurately South Asian. The restaurants, grocers, CD shops, and colorful sari stores here represent the cultures of the Bengalis, Pakistanis, Sikhs, and Sri Lankans, as well as the Indians who lived here at one time. Few still live in the area, but instead arrive from the suburbs to shop and socialize on the weekends. During the summer, stop for a snack of grilled corn on the cob or sticks of a slightly grainy ice cream called *kulfi.* If the kids are thirsty, treat them to a glass of freshly squeezed sugar cane and fruit juice.

Little Italy With the largest population of Italians outside Italy, it's not surprising that Toronto has two Italian neighborhoods. The older one, known as **Little Italy,** runs along College Street between Euclid and Shaw streets. Although much of the Italian population has moved north, this area is enjoying a renaissance as the new hip spot in the city. Twenty-somethings have laid claim to the busy club scene here, but families still stroll the neighborhood and frequent the traditional Italian restaurants and cafes. Indulge the kids' (and your own) sweet tooth in one of the Italian bakeries while you're here.

Corso Italia On St. Clair West between Bathurst Street and Old Weston Road, is the newer Little Italy. With its charming Italian street lamps and potted plants, this area is a shopper's paradise of bridal shops, men's clothing stores, children's boutiques, and textile stores. You'll also find some of the city's finest Italian restaurants here.

3 Indoor Playgrounds

Toronto has scores of indoor playgrounds. Some are disguised as museums, such as the **Children's Own Museum** (see chapter 6, "What Kids Like to See & Do"); others are to be found in hotels, such as **Where Kids Play** in the Sheraton Centre, or in stores, such as at **Bean Sprouts** consignment clothing store (see chapter 9, "Shopping for the Whole Family"). There are also several "pay-as-you-play" indoor playgrounds in the city. Most have similar rules: Socks are a must, chewing gum is a no-no, and parents are responsible for supervising their own children.

Amazon Indoor Playground   **Ages 1 to 12.** This jungle-themed indoor play space appeals to kids' imagination as well as to their adventurous spirit. There is the requisite two-story jungle climber, with extra-large tubes that allow Mom and Dad to come to the rescue if necessary. There is also a theater zone with plenty of costumes for aspiring thespians to choose from and a stage on which they can display their talents. For kids who would rather stay behind the scenes, there is also a great puppet theater.

Snack foods are sold at the playground, but families are welcome to bring their own snacks and lunches.

21 Vaughan Rd., Unit 108. ✆ 416/656-5832. www.amazonindoorplayground.com. Admission C$6.50 (US$4.30) 1 child, C$8 (US$5.30) 2 siblings, C$10 (US$6.60) 3 siblings, free for adults. Weekdays 10am–3pm; weekend hours vary—call ahead. Subway: St. Clair West, then walk south on Bathurst St. to Vaughan Rd.

Fantasy Fair   **Ages 2 to 10.** Amusement parks are usually a wash on a rainy day, but not this one. Fantasy Fair's nine full-size midway rides, arcade, children's play village, and midway games are all housed inside the Woodbine Centre shopping mall. In a complex designed to resemble a Victorian town, you'll find traditional favorites such as the old-fashioned carousel and Ferris wheel. When you arrive, definitely start with a tour of the fairgrounds by Fantasy Express train. The bumper boats and bumper cars are a hit with most youngsters, but older kids may find the park a little tame.

500 Rexdale Blvd. ✆ **416/674-5437.** http://members.tripod.com/~fantasy_fair. Free admission; midway rides C90¢ (US54¢) and under per ticket, or C$22.95 (US$15.15) for 30 tickets; day pass C$8.95–$11.95 (US$5.90–$7.90). Sat–Wed 11am–7pm; Thurs–Fri 11am–8pm; holidays 12–6pm. By car: Hwy. 401 west to Hwy. 427 northbound. Take Rexdale Blvd. exit east.

Funstation Funpark   **Ages 5 and up.** If your energetic kids are looking for a little action, take them here. Adventurous youngsters can choose from riding the bumper cars, racing the go-carts, or swinging at a few balls in the batting cages. There are also two 18-hole miniature golf courses with a railway theme, an arcade, a merry-go-round, and several other small rides.

4150 Jane St. (at Finch Ave.). ✆ 416/736-4804. Prices vary per activity. Open Apr 1–Oct 1 10am–midnight. Subway: Finch, then any no. 36 bus west to Jane St.

Kidsports Indoor Playground   **Ages 1 to 12.** A whimsical dragon watches over the fun as your kids explore their way through a series of tunnels, nets, ball pits, and slides. The bonus, especially for families like ours with a wide range of ages, is that there is something for almost everyone here. The main play structure, Adventure Challenge, is probably too tough for smaller children—have them try the Wee Challenge instead. You'll also find a gymnasium, an arcade, and a snack bar that offers reasonably priced kid favorites such as hotdogs and french fries.

4500 Dixie Rd., Unit 8, Mississauga. ℂ **905/624-9400.** Admission C$8 (US$5.30) children 3 and older, C$5 (US$3.30) children under 3, C$2 (US$1.30) children under 1, free for adults. Sat–Thurs 10am–8pm, Fri 10am–9pm. By car: Hwy. 401 west to Dixie Rd., then Dixie Rd. south to 2 traffic lights past Eglinton Ave. E.

The Peanut Club **Ages 1 to 6.** If your hotel lacks a children's activity center, bring the gang here. There are some small climbing structures and a ball pit, but the main appeal is the oodles of Little Tykes toys scattered around the facility. This is a wonderful place to bring the 5-and-under crowd, but there isn't much to interest older kids.

1500 Royal York Rd., Etobicoke. ℂ **416/245-1459.** Admission C$5 (US$3.30) 1 parent and 1 child for the first hour, then C$3 (US$2) for the rest of the day; C$8 (US$5.30) family (3 children) for the first hour, then C$3 (US$2) for the rest of the day. Mon–Fri 9:30am–3:30pm, Sat 9:30am–noon. Subway: Royal York, then any no. 73 bus north to Royal York Plaza (north of Eglinton Ave. W.).

4 Sports

BOATING & SAILING

Lake Ontario offers magnificent views, and its extreme depth and good winds make it a sailor's dream. For a great adventure, take your family on a boat trip to the Toronto Islands, or if you prefer a more sedate afternoon, explore the shoreline by canoe or paddleboat.

To rent a sailboat or powerboat, head to **Queen's Quay Yachting,** 283 Queens Quay W. (ℂ 416/203-3000; www.queensquayyachting.com). They also offer weekend and weeklong sailing lessons. Rates depend on the boat size, starting at C$60 (US$39.60) for a three-hour sailboat rental. Powerboats cost C$95 (US$62.70) and up.

If you're interested in going on a guided day or overnight canoe trip, taking kayaking lessons, or simply renting a canoe or kayak for a few hours, contact **Harbourfront Canoe and Kayak School,** 283A Queens Quay W. (ℂ 416/ 203-2277; www.paddletoronto.com). Canoes start at C$15 (US$9.90) per hour or C$40 (US$26.40) per day. Kayaks start at C$18 (US$11.90) per hour or C$50 (US$33) per day.

You can also rent canoes, punts, sailboats, and paddleboats at **Grenadier Pond** in High Park, at **Ontario Place,** and on **Centre Island** in the Toronto Islands.

BOWLING

If your kids haven't tried five-pin bowling, now's the time to take them—it's a perfect sport for kids. The ball is small and there are five pins to knock over, each worth different points. My four-year-old had no trouble mastering five-pin bowling, and even my two-year-old has tried it, albeit with mixed results.

There are many alleys in Toronto offering both 5- and 10-pin bowling. Try **Bowlerama** at one of its five locations: 2788 Bathurst St. south of Lawrence Ave. W. (ℂ 416/782-1841); 851 Jane St. (ℂ 416/769-1200); Lawrence Ave. E. (ℂ 416/759-6181); 115 Rexdale Blvd. (ℂ 416/743-8388); and 45 Overlea Blvd. (ℂ 416/421-2211).

In Mississauga, head to **Planet Bowl,** 5555 Eglinton Ave. W. between Renforth Dr. and Dixie Rd. (ℂ 416/695-2695), and in Downsview, **Wilson Pro Bowl,** 877 Wilson Ave., between Dufferin and Keele streets (ℂ 416/638-1743).

CROSS-COUNTRY SKIING

When snow blankets the walkways and trails, cross-country skiers flock to nearly all of the city's parks. In North York, **Sunnybrook Park** and **Ross Lord Park** are good bets, and in the west end, **High Park** offers miles of trails. **Earl Bales Park,** on Bathurst Street south of Sheppard Avenue; **Tommy Thompson Park,** at the south end of Leslie Street; and the **Toronto Islands** are also good choices for skiers. If you need to rent equipment, contact **Trakkers Cross-Country Ski Club,** 2336 Bloor St. W. (✆ **416/763-0173**), or **Sports World Sales and Rentals,** 2229 Queen St. E. in the Beaches (✆ **416/693-7368**).

CYCLING

Toronto is one of the best cities for cycling in North America, with over 50 kilometers (31 miles) of bicycle lanes along the city streets and 125 kilometers (77.5 miles) of bike trails. Beautiful trails wind along the waterfront and in the city parks, and many are suitable for young cyclists. You can obtain maps of bicycle routes from the *Toronto Star* (✆ **416/367-2000**), **Toronto Parks and Recreation** (✆ **416/392-8186**), or **Ontario Cycling** (✆ **416/426-7242**). Toronto Parks and Recreation also posts downloadable route maps on its website (www.city.toronto.on.ca).

You can transport bikes on any public transit system in the city except during the morning and afternoon rush hours. If you didn't bring your own bikes, numerous shops in the city rent them out, including **Wheel Excitement,** 5 Rees St. near Harbourfront (✆ **416/260-9000**); **McBride Cycle,** 180 Queens Quay W. at York St. (✆ **416/203-5651**); **High Park Cycle and Sports,** 24 Ronson Dr. (✆ **416/614-6689**); and **Toronto Islands Bicycle Rental,** 1 Island Airport on Centre Island (✆ **416/203-0009**). The cost is generally C$12 to $24 (US$7.90 to $15.85) per day.

GOLF

Torontonians are mad for golf—there are more than 75 golf courses within a one-hour drive of the city center, as well as many miniature golf courses.

Right at the center of town is **City Place Golf Course,** a 9-hole course just across from the SkyDome. Located at 2 Spadina Avenue (✆ **416/640-1888**), you can take in the city skyline as you swing. Heated tees allow the course to stay open year round. Adult green fees are C$27 (US$17.60) for 9 holes and C$45 (US$29.35) for 18 holes. Junior rates are available. Free parking and a patio restaurant complete the urban golf experience.

The **Don Valley Golf Course,** on Yonge Street south of Highway 401 (✆ **416/392-2465**), is a scenic par-71 with some challenging elevated tees. The par-3 13th hole is nicknamed Hallelujah Corner because it takes a miracle to make par. It's a good place to introduce your kids to the sport. Adult green fees are C$45 (US$29.70) weekdays, and C$49 (US$32.35) weekends; junior green fees are C$25 (US$16.50) weekdays, C$28 (US$18.50) weekends.

The relatively flat **Humber Valley** par-70 course is easy to walk and another good choice for kids. Located on Albion Road at Beattie Avenue (✆ **416/392-2488**), this course has many towering trees that offer a lot of shade. Adult green fees are C$36 (US$23.75) weekdays, C$42 (US$27.70) weekends; junior green fees are C$20 (US$13.20) weekdays, C$22 (US$14.50) weekends.

The **Glen Abbey Golf Club** championship course, located at 1333 Dorval Dr. in Oakville (✆ **800/661-1818** or 905/841-3730), is the most famous in Canada. Designed by Jack Nicklaus, the par-73 often hosts the Canadian Open.

It was here in 2000 that Tiger Woods' 181-yard 6-iron from a fairway bunker on the 18th hole set up the birdie that clinched the Bell Canadian Open and professional golf's Triple Crown. Green fees range from C$125 to $230 (US$82.50 to $151.80). There are no junior green fees but there are reduced rates for everyone in April, at C$97 (US$64).

There are also **miniature golf** courses at many locations across the city, including **Cullen Gardens and Miniature Village,** 300 Taunton Rd. W. in Whitby (© **905/686-1600**); **Funstation FunPark,** 4150 Jane St. at Finch Avenue (© **416/736-4804**); and **Golf Etc.,** 3670 St. Clair Ave. E. (© **416/ 267-5013**). **Putting Edge,** an 18-hole indoor miniature golf course with glow-in-the-dark golf, has several locations: 9625 Yonge St. (© **905/508-8222**); 241 Clarence Ave. in Brampton (© **416/455-3399**), and 60 Interchange Way in Vaughan (© **905/761-3343**).

HORSEBACK RIDING

With Toronto's emphasis on green space, it comes as no surprise that a riding stable is located within 15 minutes of downtown, in Sunnybrook Park. For beginners, **Central Don Riding Academy** (© **416/444-4044**) offers indoor and outdoor riding rings. For more experienced or more adventurous riders, the academy provides trail rides along the 19 kilometers (12 miles) of bridle trails in the park. The academy is open Monday to Thursday 1 to 5pm and Saturday to Sunday noon to 5pm. Reservations are required. Rates vary depending on the level of instruction required; a one-hour trail ride costs C$25 (US$16.50).

ICE SKATING

There are free ice-skating rinks in more than 25 city parks. Call the **City Parks Department** for information on which rinks are open and what facilities they offer (© **416/392-1111**). For ice conditions, call © **416/395-7584.**

Grenadier Pond, in High Park, is easily the most romantic skating pond in the city, with a bonfire and vendors selling roasted chestnuts. British soldiers drilled on the ice early in the 19th century and local lore maintains that many of these "Grenadiers" ended up at the bottom of the pond, lost and forgotten.

During the winter months, the giant reflecting pool at **Nathan Phillips Square,** 100 Queen St. W. in front of City Hall, is converted into a skating rink. Rentals are available and there are usually several vendors selling both hot and cold refreshments. Call the **Toronto Parks Department** for details at © **416/392-1111.**

The largest artificial ice rink in Canada, **Natrel Skating Rink** at Harbourfront, is also one of Toronto's most popular rinks. An indoor change room is on-site, and if you didn't bring your own skates, they'll rent you a pair. A DJ plays music while you skate, and when you're tired you can warm up with a cup of hot chocolate and some snacks at **Lakeside Eats** next door. The rink is open 10am to 10pm daily from early December until late March, weather permitting. Hours may vary. Call © **416/973-4866** for details.

IN-LINE SKATING/ROLLER SKATING

Toronto's parks have numerous paths for in-line skating, but you'll also see skaters on the streets (not recommended for kids) and sidewalks. Some of the best sites for family skating are along the Beaches boardwalk, at Harbourfront, and on the Toronto Islands. You can rent skates for the family at several shops, including **Wheel Excitement,** 5 Rees St. near Harbourfront (© **416/260-**

9000), and **Planet Skate,** 2144 Queen St. E. in the Beaches (✆ **416/690-7588**). One-day rentals cost C$18 to $24 (US$11.90 to $15.85), or you can rent skates for a couple of hours for C$14 (US$9.25) and up.

If indoor skating is more to your kids' liking, try **Scooters Roller Palace,** 2105 Royal Windsor Dr. in Mississauga (✆ **905/823-4001;** www.scooters. on.ca). This rink hosts family skating times as well as scheduled lessons. Rentals are available for both in-line and roller skates. It's open most evenings and weekend afternoons and evenings but is closed to the public on Mondays. Admission is C$5 (US$3.30), rental of roller skates costs C$1.50 (US$1), and rental of in-line skates is C$3.50 (US$2.30).

SNOWBOARDING

The snowboarding craze that followed the last Winter Olympics captured Toronto as well. It's an extremely popular sport, especially with kids, and although the best snowboarding venues are outside the city at spots like **Glen Eden Ski Area** (✆ **905/878-5011**) in Milton and **Caledon Ski Club** (✆ **905/453-7404**) in Caledon, there are also a few good places within the city. Popular sites for young boarders include **High Park, Earl Bales Park,** and **Centennial Park Ski Hill** in Etobicoke.

You can rent boards at **Earl Bales Park** (✆ **416/395-7931**), at **Centennial Park Ski Hill** (✆ **416/394-8754**), or from **Winward,** 5015 Yonge St. (✆ **416/512-8506**).

SWIMMING

Despite the abundance of beaches along the waterfront, Lake Ontario is not recommended for swimming. First, the water tends to be quite cold, even in midsummer. But a more serious problem is that the water, which is monitored closely by the Toronto public health department, is plagued by high bacteria counts and, more often than not, closed to swimmers. If you still think you'd like to try the water, call the **Beaches Water Quality Hotline** at ✆ **416/392-7161** to find out which, if any, beaches are open to the public for swimming. Keep in mind that kids tend to be even more susceptible than adults to bacterial infections.

BEACHES

If playing in the sand and sunbathing are what you have in mind, there are several Toronto beaches worth visiting. **Hanlan's Beach** on the Toronto Islands and the **Beaches** area (see "Neighborhood Strolls," earlier in this chapter) are wonderful spots to sit and enjoy the sun and sand, if not the water.

PUBLIC POOLS

The city's many indoor and outdoor swimming pools might be a better bet if the kids feel like taking a dip. The City of Toronto operates well over a dozen swimming pools, outfitted with lockers and change rooms. These include the Donald D. Summerville Olympic Pool at Woodbine Beach (at Woodbine Ave. and Lakeshore Blvd. E.) and the pools in Riverdale Park (Broadview and Danforth aves.), High Park (Bloor and Keele sts.), and Eglinton Park (Eglinton Ave. and Avenue Rd.). Many of the city parks also have wading pools that are open during July and August. Admission is free or there is a nominal fee. For schedules and prices, call the **South Central Region Pool Hotline** at ✆ **416/392-7838.** For pools in other regions, call the **Department of Parks and Recreation hotline** at ✆ **416/392-1111.**

The **University of Toronto Athletic Centre,** 55 Harbord St. at Spadina Avenue (✆ **416/978-3437**), offers free swimming to the public on Sundays from noon to 4pm.

WAVE POOLS/WATER PLAYGROUNDS

Ontario Place and **Paramount Canada's Wonderland** (see chapter 6, "What Kids Like to See & Do") and **Wild Water Kingdom** (see chapter 10, "Easy Side Trips from Toronto") all offer water fun for kids, but there are some less pricey options in and around the city. Several municipal pools in the outskirts of the city are notable for their original designs; for a plunge into the extraordinary, try the following pools.

Agincourt Leisure Pool (*Value* With its coconut trees, leafy palm trees, and turquoise water, this pool is definitely not one of the usual staid municipal varieties. For toddlers there is a small wading pool with a shipwreck-shaped slide. The coconuts on the trees surrounding the shipwreck fill up with water and then gently pour onto the bathers below. The intermediate pool is open to children 7 years and older (and at least 106cm or 42 in. tall). A huge water slide (for kids at least 122cm or 48 in. tall) splashes down into its own small pool. Mom and Dad (and kids over 12) can kick back in a large Jacuzzi called the Conversation Pool. Both life jackets and pool toys are provided, and if you've forgotten any essentials, a shop at the entrance sells everything from bathing caps (not mandatory) to swimsuits.

31 Glen Watford Dr. (just east of Midland Ave.), Scarborough. ✆ **416/396-8343**. Free admission for families, C$2.50 (US$1.65) adults on their own. Hours vary widely but usually include day and evening recreational swims—call for details. Subway: Sheppard, then any bus east to Glen Watford Dr. By car: Hwy. 401 east to Brimley Rd. exit, then Brimley Rd. north just past Sheppard Ave.

Birchmount Leisure Pool (*Value* The facilities here are exactly the same as those at the Agincourt Leisure Pool—water jets, a large water slide, a Jacuzzi, a large recreational pool, and a smaller tot pool. This site also offers some cool animal-shaped slides that are a big hit with toddlers.

93 Birchmount Rd. (south of Danforth Ave.). ✆ **416/396-4310**. Free admission for families, C$2.50 (US$1.65) adults on their own. Hours vary widely but usually include day and evening recreational swims—call for details. Subway: Warden, then no. 69 via Birchmount bus south to Danforth Ave.

The Wave Pool Richmond Hill This indoor wave pool, the only one in the Toronto area, is a fun place to take the kids on a rainy day or during the winter months. It's also surprisingly affordable. Life jackets are provided free of charge, and the observant lifeguards and gradual incline pool make it a fairly safe place for little ones, who can frolic in the shallow area under the rain cloud that occasionally drizzles on bathers, much to their delight. Older kids will be more interested in the 1.2-meter (4 ft.) waves and the 49-meter (160 ft.) twisting water slide.

5 Hopkins St., Richmond Hill (southwest corner of Yonge St. and Major Mackenzie Dr.). ✆ **905/508-WAVE**. Admission C$5.50 (US$3.65) adults, C$3 (US$2) seniors and children, free for children under 3; no reentry privileges. July 1–Labour Day Mon–Fri 1:30–4:30pm, Sat–Sun 1–4pm and 4:30–7:30pm. Hours vary during the rest of the year but are often extended during Christmas and spring break holidays—call for details. By car: Hwy. 401 west, then Hwy. 404 north to Major Mackenzie Dr. exit and west to Yonge St.

TENNIS

The city operates hundreds of tennis courts, all free and many floodlit at night. Parks with courts open from 7am to 11pm, in season, include **High Park** in the west end; **Stanley Park** on King Street West, three blocks west of Bathurst Street; and **Eglinton Park** on Eglinton Avenue West, just east of Avenue Road.

For information call the **Ontario Tennis Association** at © 416/426-7135 or the Parks Department at © 416/392-8186.

TOBOGGANING

The best parks for tobogganing include **High Park** in the west end and **Winston Churchill Park** at Spadina Road and St. Clair Avenue West, just two blocks from Casa Loma. You may want to limit the latter to the older kids—the steep hill in this park, built on top of a water reservoir, is sheer terror.

5 Classes & Workshops

On weekends and holidays during the school year and throughout the summer, Toronto's major venues offer both drop-in and registration-based classes and workshops for kids. The City of Toronto Department of Parks and Recreation and Department of Culture (© 416/392-8674) and the Greater Toronto YMCA (© 416/928-9622) sponsor children's workshops and programs in parks and other venues around the city. Some original offerings are listed below.

George R. Gardiner Museum of Ceramic Art Drop-in clay art workshops are offered on Sundays from 1 to 4pm, at a cost of C$8 (US$5.30) for adults and C$5 (US$3.30) for children; glazing and firing are extra. There are also regularly scheduled children's art classes at varying prices—call for dates and times. The drop-in workshops fee includes admission to the museum, at 111 Queens Park (© 416/586-8080).

Harbourkids Creative Workshops Harbourfront (Value) It's not surprising that the city's arts and culture center offers some pretty amazing crafts for kids. The art workshops here are designed to coincide with activities at Harbourfront and thus reflect a wide range of cultures, art forms, and materials. Past projects have included everything from blow painting to wind socks and peek boxes to wire sculptures. There is no need to register for the workshops—your kids can just show up and start crafting. The price is right, too: Kids are charged a mere C$2 (US$1.30). The workshops are held Sundays and holidays in the Lookout or occasionally in the Community Gallery, at the south end of York Quay Centre, 235 Queens Quay West. In the summer they move to a tent in Ann Tindal Park, just west of York Quay Centre.

Call Queens Quay at © 416/973-3000 or 416/973-4000 (box office) for information on special events, or visit their website at www.harbourfront.on.ca.

Medieval Times In the Young Knights School, kids learn what it was really like to be a medieval knight. The school is offered periodically, normally prior to Sunday performances at Medieval Times, Exhibition Place, Dufferin Gate (© 416/260-1234). Call for details.

Off the Wall! Art Gallery of Ontario (Value) A wide variety of high art projects are offered Saturdays and Sundays from 1 to 5pm at the AGO's children's creative art center. Expect the unexpected. We've seen the kids dress up as a painting and take imaginary sketching trips to the northern Ontario wilderness. Open. The workshops are free with pay-what-you-can admission to the AGO, 317 Dundas St. W. (© 416/977-0414).

Ontario Science Centre The science center, 770 Don Mills Rd. (© 416/696-3127), offers regular children's and family workshops that have included K'nex-building workshops, nature walks, and even science-themed overnight camps. Call for prices and details.

Royal Ontario Museum   The Saturday Morning Club at the ROM, 100 Queens Park (© 416/586-5797), offers a wide variety of children's workshops on everything from historical subjects to science and nature. Highlights from past workshops have included Dungeons and Dragons, Architects and Engineers, and Backyard Astronomy. Regular family workshops on similar themes are also offered on Saturday afternoons.

Square in Motion   Nathan Phillips Square   A wide variety of children's arts and crafts workshops are offered in conjunction with the Kids Tuesday free concerts at the square, located at 200 Queen Street West (© 416/395-7350). The square is busy during these free entertainment afternoons so there are usually lineups, but things move along quickly and there is plenty going on to keep the kids entertained while they wait. Programs run from mid-July to early August, 11am to 1pm.

Toronto's Historic Homes   Hands-on classes held on weekends teach the skills and crafts of centuries past. Most popular are the Historic Hearth cooking classes for kids, which teach kids how to cook the meals their ancestors enjoyed. Call individual homes for classes and prices: **Gibson House Museum,** 5172 Yonge St. (© 416/395-7432); **Historic Fort York,** Strachan and Fleet streets (© 416/392-6907); **Montgomery's Inn,** 4709 Dundas St. W. (© 416/394-8113); and **Spadina House,** 285 Spadina Rd. (© 416/392-6910).

Toronto Zoo   If spending an evening in the African savanna appeals to your kids, sign them up for one of the zoo's Serengeti Bush Camps. From May 19 to August 30 on specific family dates, you and the kids can stay overnight in tents set on platforms inside the savanna exhibit. Bush Camps are restricted to children ages 6 and older and include zoo admission, meals, sleeping cots, and a full program of tours, hikes, and a late-night campfire. Each family is assigned its own tent. The cost for adults and children 12 and older is C$90 (US$59.40), and for children ages 6 to 11 is C$80 (US$52.80).

Ⓒ Toronto the Big

As Canada's largest city, Toronto has a natural fondness for having the biggest and largest. Here are a few examples:

- Yonge Street is the longest street in the world (1,900 kilometers/1,180 miles), starting at the shore of Lake Ontario and ending beyond Lake Superior.
- The CN Tower, which opened in 1976, is the tallest freestanding structure in the world, at a height of 553.3 meters (1,815 ft., or 185 stories).
- The Italian population of Toronto is the largest outside Italy.
- Toronto has more golf courses per capita than any other place in North America.
- Agatha Christie's *The Mousetrap* has been playing here for 22 years, longer than any other show in North America.

8

Entertainment for the Whole Family

Once known as Toronto the Good— the place where they rolled up the sidewalk on Sundays—the city certainly has grown up. As the world's third-largest entertainment center, after New York and London, Toronto is the premier Canadian destination for musicals, top rock musicians, and talented dance troupes. Many of the plays currently on Broadway stages began their run in Toronto, and homegrown talent, from the Toronto Symphony Orchestra to the National Ballet of Canada, abounds.

However, in growing into an entertainment mecca, Toronto hasn't forgotten its youngest and often most appreciative audiences. The city has an enviable collection of entertainment geared specifically toward children. Many of the big venues host regular children's performances, as do the smaller independent players. Both

Beauty and the Beast and *The Lion King* have enjoyed long runs here. You don't have to worry about the major venues being unsuitable for children —most offer booster seats for their smaller patrons, and at intermission you can usually grab some chocolate chip cookies and a late-night glass of milk for the kids.

There are film, storytelling, and reading festivals just for kids, and the sports teams throw in a lot of kid-friendly entertainment with the price of a ticket. However, it is in the vibrant children's theater, dance, and music companies that Toronto's kid-friendly attitude really shines through. Children's opera, classical choruses, symphonies, ballet, modern dance, and theater troupes offer professional and entertaining productions directed toward young audiences.

FINDING OUT WHAT'S ON

For listings of local performances and events, check out **Where Toronto,** found in most hotel rooms in the city, or **Toronto Life,** the city's lifestyle magazine. The free entertainment weeklies, **Now** and **Eye,** available around town in boxes on street corners and at bars, cafes, and bookstores, list and review the various productions being staged around the city. The daily newspapers the **Globe and Mail,** the **National Post,** the **Toronto Star,** and the **Toronto Sun** all have entertainment sections.

On the Internet, *Toronto Life*'s website (**www.torontolife.com**) has great reviews as well as an event listing and the *Toronto Star* site (**www.toronto.com**) includes a lengthy and in-depth listing of performances. The Toronto Theatre Alliance has a comprehensive listing of dance, comedy, music, and theatrical performances that is updated weekly on its website (**www.theatreintoronto.com**).

THEATER DISTRICTS

There are three main theater districts in Toronto. The downtown theater district has the highest concentration of Toronto's largest and most prestigious theaters. The east end theaters are an eclectic mix of perhaps lesser known, but nonetheless high-caliber theaters. Finally, the Annex neighborhood and Bathurst Street strip are home to a number of alternative and avant-garde, lower-priced theaters.

GETTING TICKETS

Full-price theater tickets can cost anywhere from C$20 to $95 (US$13.20 to $62.70); major concerts usually run around C$40 (US$26.40) per ticket. Theaters and concert venues regularly hold pay-what-you-can (PWYC) days, usually on Sundays and occasionally on other slow nights. Call the venue directly to inquire about PWYC.

You might also consider booking tickets directly through your hotel. Many of the city's major hotels sell some good-value package deals that include tickets to events with the rooms.

Another option is **TicketMaster** (✆ **416/870-8000;** www.ticketmaster.ca), which sells tickets to almost all theater, music, dance, and sporting events. There is a service charge on every ticket (rather than on every order) sold over the phone. To avoid the charge, head to one of the TicketMaster ticket centers scattered across the city—call the information line for a lengthy list of locations. **Ticket King** also acts as a sales agent for many performances in the city. They can be reached at ✆ **416/872-1212.**

DISCOUNT TICKETS

The best bet for obtaining same-day discount tickets is **T.O. Tix,** run by the Toronto Theatre Alliance, a group representing most of the major venues and entertainment organizations in the city. During the 2000 season, close to 300 productions sold half-price tickets through T.O. Tix. Many of the leading performing arts companies guarantee T.O. Tix at least two tickets per show, so it's not uncommon for this booth to have the last two tickets for a sold-out performance—and you can get them for half price!

The booth is located in the Eaton Centre. For a complete list of available tickets call ✆ **416/536-6468,** ext. 40.

A CAUTIONARY NOTE

Avoid buying tickets from the many **scalpers** outside the major sporting events. Unless they are for a World Series or Stanley Cup game or a sold-out performance, you are bound to end up paying far too much for a ticket you could buy just as easily elsewhere.

The **rickshaws** that crowd the streets following many performances will look like a lot of fun to the kids, and they are, but be wary and demand a price up front. If they hedge on a firm price, go to the next driver—they are notoriously competitive. You'll still pay a lot for the ride, though, so your best bet might be to talk the kids out of it beforehand and use the money to treat them to a late-night snack instead.

1 The Big Venues

From the turn of the century, when vaudeville acts and later silent films attracted crowds to the city's theaters, to today, when Broadway hits such as *Showboat* and *Ragtime* open the season, Toronto has always had a vibrant entertainment scene.

The city's professional sports venues are also thriving, with NBA and NHL franchises as well as professional baseball, lacrosse, and Canadian football teams playing here. If you decide to treat the family to a big night (or day) on the town, you'll find lots of major venues to choose from.

Air Canada Centre   The C$265-million (US$175 million) Air Canada Centre can seat between 18,000 and 22,000 fans of the Toronto Raptors basketball team, Toronto Maple Leafs hockey team, and Toronto Rock professional lacrosse team. It is also a popular venue for concerts and other events. The four Sony JumboTrons and 640 televisions scattered through the building ensure you don't miss any of the action.

The Air Canada Centre also offers some pretty nifty entertainment on the public concourses inside the building, including video games that the kids can play while waiting for the game or concert to begin. There are several kid-friendly restaurants inside the building but your best and least expensive bets are probably the Pizza Pizza, Mr. Sub, Shopsy's Deli, and Tim Hortons outlets located along the concourses. Tours are available on the hour, every hour, Monday to Saturday 10am to 3pm and Sunday 11am to 3pm. A 4pm tour is available from June 1 to September 1. However, unless your kids are avid sports watchers you may want to skip the tour, which is pretty pricey at C$9.50 (US$6.25) for adults, C$6.50 (US$4.30) for children under 12, and $7.50 (US$4.95) for seniors and students. Ticket prices for events vary widely and are sold through TicketMaster (© **416/870-8000**). 40 Bay St. © **416/815-5500**. Subway: Union.

Harbourfront   Something always seems to be going on at this complex on Lake Ontario. Harbourfront hosts Toronto's premier children's festivals for all ages—the **Milk International Children's Festival** and the **International Festival of Storytelling**—as well as many ethnic celebrations throughout the year.

In the summer, free concerts are held every Sunday, and the **Rhythms of the World** festival series offers international entertainment, including dance performances, films, and food tastings, throughout the summer. Harbourfront is also the setting for the **Cushion Concerts,** a series of musical performances and interactive stories held at the DuMaurier Theatre and geared toward families with children aged 5 to 12.

In addition to the **International Festival of Authors,** Harbourfront hosts a year-round reading series, which has featured more than 2,500 of the world's foremost writers since its inception in 1974. Call to see if any children's authors or performers are taking the stage while you're in town.   235 Queens Quay W. © **416/973-3000** (information) or 416/973-4000 (box office). www.harbourfront.on.ca. Subway: Union, then no. 509 or no. 510 streetcar.

Hummingbird Centre for the Performing Arts   As a child I was first introduced to live theater at the Hummingbird, which was then known as the O'Keefe Centre. It was a magical experience. With 3,155 seats, this is the largest multi-use facility in Canada. Unlike most other major venues in the entertainment district, the Hummingbird frequently hosts productions that appeal to the youngest kids. All the major names in showbiz have played here at least once, and this is the venue of choice for favorite children's productions such as *Franklin the Turtle* and shows that entrance both adults and kids, such as Riverdance. Built in 1960, this was Toronto's first permanent venue for the performing arts. It is home to both the National Ballet of Canada and the Canadian Opera Company, as well as host to a wide range of visiting Broadway productions, including *Beauty and the Beast* and *The Wizard of Oz.* Ticket prices vary widely, depending on the event, and are sold through TicketMaster (✆ 416/872-2262). 1 Front St. E. ✆ 416/393-7474. www.hummingbirdcentre.com. Subway: Union.

Royal Alexandra Theatre   This national historic landmark has been the top stage for touring theater in Toronto since it opened in 1907. It is now operated by Ed and David Mirvish, who also own the Royal Alexandra's equally regal sister, the **Princess of Wales Theatre,** and the Old Vic in London, England.

The Royal Alex is Victorian opulence at its best, from the private boxes lining the upper walls to the plush red velvet seats for the rest of the audience. The atmosphere is formal, and watching a play here can be a wonderful dress-up occasion for the kids. A number of long-running Broadway and West End London musicals have taken the stage at the Royal Alex, including *Les Miserables, RENT,* and *Mamma Mia.* Tickets are sold through TicketKing (✆ 800/461-3333 or 416/872-1212) and vary from C$25 to $75 (US$16.50 to $49.50), depending on the production.   260 King St. W. (at Simcoe St.). ✆ 416/872-1212. Subway: St. Andrew.

Roy Thomson Hall   By day it looks like a giant thimble, but at night the hundreds of panes in the gem-like exterior become transparent, turning the 2,812-seat Roy Thomson Hall into a concert hall under glass. Currently, both the **Toronto Symphony Orchestra** and the **Toronto Mendelssohn Choir** are based here, and the hall also books an astonishing array of visiting performers, from children's entertainers to jazz quartets.

To wear off some of their energy prior to the performance, take the kids for a quick tour of the **North Court Patio,** a beautiful terraced garden complete with a reflecting pool and designed by the Toronto Garden Club. There is also a music store, which leans heavily toward the classical and sells recordings of the Toronto Symphony Orchestra and the Toronto Mendelssohn Choir. Once you're seated, be sure to point out the huge full-concert pipe organ that dominates the center of the stage.   60 Simcoe St. (at King St. W.). ✆ 416/872-4255. Subway: St. Andrew.

⌒ *Fun Fact* Theater Town

Each year over 7 million people attend the theater in Toronto, more than half of whom are visitors to the city.

SkyDome   When it was built in 1989, the 34,000-seat SkyDome was the first domed stadium with a fully retractable roof. The facility now hosts rock concerts and sporting events, and last year even presented a live J.K. Rowling reading to 20,000 Harry Potter devotees. Fans of the Toronto Blue Jays baseball team or the Toronto Argonauts football team can even get prime seats without having to leave the dinner table or their hotel room: both the **Hard Rock Cafe** and the SkySuites at the attached **Renaissance Toronto SkyDome Hotel** overlook the field.

No matter where you sit you are guaranteed a view, although if you sit in levels 400 (Upper Sky Box) or 500 (Skydeck) it will be from a JumboTron screen, unless you bring binoculars. Definitely avoid sitting too close to the JumboTron.

Sports enthusiasts in your family will enjoy the public tours, which give visitors an inside peek into the visiting team's dressing room, the broadcast booth, and the private Skyboxes, which were originally sold for more than C$1 million

(US$660,000) apiece. Sitting in the dugout, running on the Astroturf, and winding up on the hydraulic pitcher's mound are always big hits with kids during the tour.

Kids seem to find endless entertainment in watching the retractable roof open or close (it takes 20 minutes), but if little ones grow bored with the game you can take them to the small indoor playground located on level 1. Lots of kid-friendly stadium-type food is available, including the cheapest (C99¢, US60¢) and arguably best hot dogs in the league.

Ticket prices vary widely and are sold through TicketMaster (© **416/870-8000**). 1 Blue Jays Way (at Front St.). © **416/341-3663**. Subway: Union.

Fun Fact **Weiners & Elephants**

If you lined up all the hot dogs served at SkyDome in one year, they would cover the distance of 3,241 stolen bases. If that bit of trivia doesn't thrill the kids, here is another astonishing tidbit of information: 516 African or 743 Indian elephants could fit on SkyDome's field.

---

2 Seasonal Events

As noted in chapter 2, "Planning Your Family Trip to Toronto," Toronto offers a year-round calendar of events for the whole family.

Canadian Children's Reading Festival   **Ages 3 to 12.** This event is held in May at Ontario Place and is sponsored by *City Parent,* one of Toronto's parenting magazines. The festival celebrates children's literature, emphasizing the work of Canadian children's authors.

Activities include author readings and book signings. The Yellow Dot stage offers entertainment during the festival and the literary marketplace includes some lively interactive exhibits, a sales venue for the work of featured authors, and a chance to enter contests to win some of the featured books. Ontario Place, 955 Lakeshore Blvd. W. © **866/663-4386** or 416/314-9900. Free with admission to Ontario Place. Subway: Bathurst, then Bathurst streetcar south.

Canadian National Exhibition   **Ages 2 and up.** For two weeks in late August and early September, Exhibition Place on Lakeshore Boulevard is home to the CNE, the largest outdoor exhibition in Canada. With its large midway the CNE has plenty to appeal to kids, but it also offers **Kidsworld,** a separate area designed just for kids, with rides, Kidstreet, and Kidscience. The highlight of **Kidstreet** is the playhouse theater, which features performances by many of Toronto's leading children's entertainers and theater troupes. The family center offers changing and nursing rooms. In the craft studio, kids can learn and try for themselves the techniques of clay sculpting, basket weaving, and papermaking. **Kidscience,** an extension of Kidsworld in the domed horticulture building, demonstrates the fun and often strange aspects of science to youngsters through interactive exhibits and demonstrations. Animal-loving kids will want to visit the children's area in the **Farm, Food and Fun** show, held every day of the fair, and catch the SuperDogs performance. Exhibition Place, Lakeshore Blvd. © **877/676-7466**. www.theex.com. Tickets C$9 (US$5.95) general admission, C$6 (US$3.95) seniors and children 6 and under, C$23 (US$15.20) unlimited midway rides. Subway: Bathurst, then Bathurst streetcar south.

Caribana   Ages 2 and up. This festival, held over two weeks in late July and early August, celebrates Caribbean song, dance, music, and food through concerts, ferry cruises, island picnics, and arts and crafts demonstrations. The highlight is the wild and colorful Caribana parade, where participants show off the lavishness of their costumes and bands compete for the title of band of the year. The celebration attracts more than 1 million people every year, but if kids find the crowds too overwhelming, they have their own parade and special day— **Caribana Jr.**—to attend, with a parade of costumed kids and a children's carnival. Various locations. ℭ **416/465-4884.** Free admission to parade, but varying ticket prices for seats in the stands, shows, and special events.

Dream in High Park   Ages 8 and up. Even if your kids haven't yet discovered the Bard, they'll enjoy this experience. There is something incredibly magical about watching Shakespeare performed beneath the stars. Each summer the Canadian Stage Company produces Shakespearean and Canadian plays at this outdoor theater in High Park. Performances begin at 8pm, but you may want to bring a picnic and arrive early to secure the best seats. High Park (Bloor and Keele sts.). ℭ **416/367-1652,** ext. 500. Tickets pay what you can, with suggested donation of C$14 (US$9.25) for adults. Subway: Keele.

First Night Toronto   Ages 2 and up. An astonishing array of events and activities provides a family-friendly way to ring in the New Year for Torontonians and visitors to the city. Street performers mingle with the public, and activities include crafts, magic shows, concerts, and even a children's village complete with child-sized rides and a petting zoo. Various venues. ℭ **416/362-3692.** Tickets C$12 (US$7.90) adults, C$8 (US$5.30) children 6 and up, free for children 5 and under.

Garden Bros. Circus   Ages 2 to 9. Most of the big circus acts, including the Ringling Bros. and Cirque du Soleil, pay frequent visits to Toronto, but the Garden Bros. is the only act that regularly puts up its tents each spring at SkyDome and in early September in Brampton.

This traditional three-ring circus is Canada's largest and has been operating for 65 years. The emphasis is on a death-defying high-wire act, but there are also the requisite clowns, elephants, and tigers. Like most circus acts, the real expense lies not in the admission fee but in the huge selection of souvenirs. You might want to come to some agreement with the kids about spending limits before you walk inside the big top. SkyDome, 1 Blue Jays Way (at Front St.). ℭ **905/671-4111.** Tickets C$17–$19 (US$11.20–$12.55) adults, C$8–$10 (US$5.30–$3.95) seniors and children 4 and up, free for children 2 and under. Subway: Union.

Harvestfest   All ages. Held each Thanksgiving weekend (the first weekend in October), this event at Harbourfront features a variety of down-home activities that, in previous years, have included a Wild West show, pony rides, and country dancing. Harbourfront, 235 Queens Quay W. ℭ 416/973-3000 (information) or **416/973-4000** (box office). Free admission.

Kids' Tuesdays (Value   **Ages 3 to 12.** On Tuesdays from 11:30am to 1pm during the summer, Nathan Phillips Square hosts free concerts for kids. The concerts usually have a theme and offer related arts and crafts, activities, and games. There are generally lineups, but since this is one of the few places where children of all ages are inspired to get involved in the action, it is well worth the wait. Nathan Phillips Square (Queen St. W. at Bay St.). ℭ **416/395-7350.** Free admission. Subway: Queen.

Milk International Children's Festival *(Finds)*   **Ages 7 and up; some events all ages.** Featured performers at this children's art festival, held over nine days in May, include Chinese acrobats, African dancers, and Spanish bands. Kids can take part in workshops themselves or can watch master craftspeople at work, such as the Japanese candy maker who molded fanciful dragons, dolphins, and birds. The Brave New Worlds series also presents inspiring lectures by famous adventurers and athletes—the 2001 festival featured Marnie McBean, three-time Olympic Gold rower, and Timothy Treadwell, who spends several months each year living among the Alaska grizzlies.   Harbourfront, 235 Queens Quay W. ✆ **416/973-3000** (information) or 416/973-4000 (box office). Tickets C$7.50–$12 (US$4.95–$7.90). Subway: Union, then no.509 or no.510 streetcar.

Renaissance Festival   **Ages 3 and up.** This trip back to Renaissance England is a huge hit with kids of all ages. Actors in period costume stroll around the site, discussing the latest court gossip and other timely subjects. Visitors often dress up in Renaissance garb as well, so it's difficult to tell the actors from the guests. Don't be surprised if a frantic maiden stops to ask your help or a peddler tries to interest you in his wares. About 50 artisans participate, selling everything from handblown glass to flower crowns for little ones.

The real excitement for many kids lies in the demonstrations of knightly arts, including a jousting match and falconry exhibition. There is even a human chess match with "pieces" chosen from the audience. Much of this event takes place in direct sun, so put hats on the kids. This summer event, held on weekends in Milton, northeast of Toronto, is a bit of a drive from downtown and seeing it all will take up an entire day, but it's well worth the effort.   Britannia Rd., Milton. ✆ **905/878-6948.** www.renfest.com. Tickets C$16.95 (US$11.20) adults, C$8.95 (US$5.90) children 15 and under. By car: Take Hwy. 401 west to Trafalgar Rd. exit. Drive south on Trafalgar Rd., turn left onto Derry Rd., and then turn right onto the Eighth Line and continue for about 1.5km (1 mile).

Royal Agricultural Winter Fair   **Ages 2 and up.** Country comes to the city when the Royal Winter Fair rolls into town in mid-November. Since 1922, this celebration of rural life has been a preeminent Toronto event. Kids will enjoy seeing the giant vegetables and the livestock and visiting the animals in the well-stocked petting zoo. Education centers are set up around the site to teach kids about everything from biotechnology to beekeeping and horse grooming to cattle care.   The Coliseum, National Trade Centre (at the corner of Lakeshore Blvd. W. and Strachan Ave.). ✆ **416/263-3400.** Tickets C$15 (US$9.90) adults, C$9 (US$5.95) children 5–17, free for children 4 and under, C$34 (US$22.45) family pass for 4. Subway: Bathurst, then Bathurst streetcar south.

Sprockets Children's International Film Festival   **Ages 6 to 12; some films 8 and up.** Like adult film festivals, this one, held in April, screens high-quality foreign films with subtitles. The difference is that this festival is devoted solely to films for children from Canada, Denmark, Sweden, Germany, and many other countries. There are Q&A sessions following each film, and for an additional charge of C$20 to C$45 (US$13.20 to $29.70) kids can learn the filmmaker's craft through various workshops, from trying their hand at TV production of the show *Zoom* in the Youth Television Network (YTV) studio downtown, to learning the basics of film animation. Most screenings take place at the Cineplex Odeon Varsity Cinemas in the Manulife Centre, 55 Bloor St. W. Various venues. ✆ **416-967-7371.** www.e.bell.ca/filmfest/sprockets. Tickets C$8 (US$5.30) adults, C$5.50 (US$3.65) children under 18.

Toronto Festival of Storytelling **Ages 2 and up.** Organized annually by the Storytellers School of Toronto, this event features storytellers from around the world. A special children's stage presents a wide variety of tellers of children's tales. The festival takes place during the last weekend in February at a various venues in the downtown core, culminating in a weekend event at Harbourfront. Various venues. ℂ **416/656-2445.** Tickets C$12 (US$7.90) adults, C$10 (US$6.60) children.

Toronto International Festival Caravan **Ages 5 and up.** In a city where more than 40% of the residents were born in another country, it's obvious why this annual multicultural festival is an event that is second to none. Held in late June, Caravan is the Toronto's salute to internationalism and features over 30 pavilions, each representing a different part of the world. Kids get their own passports and receive a different stamp at each pavilion. Families can sample exotic native dishes in the pavilions or try their hand at a variety of ethnic crafts such as egg painting in the Ukrainian pavilion. They can also enjoy dances from Polynesia, Canada's First Nations, or the Philippines, as well as Indian sari-wrapping demonstrations. Over 200 shows are staged during the 9-day festival. Pavilions are located at various points around the city. You can pick up your maps and passports at the CN Tower, at various retail stores, or in advance by calling the Caravan office. Various locations. ℂ **416/977-0466.** Tickets C$16 (US$10.55) in advance, C$20 (US$13.20) at the door, ages 13 and up, free for children 12 and under.

Winterfest **Ages 4 and up.** Since Torontonians cannot escape winter, they have chosen, instead, to celebrate it. Winterfest is a family-centered winter festival held during the second weekend in February. Events take place in North Toronto at Mel Lastman Square (5100 Yonge St.), uptown at Yonge and Eglinton, and downtown at Nathan Phillips Square (100 Queen St. W.). Entertainment includes professional ice shows and a midway, and multiple stages present children's entertainers who thrill the kids with music, magic, puppetry, and dance. Various venues. ℂ **416/395-7350.** Free admission. Subway: Downtown, Queen; uptown, Eglinton; North Toronto, North York Centre.

Word on the Street's Kidstreet **Ages 4 and up.** Word on the Street (WOTS) is an annual book and magazine publishing fair that takes place in late September along seven blocks of Queen Street West. For families, WOTS presents Kidstreet, on Queen between Soho and Beverley streets, with booths for kid-friendly book and magazine publishers. There are plenty of giveaways and author readings by such famed children's authors as Robert Munsch and concerts by leading children's entertainers. The entire festival is free. Queen St. W. (between University and Spadina aves.). ℂ **416/504-7241.** Subway: Osgoode.

3 Theater

More than 70 theater venues and well over 100 professional theater companies in Metro Toronto stage stunning productions of classical and contemporary works, Broadway hits, and avant-garde productions. I've listed the venues that most frequently host productions suitable for kids and several production companies that offer performances targeted to children.

Most of the major theater venues offer behind-the-scenes tours, which will give kids a glimpse into theater history as well as an up-close look at props, costumes, and other backstage secrets.

🎭 Sidetrips: Shakespeare & Shaw (Ages 8 & Up)

Within a few hours' drive of Toronto are two of Canada's most illustrious seasonal theater events: the Shaw Festival in Niagara-on-the-Lake and the Stratford Festival in Stratford.

The **Stratford Festival** bases its season on live performances of Shakespearean plays but also stages other classic and modern productions. This is a wonderful way to give your children a lasting appreciation for Shakespeare. There is usually a mix of Shakespearean dramas, comedies, and histories on the playbill at each of the three venues, and additional presentations have included *The Sound of Music, The Mikado, and Who's Afraid of Virginia Woolf?* In addition to watching award-winning theater, families may want to attend the backstage tours and actor chats. The town of Stratford is also worth strolling around—with the Avon River meandering through it and swans flocking along the banks, it has the feel of a British country village. There are many places to picnic and a wide range of restaurants in town. 55 Queen St., Stratford. ☎ **800/567-1600** (festival theater and offices) or 519/273-1600. Tickets C$39 to $64 (US$25.75 to $42.25).

The **Shaw Festival** centers its playbill on the works of George Bernard Shaw and his contemporaries. Recent productions have included *The Matchmaker, Lord of the Flies,* and *She Loves Me.* The Shaw hosts its productions in three very different venues: the elegant Festival Theatre, nestled within a beautiful formal garden, the intimate Court House Theatre, and the Edwardian-inspired Royal George Theatre. The historic town of Niagara-on-the-Lake is one of Canada's most genteel cities and recently placed second as the prettiest town in the world. It's notable for its fine Victorian architecture, abundance of gardens and parks, and vineyards and wineries. P.O. Box 794, Niagara-on-the-Lake. ☎ **800/511-7429** or 905/468-2172. www.shawfest.com. Tickets C$25–$70 (US$16.50–$46.20).

VENUES

Elgin and Winter Garden theaters   The two very different theaters housed in this double-decker venue were both built in 1913 to host traveling vaudeville acts, and in 1987 they underwent complete restoration. The Elgin is a formal theater with an abundance of gold leaf and rich fabrics, plaster cherubs, and ornate private boxes. Seven stories above, the whimsical Winter Garden was hand-painted to resemble a formal garden, with realistic beech bows and lanterns hanging from the ceiling. If kids lose interest in the production, they'll find a lot to look at in the decor. Since the grand reopening in 1989, the theaters have hosted such productions as *Joseph and the Amazing Technicolor Dream Coat, The Wizard of Oz,* and *Cats.* Tickets are sold through Ticket King (☎ **416/872-1212** or 800/461-3333). 189 Yonge St. ☎ **416/314-2901.** Tickets C$20–$85 (US$13.20–$56.10). Subway: Queen.

The Pantages   Originally this beautiful theater featured vaudeville acts and silent films. After a C$18-million (US$11.9 million) restoration, this glamorous setting hosted Andrew Lloyd Webber's *Phantom of the Opera.* After a 10-year run, the production closed in the summer of 1999. Recently, the Pantages has staged brilliant productions of classics such as *Annie* and *Cabaret*. 244 Victoria St. (at Shuter St.). © **416/364-4100**. Tickets C$51–$92.50 (US$33.65–$61.05). Subway: Dundas or Queen.

Princess of Wales Theatre Built in 1993, this was the first privately funded theater to be constructed in Toronto in almost 100 years. And what a theater it is. The facility was designed so that a real helicopter could land on the stage during performances of *Miss Saigon,* the theater's first production. Each of the nearly 2,000 seats is no more than 26 meters (85 feet) from the stage. Contemporary artist Frank Stella was commissioned to paint over 929 square meters (10,000 square feet) of murals on the interior and exterior walls. Tickets can be purchased through Ticket King (© **416/872-1212** or 800/461-3333). 300 King St. W. © **416/872-1212**. Tickets: C$27–C$91 (US$17.80–$60.05). Subway: St. Andrew.

(Finds Formal Wear

Toronto's theaters do not demand formal attire, but you'll probably feel more comfortable dressing up than dressing down. If the kids have arrived in town with nothing but cargo pants and T-shirts in their suitcases, don't despair. **Kid's Wardrobe**, 2300 Yonge St. (© **416/488-5385**) rents out boys' and girls' dressy attire, created by local designer Angela Marrett.

St. Lawrence Centre for the Performing Arts In this center, the Bluma Appel Theatre is home to the Canadian Stage Company, and the smaller Jane Mallet Theatre hosts classical concerts and musicians. Both theaters also present lectures and smaller productions. 27 Front St. E. © **416/366-7723**. Tickets C$45–$85 (US$29.70–$56.10). Subway: Union.

Toronto Centre for the Arts Formerly known as the Ford Centre for the Performing Arts, this mammoth complex houses three separate venues. The 250-seat Studio Hall hosts lectures and smaller theater performances, including children's productions. The more lavish 1,850-seat Main Stage is the venue for larger productions. The 1,036-seat George Weston Recital Hall has an annual concert season and, with its top-notch acoustics, is the venue of choice for many international singers and musicians on tour. The Canadian Children's Opera Chorus and the Toronto Symphony Orchestra frequently play here. The complex also hosts the Museum of Contemporary Canadian Art. 5040 Yonge St. © **416/733-9388**. Tickets C$50–$95 (US$33–$62.70). Subway: North York Centre.

Toronto Truck Theatre *(Finds* For generations of schoolchildren around Ontario, *The Mousetrap,* the Toronto Truck Theatre's sole offering, has served as a first introduction to live theater. Canada's longest-running show, this production, based on an Agatha Christie mystery, is now in its 22nd year. Even if you know "whodunnit," it's still a great show and is most suitable for ages 7 and up. 94 Belmont St. © **416/922-0084**. Tickets C$20 (US$13.20). Subway: Rosedale.

Young People's Theatre *(Finds* This innovative theater stages quality children's theatre on par with, and sometimes excelling, adult productions in the city. YPT commissions original plays and also hosts some adaptations of classic children's stories. Most productions suit a wide range of ages, from 4 to 16; some productions are more appropriate for ages 9 and up. Previous performances have included *The Very Hungry Caterpillar, The Hobbit,* and *The Complete Works of Shakespeare,* a tongue-in-cheek romp through most of the Bard's works. YPT is housed in a building that once served as a stable for the 500 horses that pulled Toronto's streetcars, and the main stage seats 468. The annual season of five to eight plays runs from October to April. In an effort to make theater accessible to everyone, YPT reserves a number of pay-what-you-can tickets for each performance, which are made available at 10am on the day of the performance. 165 Front St. E. ℂ 416/862-2222. Tickets C$16–$28 (US$10.55–$18.50). Subway: Sherbourne, then any bus south to Front St.

THEATER COMPANIES

Solar Stage Theatre *(Value* **Ages 2 to 9.** This theater company stages its productions at the Madison Centre in North York. Past performances have included classic tales such as *Peter Rabbit,* adaptations of Robert Munsch stories, and West African folktales. Puppet shows are also frequently staged. Madison Centre, 4950 Yonge St., Concourse Level. ℂ 416/368-8031. Tickets C$8.50 (US$5.60). Subway: Sheppard, then walk 2 blocks north.

Starshine Productions   Ages 2 to 9. This company began as a thesis project by two students at downtown's Ryerson University. With some help from class-mates, the two wrote the script and music for a children's play, secured funding and a venue, sold tickets, and staged a grand performance. The project has evolved into a fully fledged theater company. Performances are multilayered and designed with an eye toward keeping both adults and children entertained. The smallest children will be wowed by the colorful costumes and lively music, older children will get more of the meaning of the play, and adults will appreciate the jokes and word play. Each performance offers 20% of tickets as pay what you can. Various venues. ℂ 416/537-7469. www.starshineproductions.com. Tickets C$15 (US$9.90) adults, C$10 (US$6.60) children.

DINNER THEATER

In addition to the brilliant and varied offerings listed above, Toronto is home to several dinner theaters, which offer a novel approach to live theater.

Famous People Players *(Finds* **Ages 3 and up.** This renowned theater troupe enchants its guests, especially small ones, with a unique blend of life-size puppets, props, and actors performing a series of vignettes in the blacklight the-ater. The Christmas show was enchanting, featuring dancing poinsettias, magic floating snowflakes, chicken ballerinas, and a sleeping Santa Claus.

The theater company, whose members are developmentally disabled, has attracted the attention of such celebrities as Liberace, who was so enchanted with the troupe's original show, which featured a puppet of the pianist, that he took the troupe with him on a Las Vegas tour. Paul Newman is a patron of Famous People's Theatre, supporting it through donations from his Newman's Own charity.

Kids of all ages will love the continuous action and wonderful music that are the trademarks of this talented troupe. They serve a great dinner as well. 30 Lisgar St. ℂ 416/532-1137. Tickets Tues–Thurs C$39.95 (US$26.35) adults, C$28.95 (US$19.10) children 10 and under, Fri–Sat C$42.95 (US$28.35) adults, C$29.95 (US$19.75) children 10 and under. Subway: Dufferin, then any bus south to Queen St. Walk 2 blocks east to Lisgar St. and then 1 block south to Sudbury St.

Medieval Times   **Ages 6 and up.** Young lords and ladies will lap up this medieval-themed feast and show, especially the part where they get to eat with their hands. Guests of this castle located on the grounds of Exhibition Place enjoy a typical medieval feast of roast chicken and ribs, delivered by costumed servers, while they cheer on the knights in their bid to become the king's personal champion. The knights compete in a series of feats of strength and horsemanship, which culminates in a search among the audience for the Queen of Love and Beauty. There is a museum of medieval torture that older kids will find gruesomely good but younger kids might find a bit frightening; an additional charge applies of C$2 (US$1.30) for adults, C$1 (US65¢) for children. When calling for tickets, ask about the young knights school, which is occasionally held prior to the feast. The free school is a fantastic way for youngsters to spend time with the knights and learn about their weapons, the games, and the horses. Exhibition Place (Dufferin Gate). ✆ **416/260-1234.** Tickets C$51.95 (US$34.30) adults, C$34.95 (US$23.05) children 11 and under. Subway: Bathurst, then Bathurst streetcar south.

Tony 'N Tina's Wedding   **Ages 12 and up.** You're invited to be a guest at the nightmare wedding of the year. Everything that can go wrong will at this interactive dinner theater where patrons are the wedding guests and experience everything from the ceremony at the Chapel of Love to the rollicking reception with live music from the 1970s and 1980s. Following the ceremony you join the cast at the Buffet of Love, a traditional Italian-Canadian dinner buffet. After dinner, the reception begins and the characters really begin to loosen up. Tickets are expensive, so this may be a better choice for older children. 56 Blue Jays Way. ✆ **416/343-0011.** Tickets C$63.50–$68.50 (US$41.90–$45.20). Subway: Union.

4 Puppet Shows

While Toronto lacks a stage dedicated solely to puppetry, the city has many talented puppeteers who perform in a variety of locations. Additional Canadian and international touring puppet shows often appear at various venues around the city. **Toronto Public Libraries** are the most popular venue for puppet shows (pick up a copy of the free *What's On* guide from any branch, or call their answer line at ✆ **416/393-7131**). The **Solar Stage Theatre** company (✆ **416/368-8031**) also frequently hosts puppet shows as part of its annual performance schedule (see "Theater Companies," above). Each year between September and November, the **Mississauga Library** system hosts an annual **Puppetry Festival**, which features puppet shows at all of the library's branches. Tickets for these performances are C$3 (US$2); free performances are also hosted by local shopping centers during the festival. Call ✆ **905/615-3500** for locations and times. Puppet shows are also typically part of the fare offered during **First Night** and **Winterfest** (see "Seasonal Events," earlier in this chapter).

For puppet shows currently playing in the Toronto area, call the following puppetry companies.

Lampoon Puppet Theatre   **All ages.** Puppeteer Johann Vandergunn presents a range of tales, many with an international flavor. *The Little Blue Hedgehog* is a Romanian puppet show, and other productions are based on folktales from Japan, Russia, and Canada. ✆ **416/967-7620.**

Merry Folklorists   **All ages.** Puppeteer Connie Calvert works with life-size marionettes and masks, reproducing much-loved children's tales such as *Goldilocks and the Three Bears* and *The Billy Goats Gruff.* The show is open concept so kids can actually watch the puppeteers work, and audience partici-pation is a part of every show. ℭ **800/667-4382** or 905/775-4304.

Puppetmongers   All ages. This unique puppet theater doesn't stick to the usual tabletop puppets and marionettes—puppeteers have been known to use bricks for characters and a dollhouse and tiny people for the set. The puppeteers themselves are always included as part of the show. ℭ **416/691-0806.**

TV Puppetree   All ages. This company specializes in teddy bear shows, with a special version for Halloween. Classics such as *Peter Rabbit* and *Aesop's Fables* are also part of the repertoire of these well-known Toronto puppeteers. ℭ **416/347-1153.**

5 Music

CONCERT HALLS & VENUES

The city of Toronto boasts many venues, both small and large, that host a wide range of musical acts, from the latest pop sensations to philharmonic orchestras. The **St. Lawrence Centre for the Arts, Harbourfront, Roy Thomson Hall,** and **SkyDome** are just a few of the venues where you and the kids might find your favorite musicians and singers performing.

Kingswood Music Theatre   This outdoor concert stage is part of Paramount Canada's Wonderland, although admission to the concerts is often charged sep-arately. This is one of the city's most popular venues for nostalgic performances from groups such as Boston and Depeche Mode; however, current favorites are featured here as well. Ticket prices vary, depending on the event, and are sold through TicketMaster (ℭ **416/870-8000**). 9580 Jane St. ℭ 905/832-8131. Subway: Yorkdale or York Mills, then Wonderland Express GO Bus.

Maple Leaf Gardens   The former home of the Toronto Maple Leafs now hosts pop and rock concerts. This isn't the most comfortable venue—the seats were designed many years ago for die-hard hockey fans—but most of the seats provide a good view. You may want to avoid the gray and green seats on either side of the stage (sections 94 to 97 and 76 to 77). Tickets are sold through TicketMaster (ℭ **416/870-8000**). 60 Carlton St. ℭ 416/977-1641. Subway: College.

Molson Amphitheatre   Jazz, blues, and classical concerts are the mainstays of this Ontario Place open-air theater, but some rock and pop groups are also booked. Aerosmith and British band Oasis have played here, as has Bryan Adams. The theater can seat up to 16,000 under the large roof and on the spacious lawn. Ticket prices vary; contact TicketMaster (ℭ **416/870-8000**). 909 Lakeshore Blvd. W. (in Ontario Place). ℭ 416/260-5600. Subway: Union, then no. 509 street-car west, or Bathurst, then any streetcar south.

St. James Cathedral Summer Sunday Concerts *(Finds*   With its 5,000-pipe organ, St. James Cathedral is an awe-inspiring setting for this series of 30-minute concerts. A different guest, usually an organist, is featured each Sunday. These brief concerts are a wonderful choice for the can't-sit-still-for-long mem-bers of your family. As a side note, many other churches throughout the city feature short concerts and are worth investigating.   65 Church St. (at King St. E.). ℭ 416/364-7865. www.stjamescathedral.on.ca. Free admission. Subway: King.

OPERA COMPANIES, SYMPHONIES & CHOIRS

Canadian Children's Opera Chorus   Ages 7 and up. In addition to performing a fully staged opera or operetta each year, this 75-member children's chorus puts on 40 performances throughout the season. The choir also works with the Canadian Opera Company at the Hummingbird Centre and has performed in conjunction with the National Ballet of Canada and the Toronto Symphony Orchestra. Ticket prices vary depending on the performance and venue. Various venues. ✆ **416/366-0467.**

Canadian Opera Company   Ages 9 and up. Canada's largest and most prestigious opera company performs its magic on the stage of the **Hummingbird Centre.** This is serious opera and, as such, is probably not a great choice for young children. Still, the company tries to make its craft accessible to all, offering pre-performance chats (45 minutes before the curtain rises) during which kids and adults can ask questions and have aspects of opera explained to them. Translation of the operas is provided by subtitles, which are projected onto an arch above the stage. 227 Front St. E. ✆ **416/363-6671.** Tickets C$38–$135 (US$25.10–$89.10) adults, C$15–$50 (US$9.90–$33) children 17 and under. Subway: Union.

Toronto Children's Chorus *(Finds*   **Ages 5 and up.** Kids love to hear and see other kids performing. The 300 children aged 7 to 17 in this chorus sing a wide variety of music, ranging from Renaissance to modern compositions, with an emphasis on the work of Canadian composers. This is a touring company that has played a wide range of venues, from Carnegie Hall in New York to the Barbican Centre in London, England. Concerts are held in a variety of locations in Toronto, including churches, the Toronto Centre for the Arts, and Roy Thomson Hall. Ticket prices vary. Various venues. ✆ **416/932-8666.**

Toronto Mendelssohn Choir   Ages 8 and up. This choir frequently performs with the Toronto Symphony Orchestra, but it's also well known for its contribution of several of the most haunting melodies for the film *Schindler's List.* The **Toronto Mendelssohn Youth Choir** is composed of 45 young singers aged 15 to 23 who perform alone and with adult choir members. Both choirs perform at a variety of venues, including **Roy Thomson Hall** and several downtown cathedrals and churches. Various venues. ✆ **416/598-0422.** Tickets C$22–$49 (US$14.50–$32.35).

Toronto Symphony Orchestra   Ages 6 and up. In addition to their regular season, the TSO has a wonderful concert series just for kids. These five one-hour concerts are held on several Saturdays from November to April. With titles like "Beethoven Lives Upstairs" and "Tubby the Tuba," this series may just turn your kids away from Barney and the Backstreet Boys and toward classical music. If nothing else, they'll leave these concerts with a new appreciation for other forms of musical expression. Be sure to arrive early so your kids can catch some of the lobby performances held prior to each concert. Performed by young musicians, these mini-concerts allow the little ones a close-up look at how each instrument is played. The TSO also hosts an annual Christmas performance, which small fry love. Most performances, including those by the youth orchestra (see below), are held at Roy Thomson Hall. 60 Simcoe St. ✆ **416/593-4828.** TSO office, 212 King St. W. ✆ 416/593-7769. Children's series tickets C$17–$20 (US$11.20–$13.20). Subway: St. Andrew.

Toronto Symphony Youth Orchestra   Ages 6 and up. Musicians under the age of 22 form this orchestra, which is associated with the Toronto Symphony Orchestra. Chamber music performances and concerts are performed by these talented young people both on their own and in conjunction with the TSO. Many of Toronto's finest classical musicians received their early training through the TSYO. Roy Thomson Hall, 60 Simcoe St. ℂ 416/593-4828. Subway: St. Andrew.

Street Performers

Toronto's street performers ply their trade in subway stations, in parks, and along the streets. In fact, Toronto's streets served as a starting point for a number of well-known Canadian performers, including the Barenaked Ladies. The best sites for catching buskers are the **Eaton Centre** and **Union Station,** where we've seen everything from a washboard band to a jazz ensemble. One classical violinist we walked by broke into a raucous rendition of "Old McDonald," much to the girls' delight. Quality ranges as widely as the music, but all subway performers must audition and apply for a license from the Toronto Transit Commission.

Buskers are part of almost all the annual festivals hosted by the city. Two popular events for Toronto's street performers are **First Night** and **Kids' Tuesdays** at **Nathan Phillips Square.** There are also three annual events devoted to street entertainment. The **Celebrate Toronto Street Festival** (ℂ 416/395-7347; www.city.toronto.on.ca) takes place downtown along Yonge Street in early July. The three-day festival features live musicians in all genres, from jazz to hip-hop, pop, and children's music. Stilt-walkers, jugglers, clowns, and a small midway add to the carnival atmosphere.

The **Toronto International Buskerfest** is a four-day festival of comedy and athletic performance sponsored by Epilepsy Toronto (ℂ **416/964-9095;** www.torontobuskerfest.com). Buskers from across North America entertain the crowd with trampoline acts, fire eating, body painting, and magic tricks. The festival is usually held the third week in June.

The **Beaches International Jazz Festival** (ℂ **416/698-2152;** www.beaches jazz.com) draws together the sounds of calypso, blues, reggae, jazz, and more in a weekend-long street festival, held in late July.

6 Dance

Canadian Children's Dance Theatre   Ages 5 and up. The membership of this modern dance repertory company includes some of the finest young dancers in the city. They hold frequent performances at the Winchester Street Theatre and the Premiere Dance Theatre, as well as at various festivals, including **Harbourfront's Milk International Children's Festival.** CCDT annually performs *Wintersong,* a collection of seasonal dances, in December, and *Teasing Gravity,* dances for the young and fearless, each year in May. Ticket prices vary depending on the performance and venue. Various venues. ℂ 416/924-5657. www.ccdt.org.

National Ballet of Canada   Ages 6 and up. If you're in town in December, the National Ballet's magical performance of *The Nutcracker* is not to be missed. The company presents a full season of classical ballet from early fall to spring. All performances are held at the **Hummingbird Centre for the Performing Arts** (1 Front St. E., ℂ **416/393-7474),** although the company does have its own rehearsal facility at the Walter Carsen Centre, 470 Queens Quay W. Various venues. ℂ **416/345-9686.** Tickets C$15–$85 (US$9.90–$56.10).

National Ballet School of Canada   **Ages 6 and up.** This school is the training ground for classical ballerinas in Canada. The Spring Showcase, held at the **Betty Oliphant Theatre** (404 Jarvis St., ℂ **416/964-3780,** ext. 2014) in late May, is a chance for you and the kids to see some of ballet's rising stars before they become famous. These young dancers also form a large part of the cast of the National Ballet of Canada's performance of *The Nutcracker* and frequently accompany performances of the Toronto Symphony Orchestra and the Canadian Opera Company.   Various venues. ℂ **416/964-3780.** Spring Showcase tickets C$18–$25 (US$11.90–$16.50).

Premiere Dance Theatre   **All ages.** Children, especially older ones, are often thrilled by the frenetic energy and pace of contemporary dance. This is the premier venue for contemporary dance in Toronto. Most of Toronto's leading contemporary dance companies perform at this theater.   207 Queens Quay W. ℂ **416/973-4000.** Tickets C$30–$95 (US$19.80–$62.70). Subway: Union, then no. 509 or no. 510 streetcar.

7 Films

Cineplex Odeon   **Ages 4 and up.** This chain has numerous locations around the city, including theaters at the Manulife Centre, each offering a changing lineup of popular movies. To find out about ticket prices and the closest theater playing the movie you want to see, call the general information number at ℂ 416/964-2463.

Cinesphere   **Ages 4 and up.** This giant dome-shaped theater is part of Ontario Place and features both IMAX films and the latest releases from Hollywood on its 20 by 24-meter (66 by 79 ft.) screen.   955 Lakeshore Blvd. W. ℂ **416/314-9900.** Tickets C$6–$9 (US$3.95–$5.95). Subway: Bathurst, then any streetcar south.

Colossus   **Ages 4 and up.** Ancient Rome meets outer space at this theater complex in Vaughan, not far from Paramount Canada's Wonderland. The complex is impossible to miss—just look for the giant spaceship. The Colossus houses 18 screens showing all the latest Hollywood flicks, as well as a six-story IMAX screen with an earth-shattering sound system that the kids will love. The complex also houses several fast-food outlets.   3555 Hwy. 7 W. ℂ **905/851-1001.** Tickets: C$4–$11 (US$2.65–$7.25). By car: Take Hwy. 401 west to Hwy. 400, then north on Hwy. 400 to Hwy. 7.

Eglinton Theatre   **Ages 4 and up.** A classic 700-seat theater with Art Deco decor and an extra-large screen, the Eglinton offers a refreshing change from multiplex theaters. This theater screens primarily first-run movies, but it's also a popular location for film festivals and special screenings.   400 Eglinton Ave. W. (at Avenue Rd.). ℂ **416/487-4721.** Tickets C$4.99–$11 (US$3.30–$7.25). Subway: Eglinton, then any bus west.

Festival Hall   **Ages 4 and up.** This entertainment complex comprises Paramount theaters, several fast-food outlets, and a huge Chapters bookstore. It also boasts an enviable location next to video game paradise Playdium. There are 13 theaters in the complex with floor-to-ceiling screens showing everything from IMAX creations to Hollywood offerings. The lobby is an attraction in itself, with a replica of a Klingon warship dominating the decor.   259 Richmond St. W. (at John St.). ℂ **416/925-4629.** Tickets C$10–$11 (US$6.60 –$7.25) adults, C$5.75–$6.75 (US$3.80–$4.45) children under 13. Subway: Osgoode.

Omnimax   Ages 4 and up. This 24-meter (79 ft.) domed theater runs IMAX and other large-format films. Part of the Ontario Science Centre, the theater has both day and evening screenings.   770 Don Mills Rd. (at Eglinton Ave.). © **416/696-1000.** Tickets C$10 (US$6.60) adults, C$6 (US$3.95) children 13–17, C$5.50(US$3.65) children 12 and under. Subway: Eglinton, then bus east to Don Mills Rd., or Pape, then Don Mills bus to St. Dennis Dr.

Hollywood North

Toronto is North America's third-largest film and production center, following closely on the heels of Los Angeles and New York. With the low Canadian dollar, tax incentives, and a locale that can transform itself into "Anycity, Anywhere," Canada's film production is a C$1.2 billion (US$792 million) industry.

In a busy month, up to 40 film crews are busy on locations around the city producing feature films, movies of the week, TV shows, and music videos. *Bless the Child, American Psycho, Loser, Knock-Around Guys, X-Men, The Sixth Day, Harvard Man,* and *The Caveman's Valentine* are just a few of the feature films recently shot in the city. Toronto has stood in for a number of cities, from New York City to Nepal, and a wide variety of time periods, from ancient Egypt to antebellum Georgia. You can check with the **Ontario Film Development Corporation** (www.ofdc.on.ca) to see what is currently being filmed and which of your favorite actors and actresses might be in town.

Toronto is also well known for its gifted animation companies. **CORE Digital Pictures** (www.core.com) was responsible for the computer-animated geese in the hit movie *Fly Away Home*. They also created digital animals for *Dr. Doolittle* and produced the monster hamster scene for *Nutty Professor II: The Klumps*. Animated series created in Toronto include Saturday-morning favorites *Monster by Mistake, Freaky Stories, Anne of Green Gables,* and *Rainbow Fish*.

8 Story Hours

Many venues across the city, including libraries, bookstores, and theaters, stage public readings and story hours throughout the year. In the summer, outdoor story hours are held in a number of locations and in conjunction with several festivals.

Another good option, especially if you're interested in doing a little book browsing yourself, is to take the kids to one of the big chain bookstores. Chapters, Indigo, and several children's bookstores all offer children's story hours, usually in the afternoon. Times vary, so call ahead. Chapters branches are located at 110 Bloor St. W. (© **416/920-9299**), 142 John St. (© **416/595-7349**), and 2400 Yonge St. (© **416/544-0625**). **Indigo** has stores in the Eaton Centre (© **416/591-3622**), Yonge-Eglinton Centre (© **416/544-0049**), and Yorkdale Shopping Centre (© **416/781-6660**). Regular story hours specifically geared toward toddlers are held at Mabel's Fables, 662 Mount Pleasant Rd. (© **416/ 322-0438**). This children's-only bookstore also frequently hosts author readings and book signings.

Children's Own Musuem   **Ages 4 to 7.** Special guests of the museum read aloud every week during the Sunday Story Session, held each Sunday at 11:30am. Museum personnel also read stories on an impromptu basis throughout the week.   90 Queen's Park Circle. ☎ 416/542-1492. Free with museum admission (C$4.75; US$3.15). Subway: Museum.

Dial a Story *(Finds*   **Ages 4 to 9.** The Mississauga Library offers this telephone bedtime story line for young children. Library volunteers read the stories, which change weekly. ☎ **905/615-3497.**

Harbourfront Reading Series   **Ages 2 to 9.** Every Wednesday at 7:30pm, the Brigantine Room at Harbourfront presents author readings. More than 3,000 authors from around the world have read here since this series began in 1974, including some noted children's authors. The series culminates each year in the **International Festival of Authors,** a salute to the literary world's best and brightest. As part of the 2000 festival, J.K. Rowling, of Harry Potter fame, read to a thrilled crowd of 20,000 fans at SkyDome.

The Harbourfront **Milk International Children's Festival** (see "Seasonal Events," earlier in this chapter), held in May, and **Cushion Concerts,** held throughout the year, feature storytellers among their numerous other entertainments.   235 Queens Quay W. ☎ **416/973-3000** (information) or 416/973-4000 (box office). www.harbourfront.on.ca. Ticket prices vary. Subway: Union, then no. 509 or no. 510 streetcar.

Toronto Public Library System *(Value*   **Ages 2 to 9.** The Toronto Public Library offers regular story hours and plenty of children's programming, including puppet shows and musical performances, at all of its branches in the city. Hours and times vary at each branch and during each season, but the library publishes a seasonal guide to its special programming called *What's On,* available at all branches. You can also call their answer line at ☎ **416/393-7131.**

9 Spectator Sports

Toronto has a thriving professional sports scene with plenty of fan support for long-term favorites the Toronto Maple Leafs and the Toronto Blue Jays, as well as for relative newcomers the Toronto Raptors and Toronto Rock. Be forewarned, though—despite the rising popularity of professional basketball, Torontonians are die-hard hockey fans, and it can be difficult, if not impossible, to get tickets for Leafs games during the playoffs.

Toronto Argonauts   **Ages 5 and up.** The Canadian game of football is basically the same as in the United States but the field is longer and teams are allowed three downs rather than four. Games are played against other teams in the Canadian Football League. Tickets are sold through TicketMaster (☎ **416/870-8000**).   SkyDome, 1 Blue Jays Way (at Front St.). ☎ 416/341-3663. Tickets C$12–$42 (US$7.90–$27.70) adults; C$8–$37 (US$5.30–$24.40) students. Subway: Union.

Toronto Blue Jays   **Ages 5 and up.** Winners of the World Series in 1992 and 1993, Toronto's professional baseball team has more to offer families than great baseball. Honda Junior Jays Saturdays, held during each Saturday home game, include face painting, removable tattoos, clowns, and interactive games. All Junior Jays can enter a draw to win the chance to announce the starting lineup, sing the national anthem, and throw the first pitch. Kids are invited to run the bases following the game. Students and seniors can also purchase tickets at a reduced rate for Saturday and weekday afternoon games. Tickets are sold

through TicketMaster (*℃* **416/870-8000**).   SkyDome, 1 Blue Jays Way (at Front St.).
℃ **416/341-3663**. Tickets C$7–$23 (US$4.60–$15.20); Junior Jays days C$5–$16 (US$3.30–
10.55). Subway: Union.

Toronto Maple Leafs   Ages 5 and up. Air Canada Centre presents NHL
hockey at its best. In addition to the game, young fans are treated to the Great
Canadian Goalie Race, where they can cheer on the goalie representing their section of the stands, and the Fan of the Game contest, in which youngsters are
photographed and entered into a contest to win a team jersey. During other pro-
motions, fans might get a chance to watch famous former Leafs take shots on a
volunteer goalie, or they may be selected to compete to see who can get their
shot closest to center ice.

Team mascot Carlton the Bear will also thrill the youngest fans with his
antics. Practices are often open and kids can watch from the stands. During the
"Move of the Game," two people in the upper bowl are moved to Platinum
seats. Tickets are sold through TicketMaster (*℃* **416/870-8000**).   Air Canada
Centre, 40 Bay St. *℃* **416/815-5700**. Tickets C$10–$130 (US$6.60–$85.80); C$330 (US$217.80)
for seats along the boards. Subway: Union.

Toronto Raptors   Ages 5 and up. According to games director Paul
McKenna, the Raptors try to get kids involved every chance they get. This
means that kids can take part in everything from a junior slam dunk to mini-
clinics during timeouts and between quarters. Toddlers can play musical chairs
with the Raptor dinosaur mascot on the court, and even babies can get in on the
act during the baby crawl held between whistles. Most of these events are held
during weekend afternoon games, when the stands are filled with families.
When you call for tickets, be sure to ask for the Sprite Zone, where tickets are
cheap and promoters are constantly working the crowd, giving away prizes and
leading the kids in cheers. Tickets are sold through TicketMaster (*℃* **416/870-
8000**). Air Canada Centre, 40 Bay St. *℃* **416/872-5000**. Tickets C$10–$130 (US$6.60–$85.80).
Subway: Union.

Toronto Rock   Ages 5 and up. Canada's official national sport rivals hockey
for its speed and basketball for the complexity of its plays. Lacrosse, long played
in minor leagues across the city, has now graduated to professional status. The
Toronto Rock plays other professional teams from the United States and
Canada. Games are held at the Air Canada Centre and the season runs from
December through April. Tickets are sold through TicketMaster (*℃* **416/870-
8000**). Air Canada Centre, 40 Bay St. *℃* **416/596-3075**. Tickets C$10–$35 (US$6.60–23.10).
Subway: Union.

10 Kids' Television

When the kids (and you) are looking for some laid-back entertainment in your
hotel room or while waiting for the pizza to arrive, the following three stations
offer daily children's programming. Of course, the US Public Broadcasting
System (PBS) is also offered on many cable systems in the city, and most stations
run Saturday morning cartoons and shows for kids.

CBC The Canadian Broadcasting Corporation is the Canadian equivalent of
the BBC in terms of radio and television broadcasting. CBC stations offer a variety of news, magazine, and prime-time programs in addition to some excellent
children's shows. CBC stations generally run children's shows weekdays in the

early morning and on Saturday mornings. If you get a chance to visit, the CBC museum (250 Front St. W., © **416/205-5574**) is free and definitely worth a look, with lots of displays of children's programming from days gone by. CBC Newsworld is broadcast live daily from the lobby of CBC Toronto.

TV Ontario   TVO is Ontario's not-for-profit television station. Mornings and after-school hours are given over to children's programming, but afternoons and weekends are generally dedicated to adult or educational programs.

YTV   The letters actually don't stand for anything, but this is a TV station solely for kids, offering a mix of shows for young and old. A variety of home-grown shows as well as imports from the United States and other countries are regular features. Tours of the studio are available—call © **416/534-6565,** ext. 444, for details.

9

Shopping for the Whole Family

Toronto is considered to be the New York of the Canadian shopping scene. Whatever you and your kids are shopping for, be it funky, vintage, or couture, one of Toronto's myriad shops will have it. Parents will especially appreciate the many high-quality discount clothing, houseware, and furniture shops.

If you're planning to take the kids toy shopping, you might want to set some ground rules for spending beforehand. The toy shops, brimming with antique reproductions and the latest high-tech toys, simply offer too much fun for kids to resist. The same is true of Toronto's many sweets shops, where even dedicated dieters may be tempted to indulge.

Toronto has some great shopping malls, most of which offer an assortment of kids' stores, the standard chains being **Gap Kids, Jacob Jr., La Senza for Girls,** and **Roots Kids.** The **Eaton Centre** is the matriarch of Toronto malls, and most visitors to

the city will spend at least some time here. Located in the center of downtown and served by two subway stops, it is also a convenient spot to get your bearings when exploring the city.

Nursing moms will find Toronto a laid-back city. I've seen moms nursing discreetly on the subway and in mall food courts. If you prefer more privacy, though, several malls, like Yorkdale and Scarborough Town Centre, offer nursing rooms, and most salespeople in the clothing shops will happily invite you to use one of the change rooms.

The majority of stores accept both Visa and MasterCard and many also accept American Express. Other credit cards are accepted far less frequently. U.S. cash is usually welcomed, though you would be well advised to either withdraw Canadian money at an ATM or exchange your cash at the bank since the exchange rate at most retail operations is less than great.

1 The Shopping Scene
SHOPPING HOURS & SALES TAX
Toronto prices tend to fall in line with those typical of large urban centers, as in you can find bargains, but most things don't come cheap. Plus, 8% provincial sales tax (PST) is levied on all goods and restaurant bills and 7% federal goods and services tax (GST) is added to all goods and services. The good news for foreign visitors is that the GST and PST are refundable for many items and the exchange rate is usually in your favor. Most shopping centers carry refund application forms, and several immediate refund centers have been set up in the city. See chapter 3, "Getting to Know Toronto," for more details.

Most stores in the city open at 10am. Closing hours vary according to the day. From Monday to Wednesday, most stores close at 6pm. On Thursdays and Fridays, many stay open until 9pm. On Saturdays, stores generally close early, either at 5pm or 6pm, and on Sundays most close by 5pm.

SHOPPING DISTRICTS

THE BEACHES

This is the perfect spot for a stroll on a sunny afternoon. Located just a few blocks from the Beaches boardwalk, this strip along Queen Street East, just east of Woodbine Avenue, has stores that tend toward the fun and casual. Because families frequent the area, there are some great kid-friendly stores, such as **Sugar Mountain, Kids Turf,** and two hair salons just for kids: **Beaches Kids Kutz** and **Little Tots Hair Shop.**

BLOOR STREET WEST

Bordered by Yonge Street and Avenue Road, Bloor Street West is home to many of Toronto's most exclusive boutiques, from **Chanel** to **Cartier.** The high-end **Holt Renfrew** department store is also prime hunting ground for well-heeled shoppers. **Gap Kids** has a store here, as well, and the three-story **Chapters** bookstore houses a vast selection of kids' books and a small play center for little shoppers who need a play break.

YORKVILLE

Once the center of Toronto's hippie counterculture, Yorkville Avenue and Cumberland Street, crisscrossed by several alley-like streets, have been transformed into Toronto's most upscale shopping area. The tony Hazelton Lanes mall is located here, and the area is well known for its designer shops and art galleries, as well as for some of the best family-friendly restaurants in the city. Kids' clothing stores include the chichi **Maison Vali** and **Tutto Chicco.** Kids will love the cool accessories at **Ice,** hip memorabilia and candy at **Retro-Fun,** and delicious bath products at **Lush.** There are great toy stores here too—**Kidding Awound** and the **Toy Shop.**

QUEEN STREET WEST

Easily Toronto's most trendy shopping district, Queen Street West from University to Spadina avenues houses an eclectic mix of vintage clothing shops and funky Canadian designer boutiques. **Chateauworks, Bluenotes,** and **Misdemeanours** are just several of the hip kids' clothing boutiques located here. When the kids are ready for a snack, nip into one of the excellent bistros in the area (Peter Pan [see p. 68], Queen Mother Cafe, Le Select or The Rivoli) and grab a window seat for people-watching.

CHINATOWN/KENSINGTON MARKET

Toronto's bustling Chinatown runs along Spadina Avenue between King and College streets, and tucked behind it is the international-flavored Kensington Market, a cluster of food and clothing shops located between Dundas and College streets and reaching west to Bathurst.

Both Kensington Market and Chinatown are great spots for hunting down bargains on designer clothing, fabric, and vintage and ethnic clothing. However, the real draw for most shoppers is the exciting array of ethnic food, seafood, fruit, and spice shops. Wares spill out onto the streets in huge bins that crowd the sidewalks. The kids will be fascinated by the exotic selections in the shops, from tables of fresh squid and octopus to crates of live crabs and barrels of multi-colored beans and grains.

SHOPPING CENTERS

Atrium on Bay   In the heart of downtown are two levels of shops selling clothing, jewelry, furniture, and more. Kid-friendly shops include the **Game Shack** and **Kiddie Kidswear.**   595 Bay St. (at Dundas St.). ✆ 416/980-2801. Subway: Dundas.

The Eaton Centre   This landmark on Yonge Street is so large it encompasses two separate subway stops. It is impossibly busy, with over 1 million people walking through its concourses every week, and it's also an unabashed tourist trap, so don't come expecting great deals. Still, it shouldn't be missed.

There are 250 stores in the Eaton Centre, anchored by the recently reopened Eatons department store. Kids' clothing stores include **La Senza for Girls, Baby Gap, Gap Kids, Roots Kids,** and the **Disney Store.** There are several toy and gadget shops and over 50 restaurants and food outlets. Also located in the mall is a **National Tax Refund Centre,** where foreign and out-of-province visitors can get instant rebates on their purchases or hotel receipts.

The geese flying over the promenade toward the fountain, created by Canadian artist Michael Snow, are an artistic delight, and the glass elevator allows young riders an awesome view of three levels of the mall.

Strollers and wheelchairs are provided free of charge. Parking is free on Sundays and C$8 (US$5.30) for four hours with any purchase over C$25 (US$16.50); make sure to validate your ticket at the store. A better option is the subway—the Dundas and Queen subway stops allow direct access to either end of the mall.

If the over 285 shops and restaurants in the Eaton Centre aren't enough, you can meander through hundreds more via Toronto's underground shopping mecca, the PATH.   220 Yonge St. ✆ 416/598-8700. www.torontoeatoncentre.com. Subway: Dundas or Queen.

First Canadian Place   This mall offers more than 120 shops and restaurants, including **Baby Gap, HMV,** and **Adelaide Sports** and the noteworthy **UNICEF Card and Gift Store.**   100 King St. W. (at Bay St.). ✆ 416/862-8138. Subway: King.

Hazelton Lanes   For unabashed luxury shopping in trendy Yorkville, Hazelton Lanes is a must. There's not much for younger kids—**Jacadi** is the only children's store here—but your teens and tweens will adore the trendy clothing and accessory shops. A courtyard in the middle of the complex is a nice place to have a bite. Parking is expensive at C$3 (US$2) per half hour to a maximum of C$25 (US$16.50), but the first hour is free with a C$25 (US$16.50) purchase from one of the stores.   55 Avenue Rd. ✆ 416/968-8602. www.hazeltonlanes.com. Subway: Bay.

Queens Quay Terminal   This unique collection of shops is housed in a converted warehouse on the waterfront. A free shuttle bus runs from Union Station, or you can take the LRT from the Union subway stop. This is a great place to hunt for that special souvenir or gift. **Dollina's Dolls and Bears** and **Oh Yes! Toronto** are both housed here, along with an eclectic mix of stores selling fine art, jewelry, and apparel. Parking is free with a minimum C$50 (US$33) purchase, but is otherwise, like most downtown venues, ridiculously expensive at C$8 (US$5.30) per hour.   207 Queens Quay W. ✆ 416/203-0510. Subway: Union, then no. 509 streetcar.

Scarborough Town Centre   This is the largest mall in northeast Toronto and a great place to shop if you are staying in that end of the city. Most of the stores are similar to those in the Eaton Centre and include **Jacob Jr., Guess, Gap Kids,** and **Club Monaco Boys and Girls.**

When the kids tire of shopping you can leave them at Where Kids Play, an in-mall baby-sitting service that charges C$4 (US$2.65) per hour for a maximum of two hours. It has a good security system and provides movies, toys, snacks, and crafts, and will let you use their facilities if you need a place to nurse. © **416/296-0901.**

The mall also offers a lost child service and, for the directionally challenged, a lost car service. There are nursing rooms off the bathrooms. Strollers are complimentary and parking is free. 300 Borough Drive, Scarborough (between McCowan and Brimley rds). © **416/296-0296.** Subway: Scarborough Town Centre.

Yorkdale Shopping Centre   This is my girls' favorite place to shop. The Rainforest Cafe and the giant kids' section in the Indigo bookstore certainly are part of the draw, but the strollers shaped like racing cars and the meticulous cleanliness of this mall also help.

All of the usual kids' stores are here, including **Gap Kids, Jacob Jr.,** the **Disney Store, Benetton, Chickaboom, Club Monaco Boys and Girls, Gymboree,** and **Panda Shoes.** There are also some interesting gift, toy, and game shops. For precious but pricey gifts, try **Holt Renfrew.**

Strollers are provided free of charge, and if you've forgotten baby's diapers, the Customer Service Centre will be happy to provide them. Family change rooms are large and clean. The one located near the Rainforest Cafe includes both adult- and child-sized sinks and toilets. Private nursing stations are also located near the Rainforest Cafe and food court.

Parking is free and the Spadina subway line and commuter GO buses both have stops at the mall. 1 Yorkdale Rd. © **416/789-3261.** www.yorkdale.com. Subway: Yorkdale.

2 Shopping A to Z

ARTS & CRAFTS

Art Gallery of Ontario Gallery Shop   For young art lovers, this boutique has books, activity sets, craft supplies, and toys. Kids will love the AGO activity book, which is packed full of fun art and logic activities related to the gallery and the artists represented there. 317 Dundas St. W. © **416/979-6660.** Subway: St. Patrick, then 3 blocks west.

Beadworks   Beads from around the world are offered at this Beaches store, which also boasts worktables, tools, and friendly, helpful staff. 2154 Queen St. E. © **416/693-0780.** Subway: Queen, then any streetcar east.

Curry's   Everything for the budding artist, young or old, is here, along with fun craft kits for rainy days. 344 Queen St. W. © **416/260-2633.** Subway: Osgoode. 490 Yonge St. (north of College St.). © **416/967-6666.** Subway: College.

Grand & Toy   The Kid Office housed within this office supply store chain has some great stuff for children. Arts and crafts materials, including some neat kits, are the mainstays, but there are also the usual school supplies and a wonderful selection of educational games. 2300 Yonge St. (in the Yonge-Eglinton Centre). © **416/ 481-5181.** Subway: Eglinton.

The City Underground: PATH

Just over 100 years ago, Eatons department store built a tunnel that would take customers to a bargain center in the basement. Twenty-five years later, the Royal York Hotel built a tunnel that would allow its wealthy guests to meet their train connections at Union Station without having to brave the winter winds or summer sun. These tunnels would eventually lead to the creation of a virtual subterranean city in Toronto's downtown.

Today, residents of downtown Toronto can go to work, do their shopping, and find their entertainment without ever venturing above ground. The PATH system of tunnels covers 12 city blocks and links 52 office towers, 2 shopping centers, and 5 subway stations. More than 1,100 retail outlets and several hotels are housed along 6 miles of attractive, air-conditioned tunnels.

Because PATH was actually built as a series of separate tunnels by several downtown businesses over a long period, it lacks the uniformity of the street system above ground, but signage is frequent and prominent maps of the system are readily available (see map, chapter 2, p. 32).

Gwartzman's Canvas and Art Supplies   Although more for the serious artist, this store still has lots of goodies for younger artists. You'll find excellent prices on everything from paper to oils.   448 Spadina Ave. (just south of College St.). ✆ 416/922-5429. Subway: Spadina, then any streetcar south.

Loomis & Toles   Alongside an array of serious art supplies are some wonderful materials and crafts for young artists and for kids looking for something to do on the way home.   2056 Danforth Ave. ✆ 416/422-2443. Subway: Woodbine.

Sassy Bead Co.   Choose from the displayed jewelry or sit down at one of the worktables and make your own keepsake by choosing from the wide selection of beads and semiprecious stones.   2076 Yonge St. ✆ 416/488-7400. Subway: Davisville, then walk north on Yonge St.

BABY & PRESCHOOLER CLOTHES

A Joaninha   This kids' clothing store primarily stocks imports from Europe, including several styles from England's David Charge. You'll find a mix of formal and casual wear in sizes newborn to 16. Colors tend toward the cool and classic, many with beautiful embroidered details.   764 College St. ✆ 416/533-9356. Subway: Queen's Park, then any streetcar west.

Amore Children's Boutique   Specializing in infant wear from Italy and France, this boutique sells wonderful baptismal outfits that can be ordered from the on-site seamstress or bought off the rack. It also carries clothing for older children up to size 16.   1242 St. Clair Ave. W. ✆ 416/654-8117. Subway: St. Clair West, then any streetcar west.

Babes   Here you'll find children's clothing from newborn to size 16, including offerings from Columbia, Ocean Pacifica, Osh Kosh, and Non-Fiction. Both dressy and casual styles are stocked.   2116A Queen St. E. (in the Beaches). ✆ 416/699-6110. Subway: Queen, then any streetcar east.

Baby Gap   The sturdy, casual style of Gap and Gap Kids comes in the smallest of sizes, from newborn to 36 months. Gorgeous cotton sweaters, denim wear, and plenty of knits and cotton line the shelves. The staff here is noted for its friendliness and willingness to assist, and the store is well organized. 220 Yonge St. (in the Eaton Centre). © **416/591-0512.** Subway: Dundas or Queen. 3401 Dufferin St. (in Yorkdale Shopping Centre). © **416/256-1176.** Subway: Yorkdale. 100 King St. W. © **416/364-9200.** Subway: King.

Baby Guess   These cute and cuddly clothes come with the Guess sense of style. Many pretty patterns such as hearts and baby bottles in pastel colors decorate everything from baby dolls to fringe-bottomed pantsuits. 77 Bloor St. W. © **416/323-9913.** Subway: Bay. 409 Queen St. W. © **416/979-1594.** Subway: Osgoode. 3401 Dufferin St. (in Yorkdale Shopping Centre). © **416/781-8192.** Subway: Yorkdale.

Bon Lieu   European children's fashions from Baby Mini, I.K.K.S., and several Canadian lines share space with strollers and other baby accessories in this Yonge Street store. If you forget to pick up the matching socks for the outfit you bought baby, don't fret: They'll deliver anywhere in North America. 890 Yonge St. © **416/963-4322.** Subway: Yonge/Bloor, then walk 3 blocks north.

Cotton Basics   Kids love the soft feel of cotton, and parents like its durability. This Kensington Market store provides clothing that is 100% cotton in 11 solid colors and fairly basic styles, including T-shirts, jumpers, socks, and hats. Newborn to extra large sizes are stocked, so if you are interested in dressing like Junior you'll be able to find matching outfits. 16 Baldwin St. © **416/977-1959.** Subway: Spadina, then any streetcar south to Baldwin St.

Jolly Tots Children's Wear and Diapers   The name explains the whole concept: Clothes at this store are bright and cheerful and primarily for the toddler set. Commerce Court, 199 Bay St. (at King St.). © **416/363-0983.** Subway: King, then 2 blocks west.

Kid's Wardrobe   Designer Angela Marett sells some original clothing, primary special-occasion stuff for girls and boys. Marett says she ships quite a lot of merchandise to the United States, and, depending on the order, she can often have your purchases shipped by the end of the week. Some off-the-rack clothes are available. There is also a formal wear rental service, so if the kids came with only shorts and T-shirts in their bags, you can rent an outfit here for your night on the town. Shopping is by appointment. 1481 Queen St. E. © **416/778-6153.** Subway: Queen, then any streetcar east.

Rebecca's Special Kids   This Oshawa store is a little out of the way but well worth the drive for baby clothes and accessories for special-needs kids. The owner is a former registered nurse who worked with special-needs kids, and her line of made-to-order clothes is fantastic. 1461 Hall St., Oshawa. © **905/720-2923.**

Scribbles and Giggles   Small kids enjoy this bright, cheerful store with its clouds on the ceiling, and older kids will be thrilled with the great selection of funky casual wear in bold oranges and more muted khakis. The store carries Pickles, Crickets, Timmy Tom Tom, Frannie Flowers, and Magi in sizes ranging from 6 months to 16. 1348 Dundas St. W. © **416/536-7264.** Subway: Dundas West, then Dundas streetcar east to Lisgar St.

BOOKS

Another Story   This alternative bookstore specializes in multicultural books and has a good selection of used titles as well. There is a good children's section of more open-minded titles. 164 Danforth Ave. © **416/462-1104.** Subway: Broadview.

Bakka Science Fiction Bookstore   If anyone in your family is interested in science fiction or horror, this is the place to take them. Offerings include science fiction, horror books, and comics. The staff is well versed in the sci-fi genre and very willing to help. 598 Yonge St. ℂ 416/963-9993. Subway: Wellesley, then 1 block north.

Book City   The last major independent bookstore in the city, Book City has four locations to serve you. Excellently stocked with hardcover and paperback fiction and non-fiction, there are also great bargains and a small but sophisticated magazine collection focusing on art and left-wing politics. There is a solid section for children and young readers. 501 Bloor St. W. ℂ 416/961-4496. Subway: Spadina. 348 Danforth Ave. ℂ 416/469-9997. Subway: Chester. 2350 Bloor St. W. ℂ 416/766-9412. Subway: Jane. 1950 Queen St. E. ℂ 416/698-1444. Streetcar: any Queen St. E. streetcar to Woodbine Ave.

Chapters   This mega bookstore has three floors of reading material. The kids' section is extensive and the staff is very knowledgeable. The store tends to concentrate on bestsellers and new releases, but there are some great finds and the business and travel sections are also well stocked. Watch for the bargain tables scattered throughout the store, especially the one in the kids' section. Then, dip into your purchases while enjoying a latte at Starbucks Coffee, located in most stores. 110 Bloor St. W. ℂ 416/920-9299. Subway: Bay, then 1 block west. 142 John St. ℂ 416/595-7349. Subway: Osgoode, then walk west to John St. 2400 Yonge St. ℂ 416/761-9773. Subway: Eglinton, then 2 blocks north.

The Constant Reader Books for Children   This shop is a great source for children's books of all descriptions; it carries a good selection of used books as well. 111 Harbord St. ℂ 416/972-0661. Subway: Spadina, then walk south.

Indigo   Canada's own megastore has an extensive array of books and magazines and a great kids' department where kids can enjoy story hours, try out computer games, and play a game of checkers at the giant board. There are some good deals to be found in the bargain bins located around the store. Book browsing can be thirsty work, and the Indigo Café on the second floor of most locations offers a great selection of fruit drinks, specialty coffees, sweet treats, and sandwiches. Most locations are open until 11pm Sunday through Wednesday and 12am Thursday through Saturday. 3401 Dufferin St. (in Yorkdale Shopping Centre). ℂ 416/781-6660. Subway: Yorkdale. 55 Bloor St. W. (in the Manulife Centre). ℂ 416/925-3536. Subway: Bay. 220 Yonge St. (in the Eaton Centre). ℂ 416/591-3622. Subway: Dundas or Queen. 2300 Yonge St. (in the Yonge-Eglinton Centre). ℂ 416/544-0049. Subway: Eglinton.

The Lion, the Witch and the Wardrobe   Aslan, the lion, guards the entrance to this treasure trove of children's books, toys, puzzles, and games. Parents can browse the adult bestseller section while the kids make their selections. 888 Eglinton Ave. W. ℂ 416/785-9177. Subway: Eglinton, then any bus west.

Mabel's Fables   This kids-only bookstore stocks infant to young adult titles. Author readings and story hours are often scheduled. 662 Mount Pleasant Rd. ℂ 416/233-8830. Subway: Eglinton, then no. 34 bus east to Mount Pleasant.

Nicholas Hoare   Remember the professor's library in *My Fair Lady*? This bookstore replicates that library right down to the ladders on wheels for reaching the uppermost shelves. Comfortable couches and a fireplace make this a cozy place to spend a rainy afternoon; young browsers can curl up on the pint-sized seats in the children's section. 45 Front St. E. ℂ 416/777-2665. Subway: Union, then walk 3 blocks east.

ParentBooks   This is the place to find books for moms, dads, caregivers, and educators on almost any parenting topic imaginable. 201 Harbord St. ✆ **416/537-8334**. Subway: Spadina, then walk south.

The World's Biggest Bookstore   The first book superstore in Canada was recently bought by Chapters, which in turn was bought by Indigo. Although the store is rather rundown and lacks the coffee shop and comfy seating that have become standard fare in newer book superstores, over 150,000 volumes line its shelves. The vast children's section includes a number of hard-to-find books, but it's the magazine section that draws me. A quarter of the bottom floor is devoted to magazines, so if someone publishes it, somewhere in the world, you'll likely find it here. 20 Edward St. ✆ **416/977-7009**. Subway: Dundas, then walk 1 block north.

CANDY, CHOCOLATE & SWEETS

Rocky Mountain Chocolate Factory   According to my daughters, the best fudge in the city is made at this store. 100 King St. W. (in First Canadian Place). ✆ **416/861-2475**. Subway: King. 2614 Yonge St. ✆ **416/482-1890**. Subway: Eglinton.

Suckers Candy Co.   This large Greektown store is usually packed with sweets lovers of all ages. You'll find a great selection of candy, with lots of old favorites such as Pez and Jelly Belly, and a cheerful if somewhat overwhelmed staff. 450 Danforth Ave. ✆ **416/405-8946**. Subway: Chester.

Sugar Mountain   If you want your kids to try the Pez or Pink Elephant Candy Popcorn you loved as child, bring them here. Huge bins contain bulk candy of every description in this lively and loud store. 1920 Queen St. E. (in the Beaches). ✆ **416/690-7998**. 320 Richmond St. W. ✆ **416/204-9544**. Subway: Osgoode, then walk west to John St. 571 Queen St. W. ✆ **416/861-1405**. Subway: Osgoode, then any streetcar west. 2525 Yonge St. ✆ **416/486-3694**. Subway: Eglinton, then walk 4 blocks north. 2299 Yonge St. (at Eglinton Ave.) ✆ **416/486-9321**. Subway: Eglinton.

Sugar Shack   We go here primarily for the awesome Jelly Belly selection, but there are heaps of other sweets. Buy a handful of the small wrapped suckers in various flavors—they're great for handing out to the kids when they have to wait in lineups. 322 King St. W. ✆ **416/435-2507**. Subway: King, then 3 blocks west.

Sugar Sugar Candy Store   The website, www.nutrientfreezone.com, pretty much says it all. You'll find a great selection of sweet stuff as well as small toys and collectibles. 515 St. Clair Ave. W. (at Bathurst St.). ✆ **416/531-1555**. Subway: St. Clair West.

The Town Dump   Remember Pop Rocks—those candies that popped like firecrackers when you put them in your mouth? I loved them and recently introduced my kids to them at this retro candy and memorabilia store celebrating the sixties, seventies, and eighties. 110 Eglinton Ave. E. ✆ **416/483-8383**. Subway: Eglinton. 2239A Bloor St. W. ✆ **416/604-0022**. Subway: Runnymede.

COMIC BOOKS/SPORTS CARDS

Dragon Lady Comic Shop   Young collectors are sure to find something they need amid the shelves and boxes piled high with new and used comics of all descriptions. Plenty of role-playing games are also available. 609 College St. (between Bathurst St. and Ossington Ave.). ✆ **416/536-7460**. Subway: Queen's Park, then any streetcar west.

Excalibur Comics   There are often good finds at this small but well-stocked comic book store. A good selection of popular role-playing games will compete for your kids' attention. 3030 Bloor St. W. ✆ **416/236-3553**. Subway: Royal York.

Hairy Tarantula Comics and Cards *(Finds)*   Serious collectors will be awestruck by the wide assortment of comics and cards. Fans of role-playing games can try out a new game or play their favorite one in the store's game room. 354A Yonge St. (at Gerrard St.). ℂ **416/596-8002.** Subway: Dundas, then 2 blocks north.

Paradise Comics   Rows and rows of both hard-to-find and popular comics fill the shelves of this small Yonge Street store. There's also a wide selection of limited edition figurines and action figures. 3278 Yonge St. ℂ **416/487-9807.** Subway: Lawrence.

Sci-Fi World   Comics are only a small part of what this north end store has to offer. Everything science fiction can be found here, including books, videos, memorabilia, and an excellent selection of computer games. 1600 Steeles Ave. W. ℂ **905/738-4348.** Subway: Downsview, then Dufferin bus north.

The Silver Snail   At this shrine to popular culture you can find almost anything comic-related from comic books to posters and collectible toys. 367 Queen St. W. ℂ **416/593-0889.** Subway: Osgoode.

Yesterday's Heroes   This store divides its offerings into a section for serious comic book collectors and a section for those interested in a quick read. This store is also well known for its collection of *Star Wars* merchandise and its assortment of collectible action figures and play sets. 742 Bathurst Ave. ℂ **416/533-9800.** Subway: Bathurst, then 1 block south.

CONSIGNMENT & OUTLET CLOTHING STORES

Bargains Group Ltd.   Located next to Yorkdale Shopping Centre, this large store stocks primarily one-of-a-kind samples and ends of lines at incredibly low prices. Sizes range from newborn to adult. Closed on weekends. 153 Bridgeland Ave. ℂ **416/785-5655.** Subway: Yorkdale.

Bean Sprouts *(Finds)*   Most nearly new stores tend to be overcrowded and disorganized, but this one is a delight to shop in. Staff offers cookies to your little ones, and the store is well lit and organized. The kids can have fun in the playroom while you look through the wide selection of gently used designer duds in sizes newborn to 16. They also carry accessories such as toys and small equipment. 616 Mount Pleasant Rd. ℂ **416/932-3727.** Subway: Eglinton, then no. 34 bus east to Mount Pleasant.

OK Kids   It's quite a hike from the city, but this discount store in Mississauga's Dixie Outlet Mall has excellent savings on casual clothes for kids aged 3 months to 12 years. Stock changes every two weeks so selections and savings vary widely. 1250 South Service Rd., Mississauga. ℂ **905/274-4779.** By car: Gardiner Expressway/Queen Elizabeth Way (QEW) west to Dixie Rd. exit. Turn left, follow Dixie Rd. south to South Service Rd.

Previously Loved Designer Kids   Gently used traditional and funky designer clothes are displayed alongside new designer duds at greatly reduced prices. 986 Bathurst St. ℂ **416/516-3613.** Subway: Bathurst, then walk 3 blocks north.

Siblings   This Dixie Outlet Mall store concentrates on great bargains primarily for girls aged 7 to 16. You'll find mostly trendy casual wear such as cargo pants, jeans, and T-shirts. As in most outlet stores, the stock changes frequently. 1250 South Service Rd., Mississauga. ℂ **905/274-2374.** By car: Gardiner Expressway/Queen Elizabeth Way (QEW) west to Dixie Rd. exit. Turn left, follow Dixie Rd. south to South Service Rd.

Spotlight Kids Manufacturers Outlet *(Value)*   If you're staying uptown or have access to a car, you may want to check out the greatly reduced prices on Frannie Flowers and Timmy Tom Tom and occasionally some Scribbles stuff.

Sizes range from 6 months to size 10. Both previous- and current-season items are stocked, many at 60% off retail price. We found some gorgeous cotton knit shorts and tops for C$8 (US$5.30) that were selling elsewhere in the city for C$27.95 (US$18.45). West Beaver Creek, Unit 15, Richmond Hill. ℅ 905/882-1113. By car: Take Hwy. 7 to Leslie St.

Twice as Nice This brightly lit store has a good selection of gently used kids' clothes, toys, and furniture. 683 St. Clair Ave. W. ℅ 416/656-9969. Subway: St. Clair West, then any streetcar west.

DANCEWEAR/COSTUMES
Dancewear Centre From ballroom to ballet, this store has everything your little dancer will need, including helpful and knowledgeable staff. 530 Wilson Ave. (just past Bathurst St.). ℅ 416/630-2292. Subway: York Mills, then Wilson bus west.

Kids Costumes and Dancewear You'll find everything your budding actor might need for dressing the part, plus a good selection of dance and skating apparel. 151 Manor Rd. E. ℅ 416/484-1940. Subway: Eglinton, then walk south to Manor Rd.

Malabar Your budding movie star will love this cool store. A great collection of costumes and accessories is complemented with some interesting gift and gag items. There is also a great selection of dancewear. 14 McCaul St. ℅ 416/598-2581. Subway: Osgoode, then 2 blocks west.

Shoe Room at the National Ballet School This is the place to shop for pointe shoes and a beautiful array of dancewear for your amateur or professional ballerina. The expert staff is very willing to assist. 404 Jarvis St. ℅ 416/964-5100. Subway: Wellesley, then walk east to Jarvis St.

DEPARTMENT STORES
The Bay Established in 1670, this is Canada's oldest retail company. Originally known for its beaver hats, the modern department store stocks designer wear, giftware, housewares, and toys, and has a good children's section. 2 Bloor St. E. (Hudson's Bay Centre). ℅ 416/972-3333. Subway: Yonge/Bloor. 176 Yonge St. ℅ 416/861-9111. Subway: Queen.

Eatons This Toronto institution was recently relaunched after a brief closure with sparkling new decor and incredibly attentive and knowledgeable staff. You'll find exclusive designer lines, jewelry, appliances, and kids' clothes and toys at numerous locations across the city. The flagship store anchors the Eaton Centre. 220 Yonge St. (Eaton Centre). ℅ 416/343-2111. Subway: Dundas. 3401 Dufferin St. (in Yorkdale Shopping Centre). ℅ 416/783-1105. Subway: Yorkdale.

Holt Renfrew With several locations in the city, this upscale department store sells items you simply can't find anywhere else. Couture lines and high-end clothing and housewares are the mainstays, but this is also the place to go for neat gifts. It's worth browsing even if you can't afford to buy. 50 Bloor St. W. ℅ 416/922-2333. Subway: Bay. 3401 Dufferin St. (in Yorkdale Shopping Centre). ℅ 416/789-5377. Subway: Yorkdale.

Sears Reasonable prices and a large selection of merchandise are the trademarks of this retail chain. 3401 Dufferin St. (in Yorkdale Shopping Centre). ℅ 416/789-1105. Subway: Yorkdale.

Value **Honest Ed's**

Honest Ed's is one of those rare retail establishments that is also a tourist attraction. You'll have no trouble spotting this store—signs with corny slogans and flashing lights decorate every inch of the building's exterior. "Welcome," the entrance sign reads, "Don't faint at our low prices, there's no place to lie down." Slapstick sales tactics aside, this 160,000-square-foot warehouse store is a true bargain hunter's delight—it's stocked to the rafters with irresistible deals on food, pharmaceuticals, clothes, toys, electronics, and housewares. We found some great souvenir T-shirts for C$5.99 (US$3.95). There is even a resident discount dentist and hair salon. When the kids get tired of bargain hunting or people-watching, they'll find respite in the kiddie playland.

This is also a fun place to simply wander around. Beside the neon-signed department store is **Mirvish Village,** a charming collection of shops and fine restaurants on tree-lined Markham Street. 581 Bloor St. W. (© **416/537-1574.** Subway: Bathurst.

DOLLS & DOLLHOUSES

Carriage Trade Dolls   The emphasis here is on collectibles but doll lovers of all kinds will find something in this specialty store.   584 Mount Pleasant Rd. (© **416/481-1639.** Subway: Eglinton, then no. 34 bus east to Mount Pleasant.

Dollina   The hundreds of dolls, dollhouses, stuffed animals, and bears artfully displayed in this Harbourfront store tempt both the young and the young at heart.   207 Queens Quay W. (© **416/203-0576.** Subway: Union, then no. 509 streetcar.

Harrison Doll Houses   This store is worth the drive from the city for serious dollhouse aficionados. In addition to its wide variety of dollhouses, the owners also sell collector-quality miniatures and teddy bears.   72 Woodhaven Park Dr. (at Lakeshore Rd.), Oakville. (© **905/827-0128.** By car: QEW west to Third Line exit, drive south and turn east on Lakeshore Rd.

Little Dollhouse Company   Everything you might need for your dollhouse, including working lights and play food, can be bought here along with a line of whimsical dollhouses exclusive to this store.   617 Mount Pleasant Rd. (© **416/489-7180.** Subway: Eglinton, then no. 34 bus east to Mount Pleasant.

DRUGSTORES

Like doughnut shops, there seems to be a drugstore on almost every corner in Toronto. Prices don't vary greatly, although the selection is probably better in larger chain stores. Most offer free delivery within the city; many are open until midnight and several are open 24 hours.

Guardian Drugs   264 Bloor St. W. (© **416/922-2156.** 658 Danforth Ave. (© **416/465-7610.**

IDA   310 Queen St. E. (© **416/363-3011.** 670 Bloor St. W. (© **416/530-0554.** 1901 Yonge St. (© **416/483-3003.** 235 Danforth Ave. (© **416/778-7780.**

Main Drug Mart   254 Queens Quay W. (© **416/260-2766.** 844 Bathurst St. (© **416/537-1900.**

Pharma Plus Drugmart 63 Wellesley St. E. ✆ **416/924-7769** (open until midnight). Commerce Court, 199 Bay St. ✆ **416/364-7824**. 2300 Yonge St. (in the Yonge-Eglinton Centre). ✆ **416/484-6750** (open until midnight).

Shopper's Drug Mart 700 Bay St. ✆ **416/979-2424** (open 24 hours). 523 St. Clair Ave. W. ✆ **416/538-1155** (open 24 hours). 2345 Yonge St. (north of Eglinton) ✆ **416/487-5411** (open 24 hours). 970 Queen St. E. ✆ **416/462-0062**.

⟮*Finds*⟯ Cool Shops

Christmas on the Beach It's Christmas year-round at this small, cheery store in the Beaches. A variety of spirit-raising ornaments, decorations, and seasonal CDs are displayed. This is the place to look for new holiday decorating ideas or to find those ornaments on your grandparents' tree you remember falling in love with.
1891 Queen St. E. ✆ **416/698-0682**. Subway: Queen, then any streetcar east.

Ice Located across the street from the Four Seasons Hotel, this funky shop stocks novel gifts and souvenirs, from red slippers like Dorothy's in *The Wizard of Oz* to baby sweaters and designer jewelry.
163 Cumberland St. ✆ **416/964-6751**. Subway: Bay.

Legends of the Game Just for sports fans, this shop carries hockey, basketball, baseball, and sports legend memorabilia. There is an impressive selection of team jerseys, cards, and other souvenirs.
322A King St. W. ✆ **416/971-8848**. Subway: King, then any streetcar west.

Lush This sweet-smelling shop is an enormous favorite with my girls, who usually gravitate to the bins of bath bombs along the back wall. Soaps are cut from huge slabs, and the wide variety of shampoos and lotion will entice. The only drawback is that you'll have a tough time convincing your kids to leave.
116 Cumberland St. ✆ **416/960-5874**. Subway: Bay. 312 Queen St. W. ✆ **416/599-5874**. Subway: Osgoode.

Oh Yes! Toronto This gift shop sells T-shirts, sweatshirts, and accessories, all with a Toronto theme. The first store opened on the waterfront selling its distinctive line of souvenirs to the Harbourfront crowd. You'll find something for everyone on your list here, from your toddler nephew to Grandma.
207 Queens Quay W. ✆ **416/203-0607**. Subway: Union, then no. 509 streetcar. 101 Yorkville Ave. ✆ **416/924-7198**. Subway: Bay. 218 Yonge St. (in the Eaton Centre). ✆ **416/593-6749**. Subway: Dundas or Queen.

Retro Fun This retail ode to decades gone by specializes in fabulous stuff from the fifties to the future. If it's fun, it's here—you'll find everything from seventies-era candy to *Lone Ranger* and *Charlie's Angels* memorabilia. Remember *Six Million Dollar Man*, *Roy Rogers*, *Bionic Woman*, and *Partridge Family* lunch boxes? They're all here, along with Beatles and KISS memorabilia and your favorite old board games like Operation and Emergency. My kids were most impressed with the original *Charlie's Angels* pics: "Look at all that hair!" And then there were the Pet Rocks: "Okay, Mom, but what do they do?"
130 Cumberland St. ✆ **416/968-7771**. Subway: Bay.

Storyville If you've ever wanted to turn back time, this is the place to go. A monument to pop culture, this Beaches store stocks clocks that run backward, wigs that grow like Chia Pets, lava lamps, and inflatable radios. They also have their own clothing line in child and adult sizes, including shirts with a choice of 500 button styles and other loungewear-type items. 1923 Queen St. E. ✆ 416/698-5406. Subway: Queen, then any streetcar east.

Three Dog Bakery If the kids are looking for something to bring home to Rover, you'll want to check out this store—offerings include toys, special baked goods, and a great selection of gift boxes. The Knead and Read Sleepy Dog Boxer is a gift box that claims to encourage quality time between your kids and their furry friends. It contains dog biscuit mix and a bone-shaped rolling pin, assorted goodies, and a goodnight book for the kids to read to their dog, *Amazing Gracie: A Dog's Tale*. 2014 Queen St. E. ✆ 416/693-3364. Subway: Queen, then any streetcar east.

ELECTRONICS

Bay Bloor Radio This 13,000-square-foot store carries all of the latest and best audio equipment, from portable units to complete in-home entertainment systems. 55 Bloor St. (in the Manulife Centre). ✆ 416/967-1122. Subway: Bay.

CDROMSTORE.COM This store stocks an amazing selection of software and games for both Macs and PCs. 345 Danforth Ave. ✆ 416/778-4048. Subway: Chester.

Replay Electronics Items returned to other retail outlets are sold at this store. Everything is new and they don't sell damaged or opened merchandise. The prices on everything from big-screen TVs to pagers are hard to beat. 1120 The Queensway (at Islington Ave.). ✆ 416/251-9096. Subway: Islington.

EVERYDAY CLOTHING

Benetton This global store is best known for its colorful ads featuring the many faces of humankind. They stock some wonderful clothes for youngsters, including selections from the Benetton, Sisley, and 0 to 12 lines. 102 Bloor St. W. ✆ 416/968-1611. Subway: Bay. 3401 Dufferin St. (in Yorkdale Shopping Centre). ✆ 416/781-9377. Subway: Yorkdale.

Bluenotes Created by Canadian jeans wear maker and retailer Thrifty's, this store carries only Bluenotes brand wear. Reasonable prices and great style abound in this shop on trendy Queen Street West. 349 Queen St. W. ✆ 416/593-2681. Subway: Osgoode.

Chateauworks Reasonable prices and stylish offerings entice the young and hip to this store. With everything from seventies spinoffs to Britney Spears–type togs, this store is sure to have something you and the kids can agree on. 340 Queen St. W. ✆ 416/971-9314. Subway: Osgoode.

Chickaboom This shop sells funky, colorful clothes for girls in sizes 8 to 14, under both their own and the Hollywood label. Stationery, jewelry, accessories, and gift items are also stocked. 3401 Dufferin St. (in Yorkdale Shopping Centre). ✆ 416/784-5262. Subway: Yorkdale.

Club Monaco Girls & Boys   This originally Canadian company sells its own line of cool, casual clothing in neutral colors, primarily for tweens and teens. They've recently launched in the United States, and their U.S. and Canadian online stores will soon be up and running. 157 Bloor St. W. (at Avenue Rd.). ✆ 416/491-8837. Subway: Bay. 403 Queen St. W. ✆ 416/979-5633. Subway: Osgoode. 3401 Dufferin St. (in Yorkdale Shopping Centre). ✆ 416/782-4428. Subway: Yorkdale. 1 Dundas St. W. (in the Eaton Centre). ✆ 416/573-7299. Subway: Dundas.

Gap Kids   With 500 stores worldwide, this younger version of the hip Gap retail chain is clearly doing the right thing. Jeans made to fit small bodies, cool styles, and attentive service geared to young shoppers make Gap Kids a great place to shop. The staff is skilled in picking out clothes that look good on your hard-to-fit child, so take them up on their offers of assistance. Clothes range from traditional jeans wear and Oxford shirts to more trendy seasonal stuff, in sizes 2 to 12. 100 King St. W. (in First Canadian Place). ✆ 416/364-9200. Subway: King. 220 Yonge Street (in the Eaton Centre). ✆ 416/591-0512. Subway: Dundas or Queen. 80 Bloor St. W. ✆ 416/515-0668. Subway: Bay. 3401 Dufferin Street (in Yorkdale Shopping Centre). ✆ 416/783-2995. Subway: Yorkdale.

Guess Kids   Classic Guess styles come in kid sizes. Girls' fashions include flower child and raver styles in bright tropical colors. Your girls will love the jeans with flower patches and pretty halter dresses, as well as the great selection of matching jewelry and handbags. Boys can select cargo pants, jeans, and T-shirts from several style groups, including Island Boy and the *Survivor*-inspired Tribal style. 77 Bloor St. W. ✆ 416/323-9913. Subway: Yonge/Bloor. 409 Queen St. W. ✆ 416/979-1594. Subway: Osgoode. 3401 Dufferin St. (in Yorkdale Shopping Centre). ✆ 416/781-8192. Subway: Yorkdale.

Gymboree   True to its name, this chain store stocks a lot of stretchy, comfortable play clothes in bright solids and patterns; sizes range from toddler to size 7. The entire collection of sturdy shirts, shorts, and other playwear is designed for mixing and matching, so the same color patterns generally are found throughout the store. We found some colorful dress and legging sets for our 4- and 6-year-olds. 220 Yonge St. (in the Eaton Centre). ✆ 416/260-2082. Subway: Dundas or Queen.

Jacob Jr.   This is style-laden attire primarily for the preteen and teen set, in boys' and girls' sizes 8 to16. 3401 Dufferin St. (in Yorkdale Shopping Centre). ✆ 416/780-0984. Subway: Yorkdale.

Kiddy Kidswear   Here you'll find fashionable clothes for babies through size 14, featuring some Asian designs in addition to more standard fare from Quebec and the United States. Colors are bright and snazzy. 20 Dundas St. W. (in Atrium on Bay). ✆ 416/506-9950. Subway: Dundas.

Kids, Cats and Dogs   Casual and comfortable kids' clothing, some sporting a cat or dog motif, is the mainstay of this store. Labels include DKNY, Ralph Lauren, and Nonfiction in both kid and adult sizes. 508 Eglinton St. W. ✆ 416/484-1844. Subway: Eglinton.

Kid's Turf   New York designer streetwear and other clothes such as Baby Adidas are sold at up to 25% off. Sizes range from newborn to young adult. 204 Augusta Ave. ✆ 416/598-5004. Subway: St. Patrick, then any streetcar west.

Kingly   This store sets out to prove that boys' wear can be funky and fashionable—and they're right! You'll also find girls' wear and a small selection of toys. 922 Queen St. W. ✆ 416/536-2601. Subway: Osgoode, then any streetcar west.

La Senza for Girls   Raver wannabes will love this store, where bright colors, bell-bottoms, and flowers rule. Separates come in a variety of styles and fabrics for girls aged 7 to 14. There's also some stuff for younger girls—my 6-year-old picked up a bright red vinyl raincoat for C$25 (US$16.50). 218 Yonge St. (in the Eaton Centre). ℂ **416/204-9396.** Subway: Dundas or Queen.

Little Ones Fashions   If your toddlers or preteens eschew Kmart togs in favor of something more exclusive, this is the place to take them. Domestic and European designer clothing, footwear, and accessories for newborns to preteens can be found at this huge store. 372 Eglinton Ave. W. ℂ **416/483-5989.** Subway: Eglinton, then 4 blocks west.

Lunatic Fringe   My preteens love the funky clothes, and the indoor basketball court is also pretty cool. This store is heavy on retro gear, and there are many items for the surfer girl look as well. 306 Eglinton Ave. W. ℂ **416/485-8789.** Subway: Eglinton, then 3 blocks west.

Popi   The store's name and lollipop-themed sign remind me of clowns, and the clothes here do tend toward the colorful and loud. However, they are definitely cute and despite the high-fashion looks the prices are excellent. There's a lot of stuff for babies and toddlers, including beautiful jumpsuits, rattles, and toys. The store outfits newborns to 8-year-olds, but my more trend-conscious, anti-cute older children weren't satisfied by the selection. Mom and the younger sisters loved it, though. 218 Yonge St. (in the Eaton Centre). ℂ **416/977-1426.** Subway: Dundas or Queen.

Rainmakers   Parasol hats are the main attraction for my kids, but this rainy day store stocks everything from rain slickers to umbrellas featuring cartoon characters. 207 Queens Quay W. ℂ **416/203-7246.** Subway: Union, then no. 509 streetcar.

Roots Kids   Kids' clothes in this Canadian chain are divided into fashions for babies (to age 2), kids (ages 2 to 8), and youths (ages 10 to 14). The selection for all age groups is excellent and concentrates on comfortable athletic wear in solid colors such as navy and, of course, Canadian red. All three sections carry the kind of clothes boys want: stylish and comfortable. You'll find lots of polo, T-, and crew shirts in cozy fleece and cotton. There are also some great selections for girls from T-shirts to cargo pants. With their DJs, geometric ceilings, and glass walls, the stores are pretty cool and have won a number of retail design awards. There are numerous branches downtown, as well as in the major malls. 181 Bay St. (in BCE Place). ℂ **416/364-0582.** Subway: Union. 220 Yonge St. (in the Eaton Centre). ℂ **416/593-9640.** Subway: Dundas or Queen. 3401 Dufferin St. (in Yorkdale Shopping Centre). ℂ **416/783-3371.** Subway: Yorkdale.

Snug   This store is well stocked with brand-name apparel for newborns to teens and includes everything from hand-knit sweaters for winter to flotation devices for summer. There are even some items here for Mom. 348 Danforth Ave. ℂ **416/463-6133.** Subway: Chester.

FASHIONS FOR KIDS

Floriane   In this classic children's retail chain store from France, you'll find tailored and functional clothes in traditional colors. Many of the clothes feature cartoon characters such as Babar and Donald Duck. Sizes start at newborn and run to age 12. 38 Avenue Rd. ℂ **416/920-6367.** Subway: Bay.

Jacadi   This selection of children's cotton and knits is imported primarily from France. Navy, red, and beige tones provide a bit of relief from the loud colors dominating other upscale children's stores. 55 Avenue Rd. (in Hazelton Lanes). ℂ **416/923-1717.** Subway: Bay.

Kid's Wardrobe   Looking for something for that wedding next summer? This store specializes in custom-made formal wear but also stocks a wide range of Canadian-made everyday wear. Shopping is by appointment.   1481 Queen St. E. © 416/778-6153. Subway: Queen, then any streetcar east.

Lovechild Children's Clothing   Kids who like to stand out from the crowd will love these designs by Jacqueline McCormack.   2523 Yonge St. © **416/486-4746.** Subway: Eglinton.

Maison Vali   Peruse the collection of designer fashions, with everything from pretty party dresses to cotton play togs and bright sundresses in sizes from toddler to age 7.   112 Cumberland St. © **416/923-3117.** Subway: Bay.

Misdemeanors   This is funky kids' wear from designer Pam Chorley, who also runs an equally stylish shop for adults, Fashion Crimes, right across the street.   322½ Queen St. W. © **416/351-8758.** Subway: Osgoode.

(Finds Bloor West Village

Tired of being cooped up in a mall? Head to Bloor West Village, a strip of shops, cafes, and fruit markets on Bloor Street West between Jane Street and Runnymede Avenue. This area is popular with the stroller crowd, not only the young families who live on the tree-lined side streets but also those who come to browse the great assortment of kids' stores.

Get off the subway at Jane station and pick up some breakfast at the **Coffee Tree Roastery,** 2412 Bloor St. W. (© **416/767-1077**). Sample the berry-packed scones and muffins and grab a cup of coffee—the beans are roasted on the premises. Walk east to **Simply Kids,** 2400 Bloor St. W. (© **416/762-5437**), where your kids can pick out a Pez dispenser and a grab bag of candy. The store also sells its own line of kids' clothing and some small toys, including ever-popular water pistols.

Mom will want to stop into **Jolanta Interiors,** 2368 Bloor St. W. (© **416/762-9638**), a kitchen gadget and glassware shop. On the next block, **Book City,** 2350 Bloor St. W. (© **416/766-9412**), has an excellent children's corner. **Roots Kids,** 2326 Bloor St. W. (© **416/763-1502**), sells casual kids' wear in sizes newborn to 14.

Pick up some golf shirts for Dad at **Down in the Village** men's casual wear, 2310 Bloor St. W. (© **416/766-6223**), then turn onto Durie Street, where you'll find **The Clothes Pony,** 262 Durie St. (© **416/762-3311**), which has designer European duds in sizes newborn to 16.

Back on Bloor Street, let your preteens and teens loose in **Animation,** 2266 Bloor St. W. (© **416/767-5234**), where they'll find hip clothing, shoes, sunglasses, and jewelry at reasonable prices. **La Cache,** next door at 2264 Bloor St. W. (© **416/760-7592**), sells linens in bright Provençal patterns, as well as cotton print dresses for little girls and moms.

Pick up some picnic supplies from the vast selection of salads at **Max's Market,** 2299 Bloor St. W. (© **416/766-6362**), along with a sweet treat from one of the many European pastry shops in the area, then walk or take the subway east to **High Park** for lunch on the grass.

Moka Designs   These couture fashions for the younger set are shown by appointment only.   1448 Dundas St. W. (near Dufferin St.). ⓒ **416/588-6779.** Subway: Dundas West, then Dundas streetcar east.

Tutto Chicco   Upscale kids' clothing from Italy is this store's specialty. 138 Cumberland St. ⓒ **416/922-0873.** Subway: Bay.

GAMES & HOBBIES

Crossed Swords   A huge collection of historical and sci-fi miniatures artfully displayed make this a fun shop for anyone to visit, but for serious game players this store has everything from paints and other restoration materials to a wide selection of board and role-playing games.   722 Annette St. ⓒ **416/604-9410.** Subway: Jane, then Annette bus.

The Game Shack   This is a great shop for young computer gamers. A wide selection of new and used computer games, video games, DVDs, and gaming cards are available, and you can trade in the games your kids don't use anymore. Atrium on Bay. ⓒ **416/351-7065.** Subway: Dundas.

The Games Workshop   This store sells plenty of adventure and war games and has a great room for trying out old and new favorites.   218 Yonge St. ⓒ **416/977-4683.** Subway: Queen.

Mind Games   Whether the kids are into a game of Risk or a session of Dungeons and Dragons, you'll find it here. This shop concentrates on stocking a perfect mix of classic and new board and role-playing games.   260 Yonge St. (in the Eaton Centre). ⓒ **416/977-8994.** Subway: Dundas or Queen.

The Sentry Models and Hobbies   Whether your kids are into building K'nex or wooden ship models, this store has it. As the name suggests, they also stock a huge assortment of military and historical miniatures.   1633 Bayview Ave. ⓒ **416/480-1687.** Subway: Eglinton, then any bus east.

ⓘ Tips Finding a Sitter

Kids tend to tire of shopping far more quickly than adults do. If you're shopping downtown, consider taking the kids to the **Sheraton Centre** for a few hours of pure playtime while you snap up a few more purchases. The Sheraton's Kid's Centre, managed by **Where Kids Play,** provides short-term bonded babysitting service for guests and walk-in clients in a well-equipped playroom. Kids are provided with snacks and parents are provided with pagers. The cost is C$8 (US$5.30) per hour for a maximum of 4 hours. 123 Queen St. W. ⓒ **416/361-1000.**

GIFTS & SOUVENIRS

Flatiron Department Store   This department/gift store has plenty of souvenir stuff that kids like, as well as a Christmas section in the back that impresses small fry. Take a few minutes while you're here to tour the fanciful, wedge-shaped building across the street, straddling the intersection of Front and Church streets, and don't miss the trompe l'oeil painting on the back—it gives the illusion of windows that were tacked up and are now falling down.   51 Front St. ⓒ **416/365-1506.** Subway: Union.

Geoasis It's not really a kids' place, but it's still worth a mention because it has a wonderful collection of semiprecious stones. Giftware includes jade and Inuit carvings, jewelry, and some interesting blown glass from Romania. 100 King St. W. (in First Canadian Place). ☎ 416/366-7070. www.geoasis.com. Subway: King.

Grimm Fans of the famous British wizard will love the huge collection of Harry Potter memorabilia at this Beaches store. Other selections include unique locally designed T-shirts as well as souvenirs and gifts. 1918A Queen St. E. ☎ 416/686-6870. www.grimminc.com. Subway: Queen, then any streetcar east.

Mr. Music Box All things musical, from singing birds to automata watches, are stocked here. Kids love this place, but with so many breakables it may not be the best spot to take toddlers. 207 Queens Quay W. ☎ 416/203-0381. Subway: Union, then no. 509 streetcar.

Rafters This store in the Hudson's Bay Centre offers an array of tasteful gifts and souvenirs, most with a Canadian theme. You'll find the usual goods—pure Canadian maple syrup, nature CDs, and works by well-known Canadian artists—as well as a large selection of Bradford Exchange pieces, Precious Moments figurines, and Beanie Babies. 20 Bloor St. E. (in the Hudson's Bay Centre). ☎ 416/975-1892. Subway: Yonge/Bloor.

The Souvenir Market Everything Canadian, from maple syrup to moose, is sold in this market shop. Roots clothing, T-shirts, jewelry, and toys round out the souvenir offerings. 91 Front St. E. (in St. Lawrence Market). ☎ 416/203-0033. Subway: Union.

UNICEF Card and Gift Store The extensive collection of Canadian-designed cards for every occasion are the focus here, but there is also an awesome array of children's games and toys. The bonus is that 50% of the purchase price goes directly toward supporting the programs of the United Nations International Children's Education Fund. 100 King St. W. (in First Canadian Place). ☎ 416/777-2294. Subway: King.

HAIRCUTS

Beach Kidz Kutz A rocking horse, toys, and friendly staff are part of the package in this kids-only hair salon. The movie videos will keep your children's minds off their falling locks. 1826A Queen St. E. ☎ 416/698-3539. Subway: Queen, then any streetcar east.

Little Tots Hair Shop Once they've visited this salon, you'll never get your kids to the neighborhood barbershop again. Cool chairs, movie videos, a playroom, and a friendly and understanding staff make getting a haircut as fun as a trip to an amusement park (well, almost!). 1926 Queen St. E. ☎ 416/691-9190. Subway: Queen, then any streetcar east.

Shortcut's Hairplace for Kids Catering to the "can't sit still" set, this innovative hair salon provides movie videos and a small play area to keep the little ones occupied. 963 Eglinton Ave. W. (west of Bathurst). ☎ 416/789-1131. Subway: Eglinton West, then any bus east.

MAGIC & GAGS

Browser's Den of Magic Magic and other performing arts materials will enthrall young and old lovers of magic. There is an unusual collection of ventriloquist dolls, as well as irresistible gag gifts. A second store is open at

Paramount Canada's Wonderland in the summer months.   875 Eglinton Ave. W. © 416/783-7022. Subway: Eglinton West, then any bus east.

Morrisey Magic   Neighborhood kids often come here to learn tricks from the magician owners, who try to stock everything both amateur and professional magicians might require. Kids will love the unicycles and easy trick kits. They'll also love, though you may not, the great selection of gag gifts, from whoopee cushions to realistic rotting skulls. This is also an awesome costume store with an unusual selection of dress-up clothes.   2477 Dufferin St. © 416/782-1393. Subway: Eglinton West, then any bus west.

MAPS
Canada Map Company   This store stocks a wide variety of maps and travel-related books and publications.   61 Front St. E. © 416/362-9297. Subway: Union.

Open Air Books and Maps   Concentrating on nature and outdoor books, this store carries a vast selection of travel-related books and maps.   25 Yonge St. © 416/363-0719. Subway: Union.

MUSIC
HMV   With locations across the city, this megastore carries recordings in every genre, in addition to music magazines and videos. Prices are generally consistent with other music stores, although there are often good sales on specific merchandise. The staff is knowledgeable and eager to assist.   333 Yonge St. © 416/596-0333. Subway: Dundas. 50 Bloor St. W. © 416/324-9979. Subway: Yonge/Bloor. 272 Queen St. W. © 416/595-2828. Subway: Osgoode.

Open City   If you or the kids have been looking for an obscure CD or book, chances are you'll find it in this used book and music store. Though the store resembles a giant flea market, merchandise is always carefully inspected before it goes on sale and comes with a three-day money back guarantee. This is the place to show your kids what records are all about—you may even pick up a copy of one of your childhood favorites.   1374 Danforth Ave. © 416/461-8087. Subway: Greenwood.

Sam the Record Man   Despite its rather retro name and the neon record on the building's façade, this longtime music emporium is still the spot for today's hottest musical talent to visit their fans while in Toronto. Both chart toppers and independent music fill the racks.   347 Yonge St. © 416/977-4650. Subway: Dundas.

Second Spin   If your kids seem to go through CDs like water or you're interested in picking up a few musical bargains of your own, this store has some great prices. The most expensive used CD in the store sells for C$7 (US$4.60), while most go for C$4 (US$2.65).   1947 Queen St. E. © 416/690-8338. Subway: Queen, then any streetcar east.

Steve's Music Store   One of the best selections of equipment for amateur and professional musicians in the city can be found here. Another bonus is the great customer service and the concerts and workshops that are routinely offered.   415 Queen St. W. © 416/593-8888. Subway: Osgoode.

Tower Records   The four floors of this chain store are filled with the latest CDs, tapes, and DVDs sorted by genre, as well as a large selection of videos, books, and movies. There are some pretty good sales bins, as well.   2 Queen St. W. © 416/593-2500. Subway: Queen.

SCIENCE STUFF

EfstonScience Inc.   Science kits of almost every description are in stock, but my kids really go for the rocket kits. Other items include everything from beakers to binoculars and microscopes to magnets. 3350 Dufferin St. ✆ 416/787-4581. Subway: Yorkdale.

Science City Inc.   Check out the huge selection of telescopes, binoculars, and other tools for your budding scientist. There are also many less technical items, such as kites and bird feeders. This store makes science fun even for non-scientists. 50 Bloor St. W. ✆ 416/968-2627. Subway: Bay.

Spy Tech   It's not strictly scientific, but this store is fascinating all the same. Amateur sleuths can find everything they need here, from night-vision scopes to necktie video cameras. The wow factor alone makes this shop worth a visit. 2028 Yonge St. ✆ 416/482-8588. Subway: Davisville.

SHOES

Browns   This chain store carries an enormous selection of designer footwear for youngsters, from Tommy Hilfiger to Hush Puppies. There's also an ample selection of Invicta school bags. 3401 Dufferin St. (in Yorkdale Shopping Centre). ✆ 416/787-0313. Subway: Yorkdale.

Little Shoe Palace   Princes and princesses, as well as rough and tumble tree-climbing tykes, will walk away with something from this store. The usual name brands are stocked and a pleasant staff will help you find the perfect pair. 3189 Bathurst St. ✆ 416/785-5290. Subway: Lawrence West, then any bus east.

Panda Shoes   A wonderful selection of shoes for kids of all sizes can be found here. Because these stores specialize in children's shoes, the staff is generally knowledgeable and helpful. 3401 Dufferin St. (in Yorkdale Shopping Centre). ✆ 416/789-5418. Subway: Yorkdale.

Petit Pied   This is the place to shop for European children's footwear, including Minibel, Buckle My Shoe, and Elefanten, in sizes newborn to 40. There are also plenty of athletic shoes. 890 Yonge St. ✆ 416/963-5925. Subway: Yonge/Bloor. 2651 Yonge St. ✆ 416/322-6067. Subway: Eglinton.

Simply the Best   This Beaches store carries Robeez footwear for tykes; the cheerful leather styles are easy for little ones to slip on, yet stay on their feet. The shoes have nonskid soles and are completely washable. 943 Kingston Rd. ✆ 416/694-3320. Subway: Main, then Main bus south and Kingston Rd. streetcar east.

SHOWER & BABY GIFTS

Absolutely Diapers   You're sure to find something for the new arrival at this shop, which stocks everything baby might need, from the practical to the frivolous. Free gift wrapping and an extremely helpful staff make gift buying a pleasure. Take a catalog with you—they'll deliver just about anywhere. 265 Queen St. W. ✆ 416/597-0006. Subway: Osgoode. 2501 Yonge St. ✆ 416/484-6666. Subway: Eglinton.

Present Place   Puzzle stools and boxes and a great selection of Ty products make this a one-stop shop for buying baby and shower gifts. 386 Eglinton Ave. W. ✆ 416/486-6332. Subway: Eglinton, then any bus west.

With Child   This small Greektown shop has lots of wonderful stuff for Mom and babes. A small but beautiful collection of maternity lingerie shares space with cloth diapers, Beanie Babies, and other toys for babies. 705 Pape St. ✆ 416/466-9693. Subway: Pape.

SPORTS GEAR

Adelaide Sports   This store stocks stuff intended primarily for runners, including everything from portable CD players to jogging suits, but there are some items of interest to racket sports players as well.   100 King St. W. (in First Canadian Place). ✆ **416/364-2772**. Subway: King.

Europe Bound Travel Outfitters   This is a one-stop shopping experience for kids' outdoor gear and accessories. The store even carries baby joggers, bikes, and camping gear.   47 & 49 Front St. E. ✆ **416/815-1043**. Subway: Union.

Mountain Equipment Co-op   This store is as much entertainment as it is a shopping venue. From camping supplies to rock-climbing equipment, everything for the outdoor enthusiast is here. There is even a rock wall for climbing practice inside the store.   400 King St. W. (at Spadina Ave.). ✆ **416/340-2667**. Subway: St. Andrew, then any streetcar west.

Nike Toronto   All things Nike are for sale at this 23,000-square-foot store. 110 Bloor St. W. ✆ **416/921-6453**. Subway: Bay.

Play It Again Sports   This superstore has new and used equipment for almost any sport your kids would like to try.   3456 Yonge St. ✆ **416/488-6471**. Subway: Lawrence, then walk north.

River City Sports   This sports shop is dedicated to official jerseys and clothing from most professional leagues such as the NFL, NHL, NBA, and AHL. 1 Dundas St. W. (in the Eaton Centre). ✆ **416/260-5055**. Subway: Dundas or Queen.

Spirit of Hockey   This small Hockey Hall of Fame gift shop stocks the usual sweatshirts and baseball caps alongside books, cards, and jerseys, all, of course, with a hockey theme.   30 Yonge St. (in BCE Place, concourse level). ✆ **416/933-8228**. Subway: Union.

SportChek   Women and Juniors   Athletic apparel and shoes for almost any sport come in a huge selection of styles and sizes. Brand names include Adidas, Nike, Reebok, and Fila.   218 Yonge St. (in the Eaton Centre). ✆ **416/979-8126**. Subway: Dundas or Queen.

Trailhead   The focus is on adventure and outdoor sports, but almost every sport is covered at this downtown store. The staff is exceptionally helpful and knowledgeable.   61 Front St. E. ✆ **416/862-0881**. Subway: Union.

STROLLERS, CRIBS & FURNITURE

K.I.D.S. Kid's Interior Design Store   If you've promised your kids their dream room, this is the place to start looking for inspiration. The selection of furniture and linens for the younger set is almost overwhelming.   1600 Steeles Ave. W. ✆ **416/784-4445**. Subway: Downsview, then Dufferin bus north.

Macklem's Baby Carriages   As the name suggests, this store specializes in prams for baby, but it also stocks a good selection of reasonably priced baby and juvenile furniture and linens. If your stroller is getting a little wobbly, this is also the place to come—they've been repairing prams for over 50 years.   2223 Dundas St. W. ✆ **416/531-7188**. Subway: Dundas West.

Nestings Kids   A home furnishing store just for kids! The exclusive furniture and beautiful custom linens for babies through teens are lovely, but be prepared to pay—this is definitely high-end stuff.   418 Eglinton Ave. W. ✆ **416/322-0511**. Subway: Eglinton, then any bus west.

A Room of My Own   Fine children's furnishings, original linens, and accessories abound alongside tot-sized computer desks and couches, and there are some wonderful fantasy beds for children and teenagers.   2111 Dunwin Dr. (at Dundas St., 1½ blocks west of Erin Mills Pkwy.), Mississauga. ☎ **905/828-2525.** By car: Queen Elizabeth Way (QEW) to Erin Mills Pkwy.

Safety Superstore   Selling everything from breathable mattresses to safety locks for cabinets, this store caters to the idea that parents are better off safe than sorry.   1600 Steeles Ave. (west of Dufferin). ☎ **905/761-7233.** Subway: Downsview, then Dufferin bus north.

THEME STORES

Barbie on Bay   This store is a find for hard-core Barbie addicts such as my 6-year-old, and the rest of us found it pretty interesting as well. Not only do they carry exclusive lines and dolls that can't be found in other shops but they will order just about anything you need. The prices are generally excellent, too. 410 Bay St. ☎ **416/861-4113.** Subway: Queen.

Disney Store   This is the kind of store that kids like to walk around in and admire. The walls are lined with scenes from Disney movies (many with moving characters), Disney music plays in the background, and animated toys are set up to blow bubbles at your children or sing them a lullaby. The Disney wares range from T-shirts to toys.   200 Yonge St. (in the Eaton Centre). ☎ **416/591-5132.** Subway: Dundas or Queen. 3401 Dufferin St. (in Yorkdale Shopping Centre). ☎ **416/782-3061.** Subway: Yorkdale.

The Hollywood Canteen   This store was launched by some dedicated movie buffs and it shows. They stock a huge selection of posters and lobby cards, from the hit flicks of the fifties to present-day blockbusters. This is also where you can find screenplays of major motion pictures or that rare video that Blockbuster no longer carries. Videos are both sold and rented. They also have an interesting collection of new and used books related to the movie industry. 1516 Danforth Ave. ☎ **416/461-1704.** Subway: Coxwell.

Wayne Gretzky's   This retail shop is part of the Great One's restaurant on Blue Jays Way. It's a hockey fan's delight, with plenty of memorabilia sporting the number 99, including T-shirts, sticks, and caps.   99 Blue Jays Way. ☎ **416/979-7825.** Subway: Union.

TOYS

Animal House _(Finds)_   If your kids just have to have a stuffed ostrich, bring them here. There are over 1,500 stuffed animals in this store, ranging from the standard teddy bear to more exotic animals, as well as collectibles such as Reiss and Gund.   1 Dundas St.W. (in the Eaton Centre). ☎ **416/593-9383.** Subway: Dundas.

Animal World   This enchanting Eaton Centre shop is for collectors of stuffed creatures. The shop carries Ty collectibles and beautiful bears from Gund, Reiss, and Merrythought, as well as many items exclusive to this chain store.   218 Yonge St. (in the Eaton Centre). ☎ **416/977-2221.** Subway: Dundas or Queen.

George's Trains   This toy train shop, one of the largest in Canada, is a must-see for train buffs. The store is a wonder for small children, with its model trains racing on their tracks around the room. Everything from Thomas the Tank Engine merchandise to models for the serious collector costing thousands of dollars can be found here.   510 Mount Pleasant Rd. ☎ **416/489-9783.** Subway: St. Clair, then Mount Pleasant bus to Belsize Ave.

The Grand River Toy Company   We bought wooden blocks for my eldest daughters here years ago and all the kids are still playing with them. A great mix of traditional and newer toys, as well as some educational toys and kits, are stocked. 276 Carlaw Ave., Unit 101. ✆ 416/469-1946. Subway: Queen, then any streetcar east.

Just Bears   As the name indicates, you'll find all things bear related here, including a magnificent collection of teddy bears created by Canadian and international designers. This store is an authorized dealer for most of the leading makers of teddy and collectible bears. They take special orders and will ship anywhere in the world. 29 Bellair St. ✆ 416/928-5963. Subway: Bay.

Kidding Awound   You might want to keep the kids away from the collection of antique playthings and music boxes in this shop, but the windup toys and gag gifts are fair game. There's plenty of neat stuff to entice even the most jaded young shoppers. 91 Cumberland St. ✆ 416/926-8996. Subway: Bay.

Kidstuff Toy Store   This store stands out for its unique collection of puppets, marionettes, and puppet theaters. Also in stock is a good selection of toys from Brio, Playmobile, and Lego, as well as art supplies, books, and tapes. 738 Bathurst St. ✆ 416/535-2212. Subway: Bathurst.

Mastermind Educational   This Beaches toy store stocks primarily educational toys, and the extremely helpful staff makes a visit worthwhile. There are also many items that are pure fun, such as the excellent selection of scooters my 8-year-old was eyeing enviously. The location at the Ontario Science Centre (✆ 416/696-1000) also sells science-related toys, gadgets, and games. 2134 Queen St. E. ✆ 416/699-3797. Subway: Queen, then any streetcar east. 3350 Yonge St. ✆ 416/487-7177. Subway: Lawrence.

Munchkinland   This store has a friendly neighborhood feel and stocks an excellent range of toys, from Groovy Girls to TV show–inspired merchandise such as Arthur, Madeline, and Blue's Clues. 294 Danforth Ave. ✆ 416/406-9911. Subway: Chester.

Royal Ontario Museum Toy Shop   The ROM boasts three gift shops, but this one is strictly for kids. You'll find educational and purely fun toys, games, and books, most of them science or history related. 100 Queen's Park Cres. ✆ 416/586-5785. Subway: Museum.

The Rubbery Warehouse Store (Value   This suburban store offers 20,000 square feet of huge backyard toys and equipment, as well as Rubbermaid, Little Tykes, and Graco toys. There is even a 1,000-square-foot playground where kids can try out some toys. 7575 Weston Rd. (Colossus Centre), Woodbridge. ✆ 905/850-4060. By car: Hwy. 400 north to Hwy. 7.

Top Banana   This fun toy store stocks everything from the latest "must have" toy to traditional favorites such as stomp rockets. 639 Mount Pleasant Rd. ✆ 416/440-0111. Subway: Eglinton, then no. 34 bus east to Mount Pleasant.

Toy Circus   This Beaches store is packed with everything from Brio to Gund bears. Despite the large inventory crammed into such a tiny space, this shop is surprisingly well organized. Many educational toys are available and there are plenty of small dime-store–type items for the wee ones. 2036 Queen St. E. ✆ 416/699-4971. Subway: Queen, then any streetcar east. 322 King St. W. ✆ 416/348-9202. Subway: King, then 3 blocks west.

The Toy Shop   Two floors of imaginative, unusual toys and books for all ages will thrill the kids, and there's a lot of educational-type stuff to please parents. The owners of this wonderful shop carefully select toys that will stand up to hours of play with even the most active child.   62 Cumberland St. (at Bay St.). © 416/961-4870. Subway: Bay.

Toys R Us   This superstore sells everything from bicycles to Barbie dolls. This is the spot to bring the kids to write out their birthday wish list—or maybe not! 195 Yonge St. © **416/866-8697**. Subway: Queen. 2300 Yonge St. (in the Yonge-Eglinton Centre). © **416/322-1599**. Subway: Eglinton.

Toys Toys Toys   From trading cards to trains, this store stocks almost every toy your children have heard of, and then some. For serious toy seekers there are intricate models and chess sets, and for those who just want to have fun the store has Barbies and sticker sets.   220 Yonge St. (in the Eaton Centre). © **416/979-1121**. Subway: Dundas or Queen.

Treasure Island Toys Limited   This small Greektown store specializes in creating loot bags for kids' parties, so there are a lot of small toys to fit the budgets of tiny shoppers.   311 Danforth Ave. © **416/778-4913**. Subway: Broadview.

10

Easy Side Trips from Toronto

If you don't mind the drive, the following attractions are great places to
visit with your kids. All are within a
two-hour drive of the city.

1 Wild Water Kingdom

40 kilometers (25 miles) NW of Toronto

Many Torontonians come here to escape the heat of the city on muggy summer
days. Wild Water Kingdom has the ambience of spring break at Daytona
Beach—a DJ plays music and cajoles young swimmers to try the water, and
older kids woosh down the seven-story speed slides, only to race back up and try
them again. Despite the wild atmosphere, this is definitely a family park. There
is a dress code (no thongs and no going topless), and profanity isn't tolerated.

Dolphin Bay, where the connected pools are no more than 45 centimeters (18
in.) deep, is the best choice for small fry. Little kids can slide down pint-sized
water slides past frogs and fish, play in the water spraying out from every angle,
and crawl through tunnels that barely skim the water surface. Life jackets are
provided free of charge. The park also offers a dry playground.

Many of the wilder rides are restricted to children 122 centimeters (48 in.) or
over, although there are three that allow kids 106 centimeters (42 in.) and over.
For the older kids who meet these requirements, there are 13 body and tube slides
and a wave pool that, with its whitecaps and rolling surf, transports you to a day
at the beach.

Parents might prefer a calmer tube trip down the half-mile Lazy River or a
lounge chair at the Caribbean Cove, which evokes a luxurious southern resort
complete with cabanas and waterfalls.

Kids will also enjoy the pay-as-you-play arcade, bumper boats, mini-golf, and
batting cages. Or, you might rent a paddleboat or canoe on the adjacent 15-acre
lake. The park tends to get crowded, especially on really hot weekends, so try to
go during the week or be prepared to share the beach with several thousand others. If you go on a busy day, plan with the kids what they should do if they lose
sight of you. There are lost children stations at the first aid station at the back
of the park and at the park gates.

Where to Eat   The park has several restaurants that offer the usual overpriced
theme-park fare, as well as several fast-food outlets such as **Pizza Pizza** and **Mr.
Sub.** Your best bet is to pack a picnic, but you'll have to enjoy it either before or
after visiting the park because you are not allowed to bring picnic supplies inside
the gates. There are, however, plenty of scenic picnic spots outside the park.

7855 Finch Ave. W., Brampton (Hwy 427 & Finch Ave.). ✆ **416/369-WILD.** www.wildwaterkingdom.com.
Admission C$21.50 (US$14.20) ages 10 and up, C$16.50 (US$10.90) seniors and children 5–10, free for

Easy Side Trips from Toronto

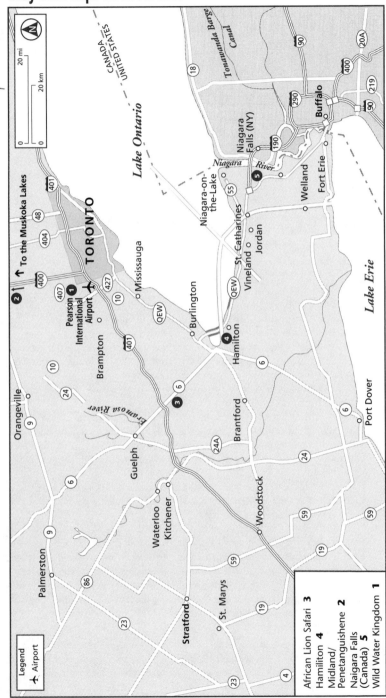

Legend
✈ Airport

African Lion Safari **3**
Hamilton **4**
Midland/
Penetanguishene **2**
Naigara Falls
(Canada) **5**
Wild Water Kingdom **1**

children 4 and under. June 1–14 Sat–Sun 10am–6pm, June 15–30 daily 10am–6pm, July1–Aug 19 daily 10am–8pm, Aug 20–Sept 3 daily 10am–6pm. Closed early Sept–June. Hours may change due to weather—call ahead to confirm. Subway: York Mills or Yorkdale, then GO Bus. By car: Take Hwy. 401 west, then Hwy. 427 north to Finch Ave.

2 African Lion Safari

90 kilometers (56 miles) W of Toronto

This attraction west of Toronto offers a twist on the traditional zoo: the people are caged while the animals roam around at will.

You have two choices for traveling on this 14.5-kilometer (9 mile) safari trail —you can either take your own vehicle or catch a ride in the air-conditioned safari bus (the trip takes about an hour). We decided to use our van and drive at our own pace, a method of travel I'd recommend with a few important caveats. First, for your own safety, keep your windows closed for much of the trip. Second, be aware that your vehicle could end up with a few dents and scratches—while the dozen or so baboons that took up residence on the roof and side mirrors of our van thrilled the girls, their father was pretty unimpressed when the curious primates hung wildly from the roof, taking much of its trim with them.

Over 1,000 animals and birds roam freely through the park, including several prides of lions. While the kids enjoyed their close-up look at these surprisingly languid predators, they were most enthralled by the giraffes that leaned down to peer in our windows and then ambled onto the path directly in front of us. Other sights included tigers, rhinos, zebra, and elands, and many other African and native species of birds and mammals.

If you have the time, take a ride on the *African Queen,* a boat that travels around the lake and affords another view of many of the park's primates and birds. The train takes you on a short ride around the park and will primarily interest the littlest members of your party. Small children will also appreciate the Pets Corner, a small zoo where they can get an up-close view of some of the park's smaller inhabitants, including pot-bellied pigs, otters, and goats.

Bring your bathing suits if it's a hot day so the kids can splash around in the jungle-themed play area. There is also an excellent dry playground where the girls wore off some of the excess energy they had stored up while driving around the park.

Older kids will appreciate the animal demonstrations. Everyone enjoyed the daily elephant bath, and our older girls were truly awed by the birds of prey demonstration. If you want to see everything, allow a minimum of five hours; the park can also be viewed in less time if you skip some of the demonstrations and curtail your time at the playgrounds. Take lots of time on the safari trail—it's definitely the highlight of the trip.

Where to Eat   There are two restaurants on-site. The **Mombassa Market Restaurant** offers plenty of inexpensive fast-food items, while the **Cabana Grill** sells barbecued foods. You can eat outdoors on the large patio at picnic tables or indoors. A better bet with kids is to carry your lunch to one of two picnic areas near Recreation Lake (where the elephants bathe). You can also pack your own picnic lunch. The park is fairly isolated, so there are no other dining options within a reasonable driving distance.

RR #1, Cambridge, ON N1R 5S2. ✆ **800/461-WILD** or 519/623-2620. www.africanlionsafari.com. Admission C$19.95 (US$13.15) ages 13–64, C$15.95 (US$10.50) ages 65 and over, C$13.95 (US$9.20) children 3–12, free for children 2 and under. Safari bus rates C$4.45–$4.95 (US$2.95–$3.25). Late Apr–late June Mon–Fri 10am–4pm, Sat–Sun 10am–5pm; late June–early Sept daily 10am–5:30pm; early Sept–early Oct daily 10am–4pm. Closed early Oct–late Apr. By car: Take Hwy. 401 west to exit 299, just past Milton. Go south on Hwy. 6 for 14km (8.7 miles), turn right on Safari Rd., and drive west for about 16km (9.9 miles).

3 Hamilton

70 kilometers (43 miles) SW of Toronto

Close enough for a quick side trip, Hamilton offers plenty of kid-friendly attractions. Hamilton is rapidly shrugging off the "Steeltown" nickname bestowed on account of its industrial roots and earning a new reputation for its family-friendly attractions. It takes less than an hour to drive here and is well worth the trip.

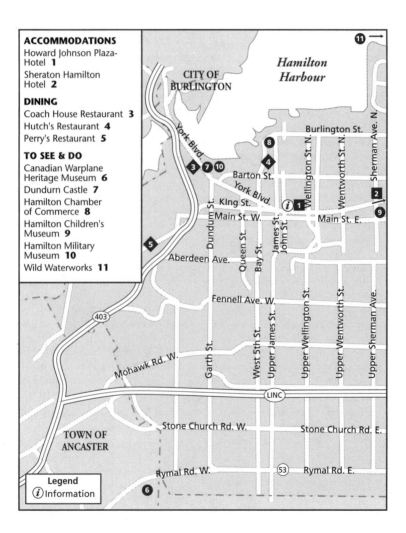

ACCOMMODATIONS
Howard Johnson Plaza-Hotel **1**
Sheraton Hamilton Hotel **2**

DINING
Coach House Restaurant **3**
Hutch's Restaurant **4**
Perry's Restaurant **5**

TO SEE & DO
Canadian Warplane Heritage Museum **6**
Dundurn Castle **7**
Hamilton Chamber of Commerce **8**
Hamilton Children's Museum **9**
Hamilton Military Museum **10**
Wild Waterworks **11**

Legend
ⓘ Information

GETTING THERE

Hamilton is about a one-hour drive southwest from downtown Toronto. From Toronto take the Queen Elizabeth Way (QEW) to Hamilton.

The GO Transit commuter train connects Hamilton to Toronto. Call ℂ **800/ 438-6646** or 416/869-3200 for information. Trains depart from Union Station as well as from several other stations in Toronto. Hamilton also has its own international airport serviced by several passenger carriers, including US Airways and WestJet.

INFORMATION

The **Greater Hamilton Tourist Information Centre** has a wealth of information on what to see and do, as well as where to dine and sleep. From early September until June 30, it is open Monday to Saturday 9am to 5pm; from July 1 through Labour Day, its hours are Monday to Saturday 10am to 5pm and Sunday noon to 5pm. The center is located at 127 King St. E., Hamilton, ON L8N 1B1 (ℂ **800/263-8590** or 905/546-2666; www.city.hamilton.on.ca/visitor.htm).

The **Hamilton Chamber of Commerce** is another good source of information on the area's attractions. It's open Monday through Friday 9am to 5pm at 555 Bay St. N., Hamilton, ON L8L 1H1 (ℂ **905/522-1151;** www. hamilton-cofc.on.ca).

TO SEE & DO IN HAMILTON

Canadian Warplane Museum **Ages 5 and up.** For kids whose experience with jets has been watching streaks of white spread across the sky, the sight of a huge CF-104 Starfighter with its nose pointed straight up in the air is awe-inspiring. This aircraft marks the entrance to the Canadian Warplane Museum. Inside, kids get a chance to sit at the controls of a real jet. Young aviators can test their piloting skills in the two-seat Flying Boxcar simulator, with its myriad switches and dials, or operate a Hawker Hurricane model aircraft. The museum houses 25 airplanes, most of which are still flyable. In fact, you can book a flight in one of two open-cockpit World War II planes for a negotiated fee.

Many of the displays in the museum are of the look-but-don't-touch variety, but kids are allowed to climb into more than enough models. An interactive global map and a variety of audio and visual displays will also keep young visitors busy. For a special treat, take the kids to the outdoor observation terrace, where they can watch the planes taking off from Hamilton International Airport.

9280 Airport Rd. (at the Hamilton International Airport). ℂ **905/679-4183.** www.warplane.com. Admission C$10 (US$6.60) adults, C$8 (US$5.30) children 8 and up, C$30 (US$19.80) family (2 adults, 2 children), free for children under 8. Fri–Wed 9am–5pm, Thurs 9am–9pm. By car: Take Hwy. 403 west through Hamilton and up the mountain. Exit at Fiddlers Green. Follow the airport signs for 8km (5 miles), pass the airport, and look for the CF-104 Starfighter jet.

Dundurn Castle **Ages 5 and up.** Translated from the Gaelic word for "fort on the water" Dundurn Castle isn't a true castle, but your kids won't care. The 43-room mansion was built in 1835 around the shell of a colonial home, with spooky underground passages that thrill older kids.

The home can be seen only by tour (unfortunately, the museum is not stroller or wheelchair accessible). Waiting in line is actually a highlight of the tour for many kids—the entry hall is stocked with early 19th-century toys, coloring books, and crosswords and activity sheets based on the castle. The guides will gear the tour toward the age of the group and do their best to include any small visitors by asking them questions, pointing out items of interest, and talking about the children who once lived in the house. The tour lasts an hour, but if you find your kids just can't hang in that long, castle staff will be happy to refund your tickets. At the end of the tour, everyone is rewarded with cookies in the castle's kitchen.

The museum gift shop stocks many unique items, including reproductions of period toys and some excellent children's books on castles.

The admission price also includes a visit to the Hamilton Military Museum on the castle grounds (see below).

Where to Eat The **Coach House Restaurant** on the castle grounds is a beautiful Victorian-themed restaurant where you can try Victorian dishes like mulligatawny soup (my eldest daughter's favorite) or spinach and mushroom pasty. There is also a good children's menu that includes more typical items such as hot dogs, chicken nuggets, and fish and chips. Kids' menu prices range from C$3 to $6 (US$2 to $3.95).

Afternoon tea is a great treat for the kids. Prices for the tea, which includes a generous supply of Victorian cakes and pastries and a selection of excellent teas, are C$9 (US$5.95) per person. Younger children can probably share the generous adult portions.

610 York Blvd., Hamilton. ✆ 905/546-2872. www.city.hamilton.on.ca/culture and recreation. Admission C$7 (US$4.60) adults, C$3 (US$2) children 6–14, C$18 (US$11.90) family (2 adults, 2 children), free for children 5 and under. Victoria Day–Labour Day daily 10am–4:30pm; the rest of the year Tues–Sun noon–4pm. By car: Take Queen Elizabeth Way (QEW) west to Hamilton and exit at York Blvd.

Hamilton Children's Museum **Ages 2 to 10.** Located in a historic home near the east end's Gage Park, this hands-on museum is one of the tiniest I've ever seen, but it packs a lot of play power into the limited space. Here your kids can dismantle and then reconstruct a house, dig up plastic dinosaur bones in a mock archaeological site, or learn about the new territory of Nunavut in the Canada exhibit. There are costumes to try on and tools to use. Older kids, even those unfamiliar with Hamilton, take great pleasure in redesigning the city by moving around the buildings in a giant model. Younger kids may prefer to play in the house or in the child-sized car.

1072 Main St. E. ✆ 905/546-4848. Admission C$2.75 (US$1.80) children 2–12, free for adults with child and children under 2. Tues–Sat 10am–4pm, Sun 1–4pm. By car: Take the QEW, then Hwy. 403 to Hamilton. Take the Main St. exit, drive through downtown, and watch for Gage Park.

Hamilton Military Museum **Ages 5 and up.** If your kids are less than thrilled by military museums, this one, on the grounds of Dundurn Castle, will probably prove to be the exception. The museum is based on exhibits, rather than hands-on displays, but the staff has done an outstanding job of adding some interactive elements for kids. The best is the Spy Game, which asks kids to comb the museum grounds for five clues that form a secret message. Another activity describes several objects in the museum and asks kids to find and identify them.

610 York Blvd., Dundurn National Historic Site. ✆ 905/546-2872. Free with admission to Dundurn Castle. Victoria Day–Labour Day daily 11am–5pm; the rest of the year Tues–Sun 1–5pm. By car: Take Queen Elizabeth Way (QEW) west to Hamilton and exit at York Blvd.

Wild Waterworks **Ages 2 and up.** This water park has something for all ages, including giant water slides that even your youngest family members can try. The older kids, those over 124 centimeters (49 in.), will undoubtedly opt for the six-story body slides—appropriately named the Demon slides. There are also two 5½-story tube slides for kids taller than 137 centimeters (54 in.). Everyone will want to take an inner-tube ride down the lazy river that meanders around the park past water jets and fountains.

The toddler pool is surprisingly large, with many cool fountains and roofs that gently spray water on the little swimmers below. The pool depth is about 46 centimeters (18 in.). The wave pool here is Canada's largest.

Where to Eat   You might try one of the two snack bars in the facility or opt for nearby **Hutch's Restaurant** (see "Dining," below).

Hwy. 20. ✆ **800/555-8775** June–Sept or 888/319-HRCA year-round. Admission C$13.50 (US$8.90) adults, C$8.50 (US$5.60) children 4–10, free for children under 4. End of June–Sept, daily 10am–8pm; the rest of the year Mon–Fri 11am–6pm, Sat–Sun 10am–6pm. Closed during bad weather. By car: Take the Queen Elizabeth Way (QEW) to Centennial Pkwy. (Hwy. 20) exit, then drive north toward the lake and follow the signs to Confederation Park.

ACCOMMODATIONS

Because Hamilton is so close to Toronto it's an ideal place for a day trip. However, if you want to stay overnight, several well-known chains have hotels here, including the Sheraton Hamilton Hope, 116 King St. W., Hamilton, ON L8P 4V3 (✆ **800/514-7101** or 905/529-5515) and Howard Johnson Plaza-Hotel, 112 King St. E., Hamilton, ON L8N 1A8 (✆ **800/263-8558** or 905/546-1111).

DINING

MODERATE

Perry's Restaurant ECLECTIC   Picky eaters are bound to find something they like on the menu, which draws its inspiration from Italian, French, Mexican, Greek, and American cuisine. Menu items include rack of ribs, sandwiches, Cajun chicken, burgers, and souvlaki. There is no children's menu per se, but kids will find lots to choose from on the main menu.

1088 Main St. ✆ **905/527-3779**. Main courses C$6–$13 (US$3.95–$8.60). MC, V. Daily 11:30am–1am.

INEXPENSIVE

Hutch's Restaurant BURGERS   This is a classic burger joint on Van Wagner Beach in Hamilton next to Wild Waterworks. It's best known for its fish and homemade chips, but the restaurant also serves great burgers, hotdogs, and milkshakes. The decor is pure 1950s, from the vinyl booths to the jukebox belting out 1950s tunes. Service is friendly and best of all, especially for tired kids, exceptionally fast.

325 Bay St. N. ✆ **905/545-5508**. Main courses C$2.95–$7.95 (US$1.95–5.25), kids' menu C$3.05 (US$2). MC, V. Spring break–Labour Day daily 11am– midnight; the rest of the year 11am–10pm.

4 Midland/Penetanguishene

143 kilometers (89 miles) N of Toronto

If you're planning a longer stay in the Toronto area, you might want to make an overnight (or longer) visit to Midland (north of Toronto). Midland, on the shore of Georgian Bay, is part of southern Ontario's cottage country. Apart from spectacular beaches and great fishing, the area offers some fun attractions for kids.

Paved walking and cycling paths hug the town's waterfront, making it a pleasant place to stroll with the kids. In the middle of town, **Little Lake Park** has a shallow, sandy beach for splashing around. Come summer when the ducks and geese arrive, however, the spot tends to get more than a little messy—you may want to opt for one of the many beaches outside of town.

Downtown is lined with quaint shops, many of which are decorated with one of the more than 30 murals in town that depict Midland's rich history. The murals are part of Midland's ongoing effort to create the largest historical mural in North America. You can pick up a free walking-tour guide of the downtown's murals and historic sights from the **Midland Chamber of Commerce** (see "Information," below).

GETTING THERE

Getting to Midland by car is simple. Take Highway 400 north to Highway 93, which leads right into town. **Penetanguishene Midland Coach Lines** runs a surprisingly fast and comfortable motor coach service from the Metro Toronto Coach Terminal and Yorkdale GO Station to Midland. Call © **888/833-2628** or 416/777-9177, or visit their website at www.midlandtours.com for departure times and prices.

INFORMATION

The **Midland/Penetanguishene Chamber of Commerce,** 208 King St., Midland, ON L4R 3L9 (© **705/526-7884;** www.town.midland.on.ca), can provide information about area accommodations, dining, and attractions. **Georgian Bay Tourism,** c/o Tourism Consortium, 208 King St., Midland, ON L4R 3L9 (© **800/263-7745**), provides similar information. Visit their website at www.georgianbaytourism.on.ca.

TO SEE & DO IN MIDLAND

Castle Village *(Finds* **All ages.** This enchanting castle—the kind Cinderella would have lived in—purports to be a gift shop, but fantasy has definitely taken over. For a modest fee, kids can peer into the cottages of Hansel and Gretel, Snow White and the Seven Dwarfs, and Goldilocks and the Three Bears. Active kids can explore the dwarf village high up in the trees, with bridges to connect the cottages and slides from almost every window. The enchanted forest offers a pretty nature trail for young explorers, while the dungeon of horror houses several horrific creatures. The ice cream shop on-site makes this a great place to stop for a treat on your way in or out of town.

701 Balm Beach Rd., Midland. © **705/526-9683.** Admission C$2 (US$1.30) all ages. Tues–Sat 10am–5pm, Sunday noon–5pm. By car: Take Hwy. 12 west to Hwy. 93, then Hwy. 93 north to Balm Beach Rd.

Discovery Harbour **Ages 4 and up.** Our kids had a lot more fun playing at being 19th-century sailors than the real sailors probably ever had. From learning to navigate a hammock to working with antique tools, this museum provides hands-on experience. The museum centers its exhibits on the life of sailors and officers in the early part of the 19th century, when a naval base was built here to defend Upper Canada (Ontario) from possible attack by Americans.

Although you can explore on your own, the guided tours are a lot of fun, especially for kids. Guides will provide all kinds of exciting tidbits of information about life in the 1820s, and are always careful to include the tour's youngest members. This is definitely a look-and-touch museum. Kids are encouraged to climb into the hammocks, play with the pots in the kitchen, and even write with a quill while sitting at a desk in the officers' quarters.

The museum consists of barracks, the intriguing officers' quarters constructed of stone, and two working full-size replicas of tall ships that were once stationed at the base: the HMS *Tecumseth* and HMS *Bee.*

For an extra fee, Discovery Harbour offers daily children's activities. Kids can make a model ship, try rowing a longboat, learn how to sling a hammock and dance a jig, enjoy a spot of tea and a game of croquet in the officers' quarters, help fire a canon, or learn how to tie complicated sailors' knots. The **Kings Wharf Theatre** is also on-site and stages several excellent productions each year. For tickets and show information call ℂ **705/549-5555.**

Where to Eat   **Captain Robert's Table** is a casual restaurant that serves buffet lunches and dinners.

93 Jury Dr, Penetanguishene. ℂ **705/549-0713.** www.discoveryharbour.on.ca. Self-guided tour C$3.50 (US$2.30) per person; guided tour C$5.50 (US$3.60) per person or C$4.50 (US$2.95) per person for a group of 4 or more, free for children 5 and under. June 30–Sept daily 10am–5pm. By car: Take Hwy. 93 north to Penetanguishene (Hwy. 93 becomes the main street). Take the main street to the bottom of the hill toward the water, turn right, and follow the Blue Ship logos to Discovery Harbour.

The Fun Stop   All ages. This giant indoor playground, located across from Little Lake in downtown Midland, is the place to take the kids if it rains or if you want to escape the sun for a little while. The complex includes a 111.5-square-meter (1,200-sq.-ft.) play structure with ball pits and slides, as well as a toddler area with a play kitchen and small toys. There are also four Nintendo stations and a games room where kids can play a variety of family games, each costing one or two tokens. If they win, they receive tickets they can redeem for prizes at the front desk. Only the playground charges an admission fee, and you can enter the playground, games room, or snack bar separately.

Where to Eat   The snack bar in the complex offers many tasty fast-food items such as hamburgers, chicken nuggets, hot dogs, and french fries. Kids' combos cost C$2.99 to $3.29 (US$1.95 to $2.15).

788 Yonge St., Midland. ℂ **705/528-7077.** Admission C$2.15 (US$1.40) children, free for adults. Game tokens C25¢ (US15¢). Mon–Sat 10am–9pm. By car: Take Yonge St. downtown. The Fun Stop is across the street from Little Lake Park.

Huronia Museum & Huron-Ouendat Village *(Value)*   **All ages.** Kids delight in being able to explore on their own, and this reproduction of a 500-year-old Huron-Ouendat village encourages them to do just that. They can duck inside the longhouses, shaman's house, and sweat lodge; imagine an enemy attack from their perch on the palisade wall lookout towers; or play some traditional Native games. Inside the Huronia Museum are a variety of local artifacts, some dating back 10,000 years. Make sure you ask the curator for a copy of the museum's treasure hunt, which asks kids to find various items throughout the museum. Special activities are occasionally offered through the summer months.

549 Little Lake Park Rd., Midland. ℂ **705/526-2844.** Admission C$6 (US$3.95) adults, C$4.50 (US$2.95) children 6–18, free for children under 6. Guided tours offered July–Aug. Open daily 9am–5pm, closed Sundays Jan–Mar. By car: Take Hwy. 93 to Yonge St. and turn right. Turn left onto 8th St. and then right onto Little Lake Park Rd.

Minds Alive   All ages. This toy store cum art supply depot defies description, but it's definitely worth visiting. The store stocks a huge selection of toys and children's educational supplies, including travel games for the trip home, kites, binoculars, Audubon bird callers, boomerangs, bug boxes, and books.

During the summer, a staff artist offers drop-in crafts each morning and evening, except Sundays. Your child might decorate a yo-yo or picture frame or make a greeting card. Crafts cost C$7 (US$4.60) and up. You can't miss the store—it's the one with the colorful sign and windmills hanging out front.

313 King St., Midland. © **705/526-6662**. www.mindsalive.on.ca. Mon–Wed 9am–5pm, Thurs 9am–6pm, Fri 9am–7pm, Sat 9am–5pm, July–Aug Sun 12–5pm. By car: Take Hwy. 12 to King St., turn left, and travel 1.5km (1 mile).

Sainte-Marie among the Hurons *(Value* **Ages 4 and up.** Over 350 years ago, French Jesuits built a fortress and mission in the midst of the lands belonging to the Huron Nation. After repeated attacks from the Iroquois, the Jesuits were forced to abandon Sainte-Marie and put it to the torch. They rebuilt on nearby Christian Island, where they endured terrible starvation and further attacks. The Iroquois nearly annihilated the Huron Nation in subsequent attacks, and two Jesuits, fathers Brébeuf and Lalemant, were martyred and are buried in a shrine on the site.

The current site is a reproduction of the fortress based on intensive archaeological digs of the area. After a 20-minute multimedia presentation that will put you and the kids in a 17th-century frame of mind, kids are invited to explore more than 20 buildings, including Huron longhouses and tepees as well as the chapels and residences belonging to the Jesuits. In a representation of archaeologists' theories about the purpose of a series of trenches traversing the site, an ingenious waterway with locks allows canoes to enter the fortress from the nearby Wye River. However, the true magic of this experience lies in the numerous costumed interpreters who perform the tasks of those who would have lived here hundreds of years ago. You'll see a Jesuit father praying in the chapel, a servant cutting wood, and a Huron Native telling stories to visitors while others pull their birch-bark canoes up to the fort.

For kids, Sainte-Marie offers daily crafts and activities, such as making cornhusk dolls, beaded bracelets, and clay figures. There are also numerous special events hosted throughout the year, many of which are geared toward kids. The museum's well-stocked gift shop offers many Native crafts, as well as unique jewelry, books, and clothes.

Where to Eat   The licensed restaurant offers a wide selection of traditional Canadian cuisine and lighter options. You can eat in the restaurant or outside in the pavilion or on the patio. There are several good options for kids on the menu.

Hwy. 12 E. © **705/526-7838**. www.saintemarieamongthehurons.on.ca. Admission C$9.75 (US$6.45) adults, C$6.25 (US$4.15) children, free for children 5 and under; C$1 (US65¢) off admission price for groups of 4 or more. Mid-May–early Oct 10am–5pm. By car: Travel east on Hwy. 12 for 5km (3.1 miles). The entrance to Sainte-Marie is across from the Martyrs' Shrine Church.

(*Fun Fact* We started small…

In 1769, the 66 Frenchmen who lived at Sainte-Marie represented one-fifth of the entire population of New France (now known as Canada)!

Wye Marsh *(Finds* **All ages.** The ostensible draw here is the resident colony of trumpeter swans—which do, in fact, trumpet quite loudly, much to the delight of watching kids. However, there is so much more to this wildlife center. A long boardwalk wends its way through the marsh, offering kids an up-close view of the marsh's plant and reptilian occupants. There are bridges from which you can view the resident wildlife and several places where you can explore the marsh bed.

Canoe rides through the marsh are available in the summer for C$5 (US$3.30) and are limited to adults and children over the age of 6. There are plenty of special programs at the marsh, many of which are geared toward the youngest visitors. Regular nature programs for parents and tots up to the age of 6 are offered through the spring and summer, including a walk, crafts, snacks, stories, and a singalong. Call the center for times and dates. On the weekends you can join one of the guided tours given by staff.

Where to Eat   The cafeteria offers the usual hotdogs, hamburgers, fries, and packaged items, as well as pancakes and maple syrup during the spring sap run.

Hwy. 12 E. *C* 705/526-7809. www.wyemarsh.com. Admission C$6.50 (US$4.30) adults, C$5.35 (US$3.55) children, free for children 3 and under. July–Sept daily 10am–6pm; the rest of the year daily 10am–4pm; closed weekends in Dec. By car: Follow Hwy. 12 east and look for the signs—it's just down the road from Saint-Marie among the Hurons.

ACCOMMODATIONS

Best Western Highland Inn   This hotel offers resort-style facilities right in the center of Midland, with a large indoor pool and a games room that will keep the kids amused.

All rooms are fairly spacious, but the family suites will give the kids some room to run and house a king-size bed, a pullout couch, and a double bed, as well as a sitting area. All of the in-room amenities you might expect in an expensive downtown Toronto hotel are included.

924 King St., P.O. Box 515, Midland, ON L4R 4L3. *C* **705/526-9307.** Fax 705/526-0099. 123 units. C$50–$100 (US$33–$66) double; C$100–$166 (US$66–$110) suite. Children under 16 stay free in parents' room. Crib free; rollaway C$10 (US$6.60). AE, DISC, MC, V. Free parking. **Amenities:** 2 restaurants (both family), 1 lounge; large indoor pool; sauna; Jacuzzi; exercise room; game room; business services; dry cleaning. *In room:* AC, TV w/ pay movies, dataport, coffeemaker, hairdryer, iron.

Comfort Inn   This hotel offers few amenities but it does provide an excellent free continental breakfast—something we've often appreciated when we travel with the kids. Rooms are fairly standard. You can squeeze a cot in here but you may want to go for an additional room if you can get a good rate.

980 King Street, Midland, ON L4R 4K5. *C* **800/228-5150** or 705/526-2090. Fax 705/526-0419. 60 units. C$82–$128 (US$54–$84). Children under 19 stay free in parents' room. Crib/rollaway C$10 (US$6.60). AE, DISC, MC, V. **Amenities:** Restaurant (family), free continental breakfast; laundry service; dry cleaning. *In room:* A/C, TV.

DINING

Midland, in typical cottage country fashion, has plenty of fast-food diners and casual restaurants. If you plan to spend most of your time sightseeing and just want to grab a quick bite before moving on, there are several options around Little Lake Park and on King and Yonge streets in downtown Midland.

MODERATE

Mom's Restaurant AMERICAN   Mom's cooks up the kind of comfort food that travelers, especially the littlest ones, crave. The setting is casual and relaxed and this is a perfect place to bring the kids after a day at the beach. Portions are always generous and the homemade bread is wonderful.

200 Taylor Dr. (at Williams St.), Midland. *C* **705/527-0700.** Main courses C$7–$14 (US$4.60–$9.25), kids' menu C$3.50–$6.95 (US$2.30–$4.60). Mon–Sat 7am–9pm, Sun 9am–9pm.

Restaurant Sainte-Marie CANADIAN Part of the Sainte-Marie among the Hurons fortress, this restaurant is designed to resemble a 17th-century banquet hall, but the kids might prefer to eat outside on the terrace or in the newly built pavilion.

Service during the day is cafeteria style and thus fairly quick, but the quality of the offerings is exceptionally high. Burgers, sandwiches, and soups are all made to order in the open kitchen. There is no children's menu per se, but kids are charged according to what they eat and the prices are extremely reasonable.

The restaurant serves dinner on Fridays and Sundays only. On Friday evenings the restaurant offers a buffet dinner, which includes a 60-piece pasta bar, prime rib, and an extensive array of seafood and salad items. On Sunday evenings the restaurant hosts a grand public barbecue, complete with a jazz ensemble.

Hwy. 12. ✆ **705/527-4162.** Lunch menu C$5–$10 (US$3.30–$6.60); Fri evening buffet C$20 (US$13.20); Sun barbecue C$11 (US$7.25). AE, MC, V. Mother's Day–Thanksgiving daily 10am–4pm, Fri evenings 5:30–10pm, Sun evenings 4:30–9pm.

INEXPENSIVE
Dairy Queen BURGERS I've had a weakness for Dairy Queen soft ice cream since I was a child, and my children seem to have inherited this trait. If feeding the kids ice cream for lunch isn't what you had in mind, they also sell made-to-order hamburgers, hotdogs, and french fries. The restaurant is right across from Little Lake, the perfect place for a picnic lunch.

776 Yonge St. ✆ **705/526-6431.** Meals C$4.00–$6.00 (US$2.65–$3.95); kids' meals C$4.00 (US$2.65). V. Daily 10am–10pm.

5 Niagara Falls

160 kilometers (99 miles) SE of Toronto

GETTING THERE
By car, take the Queen Elizabeth Way (QEW) west to Niagara Falls. The trip will take about 1½ hours. **Amtrak** (✆ **800/361-1235** in Canada, or ✆ 800/USA-RAIL in the United States) and **Via Rail** (✆ **416/366-8411**) also operate trains between Toronto and New York, stopping in St. Catharines and Niagara Falls.

GETTING AROUND
The area around Clifton Hill and the falls is especially busy and it can be exceedingly difficult to find parking. Once you do, you may be faced with a pleasant walk downhill to the falls but a tougher walk back up the hill after a day of sightseeing, when the kids are inevitably more tired and cranky.

Luckily, tourism officials in Niagara Falls have dealt with this problem. You can park your vehicle at either **Rapid View,** which is free and several kilometers from the falls, or in **Preferred Parking,** which overlooks the falls and costs C$8 (US$4.30) per day. The **People Mover** shuttle bus serves both areas and is an attraction in itself. It travels in a loop, making nine stops from Rapid View to the Spanish Aero Car from 8am to 10pm. An all-day fare costs C$5.50 (US$3.65) for adults, C$2.75 (US$1.80) for children 6 to 12. Children 5 and under ride free. Call Niagara Parks at ✆ **905/358-5781** for details.

Niagara Falls

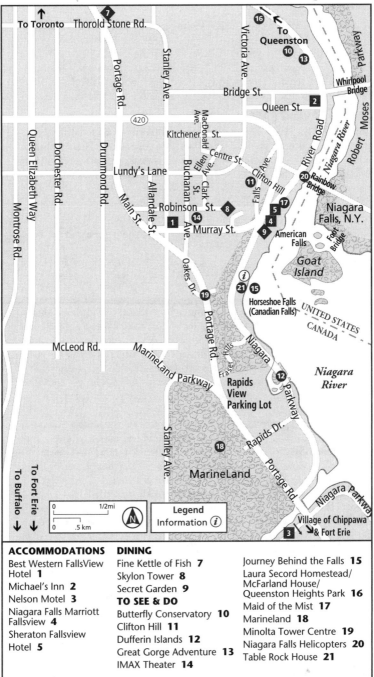

ACCOMMODATIONS
Best Western FallsView Hotel **1**
Michael's Inn **2**
Nelson Motel **3**
Niagara Falls Marriott Fallsview **4**
Sheraton Fallsview Hotel **5**

DINING
Fine Kettle of Fish **7**
Skylon Tower **8**
Secret Garden **9**

TO SEE & DO
Butterfly Conservatory **10**
Clifton Hill **11**
Dufferin Islands **12**
Great Gorge Adventure **13**
IMAX Theater **14**

Journey Behind the Falls **15**
Laura Secord Homestead/ McFarland House/ Queenston Heights Park **16**
Maid of the Mist **17**
Marineland **18**
Minolta Tower Centre **19**
Niagara Falls Helicopters **20**
Table Rock House **21**

INFORMATION

Contact the **Niagara Falls Canada Visitor and Convention Bureau,** 5433 Victoria Ave., Niagara Falls, ON L2G 3L1 (© **905/356-6061;** www.niagara tourism.com), or the **Niagara Falls Parks Commission,** Box 150, 7400 Portage Rd. S., Niagara Falls, ON L2E 6T2 (© **905/356-2241;** www.niagaraparks.com).

Summer information centers are open daily 9am to 6pm at Table Rock House, Maid of the Mist Plaza, Rapid View parking lot, and Niagara-on-the-Lake.

MONEY-SAVING PASSES

Discovery Pass Plus   This pass includes admission to the following attractions: Journey Behind the Falls, the Butterfly Conservatory, Niagara Spanish Aero Car, Great Gorge Adventure, Mackenzie Heritage Printery, Historic Fort Erie, Laura Secord Homestead, and McFarland House, plus all-day transportation aboard the People Mover. The cost is C$31.95 (US$21.10) for adults and C$16.95 (US$11.20) for children 6 to 12.

Explorer's Passport ⟨Value⟩   This passport includes admission to the Great Gorge Adventure, the Butterfly Conservatory, and Journey Behind the Falls, as well as unlimited one-day use of the People Mover bus system. It's available at information booths and costs C$24 (US$15.85) for adults and C$12 (US$7.90) for children 6 to 12. There are reduced prices for advance purchases.

SEEING THE FALLS

Although the kids may momentarily lose sight of the falls amid all the kitschy commercial attractions in Niagara Falls, the seventh natural wonder of the world is the reason you came here. And it *is* a wonder. Even my youngest children were awed by the powerful beauty of the falls and the churning water in the gorge beneath them. In the winter, the falls become icy cascades of ice bridges and other wild ice formations. Remember that the Canadian falls are also called Horseshoe Falls. There are falls on the American side too, but they're not as majestic.

Don't miss seeing the falls after dark, when they are lit by spectacular gas spotlights in shades of rose-pink, red-magenta, amber, blue, and green. Call © **800/563-2557** (in the United States) or © **905/356-6061** (in Canada) for schedules. The show starts around 5pm in winter, 8:30pm in spring and fall, and 9pm in summer. Every Friday from July through September, a spectacular fireworks display illuminates both the American and Horseshoe falls.

There are numerous ways to view the falls. The most obvious is the free view offered from the walkways that skirt **Victoria Park** and the **Table Rock** complex (see the map), and I suggest you start there. However, you may also want to pay for the more spectacular views of the falls offered by the various tour groups listed below.

IMAX Theatre   **Ages 5 and up.** In addition to other IMAX films, this theater features daily screenings of *Niagara: Miracles, Myths and Magic* on its six-story screen. Combining historical footage and scenes of death-defying stunts and heroic rescues with panoramic views of Niagara River scenery, this film serves as a great introduction to Niagara Falls.

A ticket to the theater also includes admission to the **Daredevil Hall of Fame,** a museum dedicated to remembering the daredevils (or fools, depending on your perspective) who have tumbled over the falls since the early 19th century. Your preteens will probably get a kick out of the exploits chronicled here. A variety of multimedia displays are featured.

6170 Buchanan Ave. ☎ **905/358-3611**. Admission C$10 (US$6.60) adults and children 13 and up, C$6.50 (US$4.30) children 4–12. Niagara: *Miracles, Myths and Magic* screens daily 11am, 1pm, 3pm, 4pm, 6pm, and 7pm. Open year-round.

Journey Behind the Falls   Ages 3 and up. An elevator at Table Rock House drops you 45.5 meters (150 ft.) through solid rock to the tunnels and viewing portals at this attraction, located literally behind the falls. You'll be given a disposable rain slicker to wear and you'll need it, as it's exceedingly damp—not that the kids will mind. An observation deck located within feet of the falls gives kids an appreciation for the sheer amount of water that tumbles over it—and the roar is pretty cool, too. This is a very popular attraction, so expect lineups, especially during the summer.

Table House Rock (across from the falls). ☎ **905/354-1551**. Admission C$7 (US$4.60) adults, C$3.50 (US$2.30) children 6–12, free for children under 6. June–Sept 9am–11pm, varying hours during the rest of the year.

Maid of the Mist   Ages 5 and up. Unquestionably the most exciting way to see the falls, the *Maid of the Mist* will take you to the foot of Horseshoe Falls, where 34.5 million gallons of water tumble over the 53.5-meter (176 ft.) high cataract every minute. You will get wet and your glasses will fog, but the kids will love every minute of it and you'll be given a rain slicker to protect you from the worst of it.

The boat is very safe but the deck can get slippery, so this is probably not a good choice for your less-than-sturdy toddlers. Boats leave from the dock on the parkway just down from the Rainbow Bridge. Trips operate daily, every 30 minutes.

5920 River Rd. ☎ **905/358-5781**. Admission C$12.25 (US$8.10) adults, C$7.50 (US$4.95) children 6–12, free for children under 5. Mid-Apr–Oct Mon–Fri 10am–5pm, Sat–Sun 10am–6pm.

Minolta Tower Centre   All ages. This shopping/dining amusement complex offers a wonderful view of the falls from its 99-meter (325 ft.) observation floors.

6732 Fallsview Blvd. ☎ **905/356-1501**. Admission C$6.95 (US$4.60) adults, C$4.95 (US$3.25) children 6–17, C$19.95 (US$13.15) family (2 adults, 3 children), free for children 5 and under. June–Sept 9am–1am; Oct–Dec 9am–10pm; Jan–Mar 9am–9pm; Mar–May 9am–10pm.

Niagara Falls Helicopters   Ages 6 and up. This is an expensive yet thrilling way to see the falls. Helicopters leave for a nine-minute spin over the falls from the heliport adjacent to the whirlpools at the junction of Victoria Avenue and Niagara Parkway, daily from 9am to dusk, weather permitting.

3731 Victoria Ave. ☎ **905/357-5672**. www.niagara-helicopters.com. Admission C$175 (US$115.50) for two passengers.

Skylon Tower Observation Deck *(Overrated*   **All ages.** A glass-fronted elevator (which is attraction enough for kids) takes you 158.5 meters (520 ft.) to the top of the tower, where your family is treated to an unobstructed view of the falls and the city. The observation deck is actually three decks and includes indoor and outdoor viewing areas. On a clear day you can you see the skylines of both Toronto and Buffalo, but unless the skies are bright and clear, you may find this an overly expensive view.

520 Robson St. ☎ **905/356-2651**. www.skylon.com. Summer 8am–midnight; winter 10am–10pm. Admission C$8.50 (US$5.60) adults, C$4.50 (US$2.95) children, C$23.50 (US$15.50) family.

(Fun Fact **Wow the Kids: Facts about the Falls**

- In 1848, an ice jam upriver completely dried up the Horseshoe and Rainbow (American) falls for 30 hours, the only time this has been known to happen. People walked onto the riverbed to look for artifacts.
- In 1960, a seven-year-old boy, his sister, and a family friend were boating on the river when they capsized. The sister was rescued before she reached the falls but the boy and man were swept over the falls. The man died, but the boy, still wearing his life jacket and with only minor injuries, was rescued at the base of the falls by the *Maid of the Mist*.
- Until 1912, people could walk out onto the ice bridge that spanned the river at the base of the falls as the water roared beside and underneath them. In 1888, a local newspaper reported that more than 20,000 people strolled and tobogganed on the ice on one particularly cold day.
- At one point, the falls entertainment included tightrope walkers who would balance high above the falls on a wire.
- Of the 15 people who have gone over the falls in a container, 10 have survived.
- The fine for going over the falls is C$10,000 (US$6,600).
- The first person to deliberately go over the falls was Annie Edson Taylor, a 63-year-old teacher from Bay City, Michigan, who went over in a wooden wine barrel in 1901 and survived.
- The falls are more than 12,000 years old.

TO SEE & DO IN NIAGARA FALLS
CLIFTON HILL

Terrifically tacky, this hilly street in the downtown area is home to most of Niagara Falls' kitschiest attractions. You might shudder at the profusion of fast-food restaurants, fun houses, wax museums, and other attractions, but your kids will undoubtedly lap it up. Admission fees to each attraction are not terribly steep, at C$4 to $8 (US$2.65 to $5.30), but they do tend to add up. My advice is to walk from the top of the street to the bottom to give the kids an idea of what attractions are there, then ask them to choose two or three. There is a nice park at the bottom of the hill where you can rest while they make their decision. The attractions include:

- **The Adventure Dome,** 4943 Clifton Hill (© **905/357-4330**)
- **The Fun House,** 4943 Clifton Hill (© **905/357-4330**)
- **Guinness World of Records,** 4943 Clifton Hill (© **905/356-2299**)
- **The Haunted House,** 4943 Clifton Hill (© **905/357-4330**)
- **The Mystery Maze,** Oneida Lane, off Clifton Hill (© **905/357-4330**)
- **Movieland Museum of the Stars,** 4950 Clifton Hill (© **905/358-3061**)
- **Ripley's Believe It or Not,** 4960 Clifton Hill (© **905/356-2238**)

THE NIAGARA PARKWAY
North along the Parkway

In sharp contrast to the carnival atmosphere at Clifton Hill is the natural beauty of the 56-kilometer (35 mile) parkway, with its parklands and bicycle paths. There are a number of attractions along the parkway as you travel between Niagara Falls and Niagara-on-the-Lake, a charming town that is worth a day's visit (see "Sidetrips: Shakespeare and Shaw" in chapter 8).

Great Gorge Adventure   **Ages 4 and up.** The first diversion you'll come to along the parkway is this 305-meter (1,000 ft.) boardwalk. An elevator takes you down to the boardwalk, which hugs the riverbanks and provides an amazing view of the raging and swirling rapids that travel at more than 60kmph (37.2 mph). As a bonus, there are rarely any of the lineups you'll encounter at the downtown attractions.

4330 River Rd. © **905/374-1221.** Admission C$5.75 (US$3.80) adults, C$2.90 (US$1.90) children 6–12, free for children under 6. Mar–June 9am–5pm, early June–early Sept 9am–9pm, Sept–Nov 9am–5pm, closed mid-Nov–mid-Mar.

Spanish Aero Car *(Overrated)*   Half a mile farther north is this cable car ride. Though you're actually several kilometers from the falls, the 10-minute journey over the Niagara River and giant whirlpool is a thrill for little ones. Passengers ride in a small, open car that resembles a miniature streetcar, suspended from huge cables. You'll be treated to some awe-inspiring views of the surrounding countryside and churning river below, but the ride is fairly tame and so may appeal more to easily thrilled toddlers than older kids. Lineups here are short.

On the Niagara Pkwy. 4.5km (3 miles) down-river from the falls at People Mover stops no. 8 and 16. © **905/354-5711.** Admission C$6 (US$3.95) adults, C$3 (US$2) children 6–12, free for children under 6. Mid-Apr–mid-June 9am–6pm; mid-June–early Sept 8am–9:30pm; the rest of the year hours vary.

Butterfly Conservatory   Drive past the golf club and stop at this lush tropical garden, which more than 2,000 butterflies (50 international species) call home. You can explore the garden via a 183-meter (600 ft.) network of winding pathways. Have the kids watch for Luther, Stubbs, and Waldo, the three iguanas that also reside here. Kids can also try to spot the yellow and black striped zebra butterflies and the owl butterflies with strange brown "eyes" on their lower wings. The brightly colored fish inhabiting the pools are another kid magnet.

If you have the time, take a free tour of the vast outdoor gardens on the site. They are part of the **School of Horticulture** and include an outdoor butterfly garden that attracts a wealth of native species during the summer. The other big attraction here is the 12-meter (40 ft.) floral clock holding over 25,000 plants.

In Niagara Parks Botanical Gardens, Niagara Pkwy. © **905/356-8119.** Jan–Feb 9am–5pm, Mar–Apr 9am–6pm, May 9am–8pm, June–Aug 9am–9pm, Sept–Dec 9am–5pm. Adults C$8.50(US$5.60), children 6–12 C$4 (US$2.65).

Queenston Heights Park   Your next stop north on the parkway should be this park, overlooking Queenston Heights and the Niagara River. The park is located on the site of one of the fiercest battles of the War of 1812, in which British and Canadian forces beat the invading Americans. Today, it's home to a playground, a snack bar, several picnic shelters, a wading pool, and some magnificent gardens. You can take a walking tour of the battleground, which is also a beautiful spot for a picnic lunch. There is a lot of room for the kids to run around and wear off their energy before you get back in the car to start your next adventure.

Laura Secord Homestead From her home in the village of Queenston, Laura set out on a 32-kilometer (20 mile) walk through the American lines and over wild and unsettled country to warn the British forces of an impending attack at Beaverdams. Costumed guides offer tours of the home, restored to the way it looked when Laura lived there in 1812. There is also a wonderful ice cream parlor and candy shop with the mouth-watering chocolates sold at Laura Secord stores in Toronto and Niagara Falls.

29 Queenston St., Queenston. © **905/262-4851.** Admission C$1.50 (US$1) adults and children. Daily May–June 10am–4pm, June–Sept 10am–5pm.

McFarland House Next on the parkway is this historic house, built in 1800, which was used as a hospital by both sides during the War of 1812, depending on who was in control of the area at the time. It also briefly served as a barracks for British officers during the war. Costumed guides give tours of the home and the 19th-century herb garden. If you didn't eat your picnic lunch at Queenston Heights Park, there is a charming park and playground beside the house. You can also buy a takeout picnic lunch from the quaint tearoom, along with some fresh baked goods or an ice cream for a treat.

15927 Niagara River Pkwy. © **905/468-3322.** Admission C$2 (US$1.30) adults, C$1 (US65¢) children. Late May–June daily noon–5pm, July–Labour Day 11am–6pm.

South along the Parkway

If you decide to drive south, you'll pass the **Table Rock Complex,** where you can access the **Journey Behind the Falls** (see "Seeing the Falls," above), and then the **Park Greenhouse,** a free attraction housing many gorgeous plants and a number of exotic tropical birds. There are washrooms at this site, as well, so it's a good place to stop for a quick rest. It's open July to August daily 9:30am to 7pm, and September to June 9:30am to 4:15pm.

Dufferin Islands Farther along is this free nature preserve, which is a wonderful spot to take the kids to cool off on a hot day. There are four islands joined by a series of bridges. A wonderful swimming area is maintained, and the kids can boot around in the paddleboats for extra fun. There is also a nine-hole par 3 golf course (my favorite kind) that is a great place to teach kids the rudiments of golf.

Free admission. Open second Sun in Apr–last Sun in Oct dawn–dusk.

Fort Erie Farther along is Fort Erie, a reconstruction of a fort seized by the Americans in 1814, besieged by the British, and finally blown up by the Americans in July 1814 as they retreated to Buffalo. Guards in period costume stand sentry duty, fire the cannons, and demonstrate drill and musket practice. Kids can explore the barracks and various common rooms, including the 1812 kitchen with its open hearth and huge iron pots. You'll also find a snack bar, a gift shop, and a small playground on-site.

350 Lakeshore Blvd., Fort Erie. © **905/871-0540.** Admission C$6.50(US$4.30) adults, C$4 (US$2.65) children 6–12. May 1–Labour Day daily 10am–6pm, Labour Day–Nov 30 daily 10am–4pm.

Mildred M. Mahoney Dolls House Gallery Also in Fort Erie is this amazing store, which has more than 120 fully furnished dollhouses on display, including several from the 18th century. The dollhouses represent a wide range of architectural styles and cultures. Even noncollectors will be awed by the minute crystal chandeliers, tiny Wedgewood china, and miniature oil paintings hanging on the walls.

657 Niagara River Pkwy., Fort Erie. © **905/871-5833.** Admission C$3.50 (US$2.30) adults, C$2 (US$1.30) children 6–16, free for children under 6. May 1–Dec 31 daily 10am–4pm; by appointment only at other times of the year.

MORE TO SEE & DO

Marineland   Ages 2 and up. The commercials for this attraction are infectious—once my girls heard them we had to go. As the jingle says, "everyone loves Marineland," with the possible exception of those who dislike huge crowds.

The big draw here is Kandu the killer whale. We had to watch the show twice just to make sure that everyone who wanted to get splashed did. Get there at least 15 minutes beforehand so you can choose where you want to sit—in the wet or dry section—and watch the clown who presides over the preshow—he's actually pretty funny. The aquarium shows also feature beluga whales and sea lions. Don't miss a look through Friendly Cove, where a series of walkways surrounds the whales' pool. Some lucky visitors actually get to touch one of the whales. There is also a viewing area underneath the pool where you'll get a close-up view of these graceful creatures.

You can also get close to both fish and deer at the park. Feed for both is sold near the deer paddock and the fishpond. Be forewarned, though—when the deer see you have food, they close in. My four-year-old was more than a little panicked when the deer began to press in around her. They don't bite, but 500 deer surrounding you is a little intimidating for a small child. The fish are far more polite. You can see them from the bridge over the pond, and children delight in touching them from the wharf.

There is also a bear pit and tank where the bears swim around while kids (and everyone else) pitch marshmallows to them. The kids loved it, but I found the sight of all those penned-in animals a little disturbing. There are also pens housing elk and bison.

When your kids have finished feeding and admiring the animals there are a number of rides they can enjoy. Several of the more serious rides have height restrictions, including the Flying Dragon (132cm/52 in.), Hurricane Cove (107cm/42 in.), and the Dragon Mountain Roller Coaster (122cm/48 in.). If your kids are theme-park veterans, however, these rides will likely seem pretty tame to them.

For younger kids, there is a small playground and a cute little roller coaster that my six-year-old and her four-year-old sister tackled by themselves—sitting in front, no less! The girls and Dad also had a good time on the Viking Boat Carousel and the flying swings. If you have toddlers, you can rent a dolphin-shaped stroller for C$6 (US$3.95). A facility for nursing moms, a first aid station, and lockers are also available in the complex. The gift shop is huge and stocks an assortment of toys and souvenirs, the most popular of which seemed to be the inflatable killer whales.

Where to Eat   A snack bar serves up the usual hamburgers and other fried foods at the usual high theme-park prices. You can bring a picnic, but note that your car may be parked a good distance from the front gates and you are prohibited from bringing any glass containers into the park.

7657 Portage Rd., Niagara Falls. © **905/356-9565.** Admission C$16.95 (US$11.20) ages 10–69, C$12.95 (US$8.55) children 5–9, free for children under 5. May–June 10am–5pm, July–Labour Day 9am–6pm, Sept–Oct 10am–5pm. By car: From the QEW, take the McLeod Rd. exit.

Oh Canada Eh?! (Finds   **Ages 6 and up.** This family dinner theater serves up both a wonderful meal and a hilarious lesson in Canadian history. Performances feature skits, songs, and dance, all laced with a liberal dose of humor. The skits are lively enough to keep kids happily entertained for the entire two-hour show.

The menu features simple fare that kids will like: Alberta roast beef, Atlantic haddock, and Ontario chicken, with salads, veggies, fresh bread, and potatoes representing the harvests of the other Canadian provinces. Tea or coffee and dessert are also included.

8585 Lundy's Lane, Niagara Falls. ℂ **800/467-2071** or 905/374-1995. Tickets C$42 (US$27.70) adults, C$37 (US$24.40) children 13–16, C$19.50 (US$12.85) children 6–12, free for children 5 and under. Prices do not includes taxes or gratuities. Tickets sold in advance. MC, V. May–Oct nightly 6:30pm; call for show times during the rest of the year.

ACCOMMODATIONS

Niagara Falls contains a seemingly infinite number and variety of hotels, motels, inns, and bed and breakfasts. In summer, rates tend to go up and down according to the traffic, and some proprietors will not quote rates ahead of time. Niagara Falls is increasingly marketing itself as a conference destination, and with the casino now open the city very rarely has a "down" night. However, hotels in the area often offer special package deals, including two-nights' accommodation, meals, and attraction tickets; several offer special deals for family visitors. Be sure to ask about special deals when you call.

Best Western FallsView Hotel *(Value)*   Within sight of the falls and within easy walking distance of most downtown attractions, this affordable hotel is a favorite with families. On-site amenities include a large indoor pool with a slide and an outdoor playground for the kids. Rooms are surprisingly large, with lots of space for additional cots or a crib. All rooms have either a patio or a balcony, although despite the hotel's name, none has a view of the falls. This hotel offers frequent special and package deals, so inquire when you call.

5551 Murray St., Niagara Falls, L2G 3V7. ℂ **800/263-2580** or 905/356-0551. Fax 905/356-7773. 239 units. C$79–$169 double (US$52–$112); C$10 (US$6.60) for a third adult. Children 12 and under stay free in parents' room. Crib free; rollaway C$10 (US$6.60). AE, DC, DISC, MC, V. **Amenities:** Restaurant (family), lounge; pool; sauna; Jacuzzi; small business center; valet and laundry service. *In room:* A/C, TV w/ pay movies.

Michael's Inn   This hotel is best known for its fantasy rooms (a la Scarlett O'Hara and the Garden of Paradise) catering to Niagara Falls' still-thriving honeymoon market. However, the hotel offers some surprisingly affordable and spacious accommodations for families.

Larger families will like the inn's family accommodation, which boasts three double or queen-size beds and a pullout couch, as well as a view of the Niagara River and Gorge.

Staff can arrange for fridges or cribs in any of the rooms, welcome extras when you have the kids in tow. The kids will also appreciate the indoor pool, Jacuzzi, and arcade room. The dining room features an open hearth where the kids can watch the chef cook their dinner.

5599 River Rd., Niagara Falls, ON L2E 3H3. ℂ **800/263-9390** or 905/354-2727. Fax 905/374-7706. www.michaelsinn.com. 130 units. C$59–$208 (US$39–$137) double. AE, DC, MC, V. Free parking. **Amenities:** Restaurant (family), kids' menu; pool; Jacuzzi; sauna; exercise room; arcade; babysitting. *In room:* A/C, TV w/ pay movies.

Nelson Motel   This is a great budget hotel, especially for families. There are several family units that will make the kids feel right at home, each with a double bedroom and an adjoining twin-bedded room for the kids. Keep in mind, though, that these are budget accommodations. There are no phones in the rooms, and single rooms have a shower only. Thankfully, there are baths in the family units.

10655 Niagara River Pkwy., Niagara Falls, ON L2E 6S6. ℂ **905/295-4754**. 25 units, none with phone. C$45–$55 (US$30–36) double. Crib/rollaway cot C$10 (US$6.60). MC, V. Free parking. **Amenities:** Pool. *In room:* A/C, TV.

Niagara Falls Marriott Fallsview   This hotel's name is a bit more accurate —all 400 rooms have large windows that offer a magnificent view of the falls. There are vents inside many of the rooms that, when opened, allow you to hear the falls as well. The view from the lower-level rooms is somewhat impeded by the trees, so try to get a room as high up as possible. New bi-level loft suites will open in the summer of 2001, with floor-to-ceiling windows that open so you can experience the falls without leaving your room.

Rooms are spacious enough to allow a cot or crib, and the hotel also offers two family suites with a combination of rooms that can sleep six to seven. The hotel was built in 1999, with additional renovations in 2001, so the decor and amenities still have that brand-new look.

If you happen to be in town during spring break and certain other holidays, the hotel sponsors a magnificent children's program that puts your kids to work decorating cookies with the hotel chefs, making crafts, and attending magic shows. At other times, the kids will find plenty to do in the hotel's large indoor pool and outdoor sundeck.

6740 Fallsview Blvd., Niagara Falls, ON L2G 3W6. ℂ **888/501-8916** or 905/357-7300. Fax 905/357-0490. www.niagarafallsmarriot.com. 400 units. C$89–$249 (US$59–$164) double, C$239–$850 (US$158–$561) suite. Children under 18 stay free in parents' room. Crib/rollaway free. AE, DC, DISC, MC, V. **Amenities:** Restaurant (Italian/French); indoor pool; outdoor sundeck; health club; full-service spa; concierge; tour desk; business center; room service; laundry service; dry cleaning. *In room:* A/C, TV w/ pay movies, dataport, coffeemaker, hairdryer, iron, PlayStation.

Sheraton Fallsview Hotel and Convention Centre   If you are hoping to combine a traditional romantic Niagara Falls getaway with a family vacation, the Sheraton offers families two-room suites with separate baths. The kids' room has two double beds, and the big people's room has a king-size bed and a whirlpool bath.

If you reserve early enough, you may be able to book a room with a view of the falls, but they go quickly. If you can't get one, the hotel has an observation deck with a decent view of both the American and the Canadian falls.

Though it is an expensive option, this hotel more than makes up for its price with its many extras. Kids under 7 stay for free and eat for free in the hotel restaurants, and parking, an expensive and rare commodity in Niagara Falls, is free for guests. The hotel also boasts an enviable location within 274 meters (300 yards) of the falls and within walking distance of the downtown attractions. Free children's programs are provided during most holidays.

6755 Fallsview Blvd., Niagara Falls, ON L2G 3W7. ℂ **800/267-8439** or 905/374-1077. Fax 905/374-6224. www.fallsview.com. 403 units. C$129–$289 (US$85–$191) double, C$379–$509 (US$250–$336) suite. Children under 7 stay free in parents' room. Crib/rollaway C$10 (US$6.60). AE, DC, DISC, MC, V. Free parking. **Amenities:** Restaurant (fine dining), cafe, lounge; indoor pool; Jacuzzi; exercise room; business center; room service; babysitting; laundry service. *In room:* TV w/ pay movies; dataport; coffeemaker; hairdryer; pay-per-play PlayStation.

DINING

Niagara has a plethora of dining options, from fast-food fare to expensive and impressive dining. If fast food is what you are after, Clifton Hill offers a little bit of everything. There are also several restaurants along River Road.

The **Niagara Parkway Commission** has commandeered the most spectacular scenic spots, where it operates reasonably priced dining outlets. **Table Rock Restaurant** (© 905/354-3631) and **Victoria Park Restaurant** (© 905/356-2217) are both on the parkway right by the falls and are pleasant, if crowded.

VERY EXPENSIVE

The Skylon Tower CONTINENTAL   It's undeniably expensive, but this revolving restaurant set 236 meters (775 ft.) above the falls is an unforgettable experience, especially for kids. The restaurant completes one rotation every hour, so you will get a chance to see everything during your lunch or dinner. You reach the dining room via one of two glass elevators, which afford views of either the American or the Canadian falls.

This is fine dining, so you'll have to keep a tight rein on your little ones and discourage them from running to peer out the windows on the other side of the room. The early dinner special, a discounted dinner menu, is served at 4:30pm and 5:30pm—a good time to bring the kids, as few serious diners are in the restaurant.

For lunch the daily specials, which range from braised veal to crab and sole croquettes, are usually a good choice. During dinner hours the restaurant offers an eclectic mix of fine cuisine, including an excellent filet mignon with tiger shrimps. The kids' menu also offers upscale fare, with choices such as a beef tenderloin burger at lunch or a kid's cut of prime rib for dinner. The kids' menu prices include a drink and dessert.

5200 Robinson St., Niagara Falls, ON L2G 2A3. © **905/356-2651**. www.skylon.com. Reservations required. Main courses C$34.95–$57.95 (US$23.05–$38.25), kids' menu C$22.05 (US$14.55); early-bird dinner C$32.50 (US$21.45) adults, C$13.50 (US$8.90) children. AE, MC, V. Lunch reserved seatings 11:30am, 1pm, 2:30pm; dinner reserved seatings 4:30pm, 5pm, 6pm, 6:30pm, 8:30pm, 9:00pm, 10pm.

MODERATE

Fine Kettle of Fish SEAFOOD   There is something about sightseeing all day at the falls and then eating copious amounts of seafood that goes together. If the kids aren't entertained enough watching the lobsters in the tanks by the kitchen, they'll be given crayons and coloring books to keep them amused. The menu features heaps of seafood options, and the kids' menu includes hamburgers, nugget combos, and a shrimp and chip platter my eldest daughter loved. This restaurant lays claim to the best fish and chips recipe in the city.

3641 Portage Rd., Niagara Falls, ON L2J 2K8. © **888/448-8878** or 905/357-3474. Fax 905/374-3474. Main courses C$9.99–16.99 (US$6.60–$11.20), kids' menu C$4.95 (US$3.25). AE, MC, V. Mon–Thurs 11am–9pm, Fri–Sun 11am–10pm.

The Secret Garden CANADIAN   This gorgeous restaurant with a palatial patio is nestled in the formal gardens of Oakes Garden Theatre across from the American falls. The restaurant features a distinctly Canadian menu and the decor is Canadian-themed, with Canadian artwork prominently displayed.

The braised beef served with red wine sauce and pasta is a popular dish, and in a unique twist, stir-fried vegetables are served with all entries. A wide selection of vegetarian dishes is also available. If you prefer something light, the lunch menu is served all day. Kids' menu choices are the fairly standard hamburgers, hot dogs, and chicken fingers with fries.

5827 River Rd., Niagara Falls, ON L2G 3K9. © **905/358-4588**. www.secretgarden.net. All-day menu C$6.95–$12.95 (US$4.60–$8.55), dinner menu C$14.95–$24.95 (US$9.85–$16.45), kids' menu C$3.95–$6.95 (US$2.60–$4.60). AE, DISC, MC, V. Daily 8am–9pm (later if restaurant is busy).

Index

See also Accommodations and Restaurant indexes, below.

ACCOMMODATIONS

RESTAURANTS

TORONTO IS FOR KIDS IN 2002

CHECK OUR AGENDA

Jan. International Boat Show (kids section).

Feb. Toronto Winterfest. Chinese New Year Celebrations.

March. One of a Kind Spring Canadian Craft Show. St. Patrick's Day Parade. March Break Activities (throughout the city).

May. Doors Open Toronto. Milk Children's International Festival.

June. Buskerfest. Lion Dance Festival. Dragon Boat Festival. Toronto International Caravan.

July. Canada Day Celebrations. Toronto Outdoor Art Exhibition. Celebrate Toronto Street Festival. Caribana Junior Parade.

Aug. Caribana Parade and Festival. Taste of the Danforth. Canadian National Exhibition.

Sept. Canadian International Air Show. Toronto Celtfest at Fort York.

Nov. Royal Winter Fair. Santa Claus Parade. Aboriginal Festival. One-of-a-Kind Christmas Canadian Craft Show.

Dec. Kensington Festival of Lights. First Night Toronto.

For more information, or to book a hotel, contact Toronto Convention & Visitors Association at **1-800-363-1990 or www.torontotourism.com**

TORONTO
The world within a city™

FROMMER'S® COMPLETE TRAVEL GUIDES

Alaska
Amsterdam
Argentina & Chile
Arizona
Atlanta
Australia
Austria
Bahamas
Barcelona, Madrid & Seville
Beijing
Belgium, Holland &
  Luxembourg
Bermuda
Boston
British Columbia & the
  Canadian Rockies
Budapest & the Best of Hungary
California
Canada
Cancún, Cozumel & the
  Yucatán
Cape Cod, Nantucket &
  Martha's Vineyard
Caribbean
Caribbean Cruises & Ports
  of Call
Caribbean Ports of Call
Carolinas & Georgia
Chicago
China
Colorado
Costa Rica
Denmark
Denver, Boulder & Colorado
  Springs
England
Europe

European Cruises & Ports of Call
Florida
France
Germany
Greece
Greek Islands
Hawaii
Hong Kong
Honolulu, Waikiki & Oahu
Ireland
Israel
Italy
Jamaica
Japan
Las Vegas
London
Los Angeles
Maryland & Delaware
Maui
Mexico
Montana & Wyoming
Montréal & Québec City
Munich & the Bavarian Alps
Nashville & Memphis
Nepal
New England
New Mexico
New Orleans
New York City
New Zealand
Nova Scotia, New Brunswick &
  Prince Edward Island
Oregon
Paris
Philadelphia & the Amish
  Country
Portugal

Prague & the Best of the Czech
  Republic
Provence & the Riviera
Puerto Rico
Rome
San Antonio & Austin
San Diego
San Francisco
Santa Fe, Taos & Albuquerque
Scandinavia
Scotland
Seattle & Portland
Shanghai
Singapore & Malaysia
South Africa
Southeast Asia
South Florida
South Pacific
Spain
Sweden
Switzerland
Texas
Thailand
Tokyo
Toronto
Tuscany & Umbria
USA
Utah
Vancouver & Victoria
Vermont, New Hampshire
  & Maine
Vienna & the Danube Valley
Virgin Islands
Virginia
Walt Disney World & Orlando
Washington, D.C.
Washington State

FROMMER'S® DOLLAR-A-DAY GUIDES

Australia from $50 a Day
California from $70 a Day
Caribbean from $70 a Day
England from $70 a Day
Europe from $70 a Day

Florida from $70 a Day
Hawaii from $70 a Day
Ireland from $60 a Day
Italy from $70 a Day
London from $85 a Day

New York from $80 a Day
Paris from $80 a Day
San Francisco from $60 a Day
Washington, D.C.,
  from $70 a Day

FROMMER'S® PORTABLE GUIDES

Acapulco, Ixtapa &
  Zihuatanejo
Alaska Cruises & Ports
  of Call
Amsterdam
Australia's Great Barrier Reef
Bahamas
Baja & Los Cabos
Berlin
Boston
California Wine Country
Charleston & Savannah
Chicago

Dublin
Hawaii: The Big Island
Hong Kong
Houston
Las Vegas
London
Los Angeles
Maine Coast
Maui
Miami
New Orleans
New York City
Paris

Phoenix & Scottsdale
Portland
Puerto Rico
Puerto Vallarta, Manzanillo &
  Guadalajara
San Diego
San Francisco
Seattle
Sydney
Tampa & St. Petersburg
Vancouver
Venice
Washington, D.C.

FROMMER'S® NATIONAL PARK GUIDES

Family Vacations in the
  National Parks
Grand Canyon

National Parks of the American
  West
Rocky Mountain
Yellowstone & Grand Teton

Yosemite & Sequoia/
  Kings Canyon
Zion & Bryce Canyon